Human Rights Machinery

Human Rights Machinery

Tanuj Sharma

RANDOM PUBLICATIONS
NEW DELHI (INDIA)

Human Rights Machinery

ISBN 978-93-5111-512-0

Published in 2015 in India by

RANDOM PUBLICATIONS

4376-A/4B, Gali Murari Lal, Ansari Road
New Delhi-110 002
Phone : +9111-43580356, 011-23289044, 011-43142548
e-mail: sales@randompublications.com,
info@randompublications.com, randomexports@gmail.com

Type Setting by : Friends Media, Delhi-110089
Digitally Printed at : Replika Press Pvt. Ltd.

Preface

Human rights are commonly understood as inalienable fundamental rights to which a person is inherently entitled simply because she or he is a human being. Human rights are thus conceived as universal and egalitarian. These rights may exist as natural rights or as legal rights, in both national and international law. The doctrine of human rights in international practice, within international law, global and regional institutions, in the policies of states and in the activities of non-governmental organizations, has been a cornerstone of public policy around the world.

Many of the basic ideas that animated the human rights movement developed in the aftermath of the Second World War and the atrocities of The Holocaust, culminating in the adoption of the Universal Declaration of Human Rights in Paris by the United Nations General Assembly in 1948. The United Nations has played an important role in international human-rights law since its creation. Following the World Wars, the United Nations and its members developed much of the discourse and the bodies of law that now make up international humanitarian law and international human rights law. The panoply of implementation measures that the UN has taken since 1945 has resulted in a diverse and complex set of institutional arrangements, the effectiveness of which varies widely.

This book critically examines the functions, procedures, and performance of each of the major bodies dealing with human rights, including the charter-based bodies, treaty-based bodies, security council, international court of justice, international criminal court, as well as the more specialized bodies monitoring the implementation of human rights treaties. Significant attention is devoted to the considerable efforts at reforming the UN's human rights machinery. The book will be a valuable source of information for all who are concerned about international human rights machinery.

Author

Contents

1

What are Human Rights?

Human rights are rights inherent to all human beings, whatever our nationality, place of residence, sex, national or ethnic origin, colour, religion, language, or any other status. We are all equally entitled to our human rights without discrimination. These rights are all interrelated, interdependent and indivisible.

Universal human rights are often expressed and guaranteed by law, in the forms of treaties, customary international law , general principles and other sources of international law. International human rights law lays down obligations of Governments to act in certain ways or to refrain from certain acts, in order to promote and protect human rights and fundamental freedoms of individuals or groups.

The principle of universality of human rights is the cornerstone of international human rights law. This principle, as first emphasized in the Universal Declaration on Human Rights in 1948, has been reiterated in numerous international human rights conventions, declarations, and resolutions. The 1993 Vienna World Conference on Human Rights, for example, noted that it is the duty of States to promote and protect all human rights and fundamental freedoms, regardless of their political, economic and cultural systems.

All States have ratified at least one, and 80% of States have ratified four or more, of the core human rights treaties, reflecting consent of States which creates legal obligations for them and giving concrete expression to universality. Some fundamental human rights norms enjoy universal protection by customary international law across all boundaries and civilizations.

Human rights are inalienable. They should not be taken away, except in specific situations and according to due process. For example, the right to liberty may be restricted if a person is found guilty of a crime by a court of law.

All human rights are indivisible, whether they are civil and political rights, such as the right to life, equality before the law and freedom of expression; economic, social and cultural rights, such as the rights to work, social security and education , or collective rights, such as the rights to development and self-determination, are indivisible, interrelated and interdependent. The improvement of one right facilitates advancement of the others. Likewise, the deprivation of one right adversely affects the others.

Non-discrimination is a cross-cutting principle in international human rights law. The principle is present in all the major human rights treaties and provides the central theme of some of international human rights conventions such as the International Convention on the Elimination of All Forms of Racial Discrimination and the Convention on the Elimination of All Forms of Discrimination against Women.

The principle applies to everyone in relation to all human rights and freedoms and it prohibits discrimination on the basis of a list of non-exhaustive categories such as sex, race, colour and so on. The principle of non-discrimination is complemented by the principle of equality, as stated in Article 1 of the Universal Declaration of Human Rights: "All human beings are born free and equal in dignity and rights."

Human rights entail both rights and obligations. States assume obligations and duties under international law to respect, to protect and to fulfil human rights. The obligation to respect means that States must refrain from interfering with or curtailing the enjoyment of human rights. The obligation to protect requires States to protect individuals and groups against human rights abuses. The obligation to fulfil means that States must take positive action to facilitate the enjoyment of basic human rights. At the individual level, while we are entitled our human rights, we should also respect the human rights of others.

Defining Human Rights

Human rights are commonly understood as "inalienable fundamental rights to which a person is inherently entitled simply because she or he is a human being." Human rights are thus conceived as universal (applicable everywhere) and egalitarian (the same for everyone). These rights may exist as natural rights or as legal rights, in both national and international law. The doctrine of human rights in international practice, within international law, global and regional institutions, in the policies of states and in the activities of non-governmental organizations, has been a cornerstone of public policy around the world. The idea of human rights states, "if the public discourse of peacetime global society can be said to have a common moral language, it is that of human rights." Despite this, the strong claims made by the doctrine of human rights continue to provoke considerable skepticism and debates about the content, nature and justifications of human rights to this day. Indeed, the question of what is meant by a "right" is itself controversial and the subject of continued philosophical debate.

Many of the basic ideas that animated the human rights movement developed in the aftermath of the Second World War and the atrocities of The Holocaust, culminating in the adoption of the Universal Declaration of Human Rights in Paris by the United Nations General Assembly in 1948. The ancient world did not possess the concept of universal human rights. Ancient societies had "elaborate systems of duties... conceptions of justice, political legitimacy, and human flourishing that sought to realize human dignity, flourishing, or well-being entirely independent of human rights". The modern concept of human rights developed during the early Modern period, alongside the European secularization of Judeo-Christian ethics. The true forerunner of human rights discourse was the concept of natural rights which appeared as part of the medieval Natural law tradition that became prominent during the Enlightenment with such philosophers as John Locke, Francis Hutcheson, and Jean-Jacques Burlamaqui, and featured prominently in the political discourse of the American Revolution and the French Revolution.

History of Human Rights

The modern sense of human rights can be traced to Renaissance Europe and the Protestant Reformation, alongside the disappearance of the feudal authoritarianism and religious conservativism that dominated the Middle

Ages. Human rights were defined as a result of European scholars attempting to form a "secularized version of Judeo-Christian ethics". Although ideas of rights and liberty have existed in some form for much of human history, they do not resemble the modern conception of human rights. According to Jack Donnelly, in the ancient world, "traditional societies typically have had elaborate systems of duties... conceptions of justice, political legitimacy, and human flourishing that sought to realize human dignity, flourishing, or well-being entirely independent of human rights. These institutions and practices are alternative to, rather than different formulations of, human rights". The most commonly held view is that concept of human rights evolved in the West, and that while earlier cultures had important ethical concepts, they generally lacked a concept of human rights. For example, McIntyre argues there is no word for "right" in any language before 1400. Medieval charters of liberty such as the English Magna Carta were not charters of human rights, rather they were the foundation and constituted a form of limited political and legal agreement to address specific political circumstances, in the case of Magna Carta later being recognised in the course of early modern debates about rights.

One of the oldest records of human rights is the statute of Kalisz (1264), giving privileges to the Jewish minority in the Kingdom of Poland such as protection from discrimination and hate speech. The basis of most modern legal interpretations of human rights can be traced back to recent European history. The Twelve Articles (1525) are considered to be the first record of human rights in Europe. They were part of the peasants' demands raised towards the Swabian League in the German Peasants' War in Germany. In Spain in 1542 Bartolomé de Las Casas argued against Juan Ginés de Sepúlveda in the famous Valladolid debate, Sepúlveda mainted an Aristotelian view of humanity as divided into classes of different worth, while Las Casas argued in favor of equal rights to freedom of slavery for all humans regardless of race or religion. In Britain in 1683, the English Bill of Rights (or "An Act Declaring the Rights and Liberties of the Subject and Settling the Succession of the Crown") and the Scottish Claim of Right each made illegal a range of oppressive governmental actions. Two major revolutions occurred during the 18th century, in the United States (1776) and in France (1789), leading to the adoption of the United States Declaration of Independence and the French Declaration of the Rights of Man and of the Citizen respectively, both of which established certain legal rights. Additionally, the Virginia Declaration of Rights of 1776 encoded into law a number of fundamental civil rights and civil freedoms.

> We hold these truths to be self-evident, that all men are created equal, that they are endowed by their Creator with certain unalienable Rights, that among these are Life, Liberty and the pursuit of Happiness. (United States Declaration of Independence, 1776)

These were followed by developments in philosophy of human rights by philosophers such as Thomas Paine, John Stuart Mill and G.W.F. Hegel during the 18th and 19th centuries. The term human rights probably came into use some time between Paine's The Rights of Man and William Lloyd Garrison's 1831 writings in The Liberator, in which he stated that he was trying to enlist his readers in "the great cause of human rights".

In the 19th century, human rights became a central concern over the issue of slavery. A number of reformers, such as William Wilberforce in Britain, worked towards the abolition of slavery. This was achieved in the British Empire by the Slave Trade Act 1807 and the Slavery Abolition Act 1833. In the United States, all the northern states had abolished the institution of slavery between 1777 and 1804, although southern states clung tightly to the "peculiar institution". Conflict and debates over the expansion of slavery to new territories constituted one of the reasons for the southern states' secession and the American Civil War. During the reconstruction period immediately following the war, several amendments to the United States Constitution were made. These included the 13th amendment, banning slavery, the 14th amendment, assuring full citizenship and civil rights to all people born in the United States, and the 15th amendment, guaranteeing African Americans the right to vote.

Many groups and movements have achieved profound social changes over the course of the 20th century in the name of human rights. In Europe and North America, labour unions brought about laws granting workers the right to strike, establishing minimum work conditions and forbidding or regulating child labor. The women's rights movement succeeded in gaining for many women the right to vote. National liberation movements in many countries succeeded in driving out colonial powers. One of the most influential was Mahatma Gandhi's movement to free his native India from British rule. Movements by long-oppressed racial and religious minorities succeeded in many parts of the world, among them the African American

Civil Rights Movement, and more recent diverse identity politics movements, on behalf of women and minorities in the United States.

The establishment of the International Committee of the Red Cross, the 1864 Lieber Code and the first of the Geneva Conventions in 1864 laid the foundations of International humanitarian law, to be further developed following the two World Wars.

The World Wars, and the huge losses of life and gross abuses of human rights that took place during them, were a driving force behind the development of modern human rights instruments. The League of Nations was established in 1919 at the negotiations over the Treaty of Versailles following the end of World War I. The League's goals included disarmament, preventing war through collective security, settling disputes between countries through negotiation and diplomacy, and improving global welfare. Enshrined in its charter was a mandate to promote many of the rights later included in the Universal Declaration of Human Rights.

At the 1945 Yalta Conference, the Allied Powers agreed to create a new body to supplant the League's role; this was to be the United Nations. The United Nations has played an important role in international human-rights law since its creation. Following the World Wars, the United Nations and its members developed much of the discourse and the bodies of law that now make up international humanitarian law and international human rights law.

Philosophy of Human Rights

The philosophy of human rights attempts to examine the underlying basis of the concept of human rights and critically looks at its content and justification. Several theoretical approaches have been advanced to explain how and why human rights have become a part of social expectations.

One of the oldest Western philosophies of human rights is that they are a product of a natural law, stemming from different philosophical or religious grounds. Other theories hold that human rights codify moral behavior which is a human social product developed by a process of biological and social evolution (associated with Hume). Human rights are also described as a sociological pattern of rule setting (as in the sociological theory of law and the work of Weber). These approaches include the notion that individuals in a society accept rules from legitimate authority in exchange for security and economic advantage (as in Rawls) – a social contract. The two theories that dominate contemporary human rights discussion are the interest theory and the will theory. Interest theory argues that the principal function of human rights is to protect and promote certain essential human interests, while will theory attempts to establish the validity of human rights based on the unique human capacity for freedom.

The strong claims made by human rights to universality have led to persistent criticism. Philosophers who have criticized the concept of human rights include Jeremy Bentham, Edmund Burke, Friedrich Nietzsche and Karl Marx. Political philosophy professor Charles Blattberg argues that discussion of human rights, being abstract, demotivates people from upholding the values that rights are meant to affirm. The Internet Encyclopedia of Philosophy gives particular attention to two types of criticisms: the one questioning universality of human rights and the one denying them objective ground. Alain Pellet, an international law scholar, criticizes "human rightism" approach as denying the principle of sovereignty and claiming a special place for human rights among the branches of international law; Alain de Benoist questions human rights premises of human equality. David Kennedy had listed pragmatic worries and polemical charges concerning human rights in 2002 in Harvard Human Rights Journal.

Classification of Human rights

Human rights can be classified and organized in a number of different ways, at an international level the most common categorisation of human rights has been to split them into civil and political rights, and economic, social and cultural rights.

Civil and political rights are enshrined in articles 3 to 21 of the Universal Declaration of Human Rights (UDHR) and in the International Covenant on Civil and Political Rights (ICCPR). Economic, social and cultural rights are enshrined in articles 22 to 28 of the Universal Declaration of Human Rights (UDHR) and in the International Covenant on Economic, Social and Cultural Rights (ICESCR).

Indivisibility

The UDHR included both economic, social and cultural rights and civil and political rights because it was based on the principle that the different rights could only successfully exist in combination:

> The ideal of free human beings enjoying civil and political freedom and freedom from fear and want can only be achieved if conditions are created whereby everyone may enjoy his civil and political rights, as well as his social, economic and cultural rights. (International Covenant on Civil and Political Rights and the International Covenant on Economic Social and Cultural Rights, 1966)

This is held to be true because without civil and political rights the public cannot assert their economic, social and cultural rights. Similarly, without livelihoods and a working society, the public cannot assert or make use of civil or political rights (known as the full belly thesis).

The indivisibility and interdependence of all human rights has been confirmed by the 1993 Vienna Declaration and Programme of Action:

> All human rights are universal, indivisible and interdependent and related. The international community must treat human rights globally in a fair and equal manner, on the same footing, and with the same emphasis. (Vienna Declaration and Programme of Action, World Conference on Human Rights, 1993).

This statement was again endorsed at the 2005 World Summit in New York (paragraph 121).

Although accepted by the signatories to the UDHR, most do not in practice give equal weight to the different types of rights. Some Western cultures have often given priority to civil and political rights, sometimes at the expense of economic and social rights such as the right to work, to education, health and housing. Similarly the ex Soviet bloc countries and Asian countries have tended to give priority to economic, social and cultural rights, but have often failed to provide civil and political rights.

Categorization

Opponents of the indivisibility of human rights argue that economic, social and cultural rights are fundamentally different from civil and political rights and require completely different approaches. Economic, social and cultural rights are argued to be:

- positive, meaning that they require active provision of entitlements by the state (as opposed to the state being required only to prevent the breach of rights)
- resource-intensive, meaning that they are expensive and difficult to provide

- progressive, meaning that they will take significant time to implement
- vague, meaning they cannot be quantitatively measured, and whether they are adequately provided or not is difficult to judge
- ideologically divisive/political, meaning that there is no consensus on what should and shouldn't be provided as a right
- socialist, as opposed to capitalist
- non-justiciable, meaning that their provision, or the breach of them, cannot be judged in a court of law
- aspirations or goals, as opposed to real 'legal' rights

Similarly civil and political rights are categorized as:

- negative, meaning the state can protect them simply by taking no action
- cost-free
- immediate, meaning they can be immediately provided if the state decides to
- precise, meaning their provision is easy to judge and measure
- non-ideological/non-political
- capitalist
- justiciable
- real 'legal' rights

Olivia Ball and Paul Gready argue that for both civil and political rights and economic, social and cultural rights, it is easy to find examples which do not fit into the above categorisation. Among several others, they highlight the fact that maintaining a judicial system, a fundamental requirement of the civil right to due process before the law and other rights relating to judicial process, is positive, resource-intensive, progressive and vague, while the social right to housing is precise, justiciable and can be a real 'legal' right.

Three Generations

Another categorization, offered by Karel Vasak, is that there are three generations of human rights: first-generation civil and political rights (right to life and political participation), second-generation economic, social and cultural rights (right to subsistence) and third-generation solidarity rights (right to peace, right to clean environment). Out of these generations, the third generation is the most debated and lacks both legal and political recognition. This categorisation is at odds with the indivisibility of rights, as it implicitly states that some rights can exist without others. Prioritisation of rights for pragmatic reasons is however a widely accepted necessity. Human rights expert Philip Alston argues:

> If every possible human rights element is deemed to be essential or necessary, then nothing will be treated as though it is truly important.

He, and others, urge caution with prioritisation of rights:

> [T]he call for prioritizing is not to suggest that any obvious violations of rights can be ignored. (Philip Alston)

> Priorities, where necessary, should adhere to core concepts (such as reasonable attempts at progressive realization) and principles (such as non-discrimination, equality and participation. (Olivia Ball, Paul Gready)

Some human rights are said to be "inalienable rights". The term inalienable rights (or unalienable rights) refers to "a set of human rights that are fundamental, are not awarded by human power, and cannot be surrendered."

International Protection

In the aftermath of the atrocities of World War II, there was increased concern for the social and legal protection of human rights as fundamental freedoms. The foundation of the United Nations and the provisions of the United Nations Charter provided a basis for a comprehensive system of international law and practise for the protection of human rights. Since then, international human rights law has been characterized by a linked system of conventions, treaties, organisations, and political bodies, rather than any single entity or set of laws.

United Nations Charter

The provisions of the United Nations Charter provided a basis for the development of international human rights protection. The preamble of the charter provides that the members "reaffirm faith in fundamental human rights, in the equal rights of men and women" and Article 1(3) of the United Nations charter states that one of the purposes of the UN is: "to achieve international cooperation in solving international problems of an economic, social, cultural, or humanitarian character, and in promoting and encouraging respect for human rights and for fundamental freedoms for all without distinction as to race, sex, language, or religion". Article 55 provides that:

The United Nations shall promote:

a) higher standards of living, full employment, and conditions of economic and social progress and development;

b) solutions of international economic, social, health, and related problems;

c) international cultural and educational cooperation;

d) universal respect for, and observance of, human rights and fundamental freedoms for all without distinction as to race, sex, language, or religion.

Of particular importance is Article 56 of the charter:"All Members pledge themselves to take joint and separate action in co-operation with the Organization for the achievement of the purposes set forth in Article 55." This is a binding treaty provision applicable to both the Organisation and its members and has been taken to constitute a legal obligation for the members of the United Nations. Overall, the references to human rights in the Charter are general and vague. The Charter does not contain specific legal rights, nor does it mandate any enforcement procedures to protect these rights. Despite this, the significance of the espousal of human rights within the UN charter must not be understated. The importance of human rights on the global stage can be traced to the importance of human rights within the United Nations framework and the UN Charter can be seen as the starting point for the development of a broad array of declarations, treaties, implementation and enforcement mechanisms, UN organs, committees and reports on the protection of human rights. The rights espoused in the UN charter would be codified and defined in the International Bill of Human Rights, composing the Universal Declaration of Human Rights, the International Covenant on Civil and Political Rights and the International Covenant on Economic, Social and Cultural Rights.

Universal Declaration of Human Rights

The Universal Declaration of Human Rights (UDHR) was adopted by the United Nations General Assembly in 1948, partly in response to the atrocities of World War II. Although the UDHR was a non-binding resolution, it is now considered by some to have acquired the force of international customary law which may be invoked in appropriate circumstances by national and other judiciaries. The UDHR urges member nations to promote a number of human, civil, economic and social rights, asserting these rights as part of the "foundation of freedom, justice and peace in the world." The declaration was the first international legal effort to limit the behaviour of states and press upon them duties to their citizens following the model of the rights-duty duality.

> ...recognition of the inherent dignity and of the equal and inalienable rights of all members of the human family is the foundation of freedom, justice and peace in the world. (Preamble to the Universal Declaration of Human Rights, 1948)

The UDHR was framed by members of the Human Rights Commission, with former First Lady Eleanor Roosevelt as Chair, who began to discuss an International Bill of Rights in 1947. The members of the Commission did not immediately agree on the form of such a bill of rights, and whether, or how, it should be enforced. The Commission proceeded to frame the UDHR and accompanying treaties, but the UDHR quickly became the priority. Canadian law professor John Humphrey and French lawyer René Cassin were responsible for much of the cross-national research and the structure of the document respectively, where the articles of the declaration were interpretative of the general principle of the preamble. The document was structured by Cassin to include the basic principles of dignity, liberty, equality and brotherhood in the first two articles, followed successively by rights pertaining to individuals; rights of individuals in relation to each other and to groups; spiritual, public and political rights; and economic, social and cultural rights. The final three articles place, according to Cassin, rights in the context of limits, duties and the social and political order in which they are to be realized. Humphrey and Cassin intended the rights in the UDHR to be legally enforceable through some means, as is reflected in the third clause of the preamble:

> Whereas it is essential, if man is not to be compelled to have recourse, as a last resort, to rebellion against tyranny and oppression, that human rights should be protected by the rule of law.(Preamble to the Universal Declaration of Human Rights, 1948).

Some of the UDHR was researched and written by a committee of international experts on human rights, including representatives from all continents and all major religions, and drawing on consultation with leaders such as Mahatma Gandhi. The inclusion of civil, political, economic, social and cultural rights was predicated on the assumption that all human rights are indivisible and that the different types of rights listed are inextricably linked. This principle was not then opposed by any member states (the declaration was adopted unanimously, Byelorussian SSR, Czechoslovakia, Poland, Saudi Arabia, Ukrainian SSR, Union of South Africa, USSR, Yugoslavia.); however, this principle was later subject to significant challenges.

The Universal Declaration was bifurcated into treaties, a Covenant on Civil and Political Rights and another on social, economic, and cultural rights, due to questions about the relevance and propriety of economic and social provisions in covenants on human rights. Both covenants begin with the right of people to self-determination and to sovereignty over their natural resources. This debate over whether human rights are more fundamental than economic rights has continued to the present day.

The drafters of the Covenants initially intended only one instrument. The original drafts included only political and civil rights, but economic and social rights were also proposed. The disagreement over which rights were basic human rights resulted in there being two covenants. The debate was whether economic and social rights are aspirational, as contrasted with basic human rights which all people possess purely by being human, because economic and social rights depend on wealth and the availability of resources. In addition, which social and economic rights should be recognised depends on ideology or economic theories, in contrast to basic human rights, which are defined purely by the nature (mental and physical abilities) of human beings. It was debated whether economic rights were appropriate subjects for binding obligations and whether the lack of consensus over such rights would dilute the strength of political-civil rights. There was wide agreement and clear recognition that the means required to enforce or induce compliance with socio-economic undertakings were different from the means required for civil-political rights.

This debate and the desire for the greatest number of signatories to human-rights law led to the two covenants. The Soviet bloc and a number of developing countries had argued for the inclusion of all rights in a so-called Unity Resolution. Both covenants allowed states to derogate some rights. Those in favor of a single treaty could not gain sufficient consensus.

International Treaties

In 1966, the International Covenant on Civil and Political Rights (ICCPR) and the International Covenant on Economic, Social and Cultural Rights (ICESCR) were adopted by the United Nations, between them making the rights contained in the UDHR binding on all states that have signed this treaty, creating human-rights law.

Since then numerous other treaties (pieces of legislation) have been offered at the international level. They are generally known as human rights instruments. Some of the most significant, referred to (with ICCPR and ICESCR) as "the seven core treaties", are:

- Convention on the Elimination of All Forms of Racial Discrimination (CERD) (adopted 1966, entry into force: 1969)
- Convention on the Elimination of All Forms of Discrimination Against Women (CEDAW) (adopted 1979, entry into force: 1981)
- United Nations Convention Against Torture (CAT) (adopted 1984, entry into force: 1984)
- Convention on the Rights of the Child (CRC) (adopted 1989, entry into force: 1989)
- Convention on the Rights of Persons with Disabilities (CRPD) (adopted 2006, entry into force: 2008)
- International Convention on the Protection of the Rights of All Migrant Workers and Members of their Families (ICRMW or more often MWC) (adopted 1990, entry into force: 2003)

Customary International Law

In addition to protection by international treaties, customary international law may protect some human rights, such as the prohibition of torture, genocide and slavery and the principle of non-discrimination.

International Humanitarian Law

The Geneva Conventions came into being between 1864 and 1949 as a result of efforts by Henry Dunant, the founder of the International Committee of the Red Cross. The conventions safeguard the human rights of individuals involved in armed conflict, and build on the Hague Conventions of 1899 and 1907, the international community's first attempt to formalize the laws of war and war crimes in the nascent body of secular international law. The conventions were revised as a result of World War II and readopted by the international community in 1949.

United Nations System

Under the mandate of the UN charter, the and the multilateral UN human rights treaties, the United Nations (UN) as an intergovernmental body seeks to apply international jurisdiction for universal human-rights legislation. Within the UN machinery, human-rights issues are primarily the concern of the United Nations Security Council and the United Nations Human Rights Council, and there are numerous committees within the UN with responsibilities for safeguarding different human-rights treaties. The most senior body of the UN in the sphere of human rights is the Office of the High Commissioner for Human Rights. The United Nations has an international mandate to:

> achieve international co-operation in solving international problems of an economic, social, cultural, or humanitarian character, and in promoting and encouraging respect for human rights and for fundamental freedoms for all without distinction as to race, gender, language, or religion. (Article 1–3 of the United Nations Charter).

Political bodies

Security Council

The United Nations Security Council has the primary responsibility for maintaining international peace and security and is the only body of the UN that can authorize the use of force. It has been criticised for failing to take action to prevent human rights abuses, including the Darfur crisis, the Srebrenica massacre and the Rwandan Genocide. For example, critics blamed the presence of non-democracies on the Security Council for its failure regarding.

On April 28, 2006 the Security Council adopted resolution 1674 that reaffirmed the responsibility to protect populations from genocide, war crimes, ethnic cleansing and crimes against humanity" and committed the Security Council to action to protect civilians in armed conflict.

General Assembly

The United Nations General Assembly, under Article 13 of the UN Charter, has the power to initiate studies and make recommendations on human rights issues. Under this provision, the general assembly passed the Universal Declaration of Human Rights in 1948, and since then a wide variety of other human rights instruments. The assembly has several subsidiary organs that deal with specific human rights issues, such as the Special Committee on Decolonisation and the Special Commission against Apartheid (no longer operational). In addition the general assembly has set up a number of subsidiary organs that consider human rights issues in a number of high-profile contexts: such as the UN Council on Namibia, the Special Committee to Investigate Israeli Practises in the Occupied territories and the Committee on the Exercise of the Inalienable rights of the Palestine People.

Human Rights Council

The United Nations Human Rights Council, created at the 2005 World Summit to replace the United Nations Commission on Human Rights, has a mandate to investigate violations of human rights. The Human Rights Council is a subsidiary body of the General Assembly and reports directly to it. It ranks below the Security Council, which is the final authority for the interpretation of the United Nations Charter. Forty-seven of the one hundred ninety-one member states sit on the council, elected by simple majority in a secret ballot of the United Nations General Assembly. Members serve a maximum of six years and may have their membership suspended for gross human rights abuses. The Council is based in Geneva, and meets three times a year; with additional meetings to respond to urgent situations.

Independent experts (rapporteurs) are retained by the Council to investigate alleged human rights abuses and to provide the Council with reports.

The Human Rights Council may request that the Security Council take action when human rights violations occur. This action may be direct actions, may involve sanctions, and the Security Council may also refer cases to the International Criminal Court (ICC) even if the issue being referred is outside the normal jurisdiction of the ICC.

Treaty bodies

In addition to the political bodies whose mandate flows from the UN charter, the UN has set up a number of treaty-based bodies, comprising committees of independent experts who monitor compliance with human rights standards and norms flowing from the core international human rights treaties. They are supported by and are created by the treaty that they monitor, With the exception of theCESCR, which was established under a resolution of the Economic and Social Council to carry out the monitoring functions originally assigned to that body under the Covenant, they are technically autonomous bodies, established by the treaties that they monitor and accountable to the state parties of those treaties - rather than subsidiary to the United Nations. Though in practise they are closely intertwined with the United Nations system and are supported by the UN High Commissioner for Human Rights (UNHCHR) and the UN Center for Human Rights.

The Human Rights Committee promotes participation with the standards of the ICCPR. The eighteen members of the committee express opinions on member countries and make judgments on individual complaints against countries which have ratified an Optional Protocol to the treaty. The judgments, termed "views", are not legally binding.

The Committee on Economic, Social and Cultural Rights monitors the ICESCR and makes general comments on ratifying countries performance. It will have the power to receive complaints against the countries that opted into the Optional Protocol once it has come into force. It is important to note that unlike the other treaty bodies, the economic committee is not an autonomous body responsible to the treaty parties, but directly responsible to the Economic and Social Council and ultimately to the General Assembly. This means that the Economic Committee faces particular difficulties at its disposal only relatively "weak" means of implementation in comparison to other treaty bodies. Particular difficulties noted by commentators include: perceived vagueness of the principles of the treaty, relative lack of legal texts and decisions, ambivalence of many states in addressing economic, social and cultural rights, comparatively few non-governmental organisations focused on the area and problems with obtaining relevant and precise information.

The Committee on the Elimination of Racial Discrimination monitors the CERD and conducts regular reviews of countries' performance. It can make judgments on complaints against member states allowing it, but these are not legally binding. It issues warnings to attempt to prevent serious contraventions of the convention.

The Committee on the Elimination of Discrimination against Women monitors the CEDAW. It receives states' reports on their performance and comments on them, and can make judgments on complaints against countries which have opted into the 1999 Optional Protocol.

The Committee Against Torture monitors the CAT and receives states' reports on their performance every four years and comments on them. Its subcommittee may visit and inspect countries which have opted into the Optional Protocol.

The Committee on the Rights of the Child monitors the CRC and makes comments on reports submitted by states every five years. It does not have the power to receive complaints.

The Committee on Migrant Workers was established in 2004 and monitors the ICRMW and makes comments on reports submitted by states every five years. It will have the power to receive complaints of specific violations only once ten member states allow it.

The Committee on the Rights of Persons with Disabilities was established in 2008 to monitor the Convention on the Rights of Persons with Disabilities. It has the power to receive complaints against the countries which have opted into the Optional Protocol to the Convention on the Rights of Persons with Disabilities.

Each treaty body receives secretariat support from the Human Rights Council and Treaties Division of Office of the High Commissioner on Human Rights (OHCHR) in Geneva except CEDAW, which is supported by the Division for the Advancement of Women (DAW). CEDAW formerly held all its sessions at United Nations headquarters in New York but now frequently meets at the United Nations Office in Geneva; the other treaty bodies meet in Geneva. The Human Rights Committee usually holds its March session in New York City.

Regional Human Rights Regimes

International human rights regime's are in several cases "nested" within more comprehensive and overlapping regional agreements. These regional regimes can be seen as relatively independently coherent human rights sub-regimes. Three principle regional human rights instruments can be identified, the African Charter on Human and Peoples' Rights, the American Convention on Human Rights (the Americas) and the European Convention on Human Rights. The European Convention on Human Rights has since 1950 defined and guaranteed human rights and fundamental freedoms in Europe. All 47 member states of the Council of Europe have signed the Convention and are therefore under the jurisdiction of the European Court of Human Rights in Strasbourg.

NON-GOVERNMENTAL ACTORS

International non-governmental human rights organizations such as Amnesty International, Human Rights Watch, International Service for Human Rights and FIDH monitor what they see as human rights issues around the world and promote their views on the subject. Human rights organizations have been said to “”translate complex international issues into activities to be undertaken by concerned citizens in their own community”. Human rights organizations frequently engage in lobbying and advocacy in an effort to convince the United Nations, supranational bodies and national governments to adopt their policies on human rights. Many human-rights organizations have observer status at the various UN bodies tasked with protecting human rights. A new (in 2009) nongovernmental human-rights conference is the Oslo Freedom Forum, a gathering described by The Economist as “on its way to becoming a human-rights equivalent of the Davos economic forum.” The same article noted that human-rights advocates are more and more divided amongst themselves over how violations of human rights are to be defined, notably as regards the Middle East.

There is criticism of human-rights organisations who use their status but allegedly move away from their stated goals. For example, Gerald M. Steinberg, an Israel-based academic, maintains that NGOs take advantage of a “halo effect” and are “given the status of impartial moral watchdogs” by governments and the media. Such critics claim that this may be seen at various governmental levels, including when human-rights groups testify before investigation committees.

Human Rights Defenders

A human rights defender is someone who, individually or with others, acts to promote or protect human rights. Human rights defenders are those men and women who act peacefully for the promotion and protection of those rights.

Corporations

Multinational companies play an increasingly large role in the world, and have been responsible for numerous human rights abuses. Although the legal and moral environment surrounding the actions of governments is reasonably well developed, that surrounding multinational companies is both controversial and ill-defined. Multinational companies’ primary responsibility is to their shareholders, not to those affected by their actions. Such companies may be larger than the economies of some of the states within which they operate, and can wield significant economic and political power. No international treaties exist to specifically cover the behavior of companies with regard to human rights, and national legislation is very variable. Jean Ziegler, Special Rapporteur of the UN Commission on Human Rights on the right to food stated in a report in 2003:

> [T]he growing power of transnational corporations and their extension of power through privatization, deregulation and the rolling back of the State also mean that it is now time to develop binding legal norms that hold corporations to human rights standards and circumscribe potential abuses of their position of power.—Jean Ziegler

In August 2003 the Human Rights Commission's Sub-Commission on the Promotion and Protection of Human Rights produced draft Norms on the responsibilities of transnational corporations and other business enterprises with regard to human rights. These were considered by the Human Rights Commission in 2004, but have no binding status on corporations and are not monitored.

Human Rights Violations

Human rights violations occur when actions by state (or non-state) actors abuse, ignore, or deny basic human rights (including civil, political, cultural, social, and economic rights). Furthermore, violations of human rights can occur when any state or non-state actor breaches any part of the UDHR treaty or other international human rights or humanitarian law. In regard to human rights violations of United Nations laws, Article 39 of the United Nations Charter designates the UN Security Council (or an appointed authority) as the only tribunal that may determine UN human rights violations.

Human rights abuses are monitored by United Nations committees, national institutions and governments and by many independent non-governmental organizations, such as Amnesty International, International Federation of Human Rights, Human Rights Watch, World Organisation Against Torture, Freedom House, International Freedom of Expression Exchange and Anti-Slavery International. These organisations collect evidence and documentation of alleged human rights abuses and apply pressure to enforce human rights laws.

Wars of aggression, war crimes and crimes against humanity, including genocide, are breaches of International humanitarian law and represent the most serious of human rights violations.

In efforts to eliminate violations of human rights, building awareness and protesting inhumane treatment has often led to calls for action and sometimes improved conditions. The UN Security Council has interceded with peace keeping forces, and other states and treaties (NATO) have intervened in situations to protect human rights.

Substantive Rights

Right to Life

The right to life is the essential right that a human being has the right not to be killed by another human being. The concept of a right to life is central to debates on the issues of abortion, capital punishment, euthanasia, self defense and war. According to many human rights activists, the death penalty violates this right. The United Nations has called on states retaining the death penalty to establish a moratorium on capital punishment with a view to its abolition. States which do not do so face considerable moral and political pressure.

Freedom from Torture

Throughout history, torture has been used as a method of political re-education, interrogation, punishment, and coercion. In addition to state-sponsored torture, individuals or groups may be motivated to inflict torture on others for similar reasons to those of a state; however, the motive for torture can also be for the sadistic gratification of the torturer, as in the Moors murders.

Torture is prohibited under international law and the domestic laws of most countries in the 21st century. It is considered to be a violation of human rights, and is declared to be unacceptable by Article 5 of the UN Universal Declaration of Human Rights. Signatories of the Third Geneva Convention and Fourth Geneva Convention officially agree not to torture prisoners in armed conflicts. Torture is also prohibited by the United Nations Convention Against Torture, which has been ratified by 147 states.

National and international legal prohibitions on torture derive from a consensus that torture and similar ill-treatment are immoral, as well as impractical. Despite these international conventions, organizations that monitor abuses of human rights (e.g. Amnesty International, the International Rehabilitation Council for Torture Victims) report widespread use condoned by states in many regions of the world. Amnesty International estimates that at least 81 world governments currently practice torture, some of them openly.

Freedom from Slavery

Freedom from slavery is an internationally recognized human right. Article 4 of the Universal Declaration of Human Rights states:

> No one shall be held in slavery or servitude; slavery and the slave trade shall be prohibited in all their forms.

Despite this, the number of slaves today is higher than at any point in history, remaining as high as 12 million to 27 million, Most are debt slaves, largely in South Asia, who are under debt bondage incurred by lenders, sometimes even for generations. Human trafficking is primarily for prostituting women and children into sex industries.

Groups such as the American Anti-Slavery Group, Anti-Slavery International, Free the Slaves, the Anti-Slavery Society, and the Norwegian Anti-Slavery Society continue to campaign to rid the world of slavery.

Right to a Fair Rrial

Everyone is entitled in full equality to a fair and public hearing by an independent and impartial tribunal, in the determination of his rights and obligations and of any criminal charge against him.

The right to a fair trial has been defined in numerous regional and international human rights instruments. It is one of the most extensive human rights and all international human rights instruments enshrine it in more than one article. The right to a fair trial is one of the most litigated human rights and substantial case law has been established on the interpretation of this human right. Despite variations in wording and placement of the various fair trial rights, international human rights instrument define the right to a fair trial in broadly the same terms. The aim of the right is to ensure the proper administration of justice. As a minimum the right to fair trial includes the following fair trial rights in civil and criminal proceedings:

- the right to be heard by a competent, independent and impartial tribunal
- the right to a public hearing
- the right to be heard within a reasonable time
- the right to counsel
- the right to interpretation

Freedom of Speech

Freedom of speech is the freedom to speak freely without censorship. The term freedom of expression is sometimes used synonymously, but includes any act of seeking, receiving and imparting information or ideas, regardless of the medium used. In practice, the right to freedom of speech is not absolute in any country and the right is commonly subject to limitations, such as on libel, slander, obscenity, incitement to commit a crime, etc. The right to freedom of expression is recognized as a human right under Article 19 of the Universal Declaration of Human Rights and recognized in international human rights law in the International Covenant on Civil and Political Rights (ICCPR). Article 19 of the ICCPR states that "[e]veryone shall have the right to hold opinions without interference" and "everyone shall have the right to freedom of expression; this right shall include freedom to seek, receive and impart information and ideas of all kinds, regardless of frontiers, either orally, in writing or in print, in the form of art, or through any other media of his choice".

Freedom of Thought, Conscience and Religion

Freedom of thought, conscience and religion are closely related rights that protect the freedom of an individual or community, in public or private, to think and freely hold conscientious beliefs and to manifest religion or belief in teaching, practice, worship, and observance; the concept is generally recognized also to include the freedom to change religion or not to follow any religion. The freedom to leave or discontinue membership in a religion or religious group—in religious terms called "apostasy"—is also a fundamental part of religious freedom, covered by Article 18 of the Universal Declaration of Human Rights.

Human rights groups such as Amnesty International organises campaigns to protect those arrested and or incarcerated as a prisoner of conscience because of their conscientious beliefs, particularly concerning intellectual, political and artistic freedom of expression and association. In legislation, a conscience clause is a provision in a statute that excuses a health professional from complying with the law (for example legalising surgical or pharmaceutical abortion) if it is incompatible with religious or conscientious beliefs.

Future Generations

In 1997 UNESCO adopted the Declaration on the Responsibilities of the Present Generation Towards the Future Generation. The Declaration opens with the words:

> Mindful of the will of the peoples, set out solemnly in the Charter of the United Nations, to 'save succeeding generations from the scourge of war' and to safeguard the values and principles enshrined in the Universal Declaration of Human Rights, and all other relevant instruments of international law. (Declaration on the Responsibilities of the Present Generation Towards the Future Generation)

Article 1 of the declaration states "the present generations have the responsibility of ensuring that the needs and interests of present and future generations are fully safeguarded." The preamble to the declaration states that "at this point in history, the very existence of humankind and its environment are threatened" and the declaration covers a variety of issues including protection of the environment, the human genome, biodiversity, cultural heritage, peace, development, and education. The preamble recalls that the responsibilities of the present generations towards future generations has been referred to in various international instruments, including the Convention for the Protection of the World Cultural and Natural Heritage (UNESCO 1972), the United Nations Framework Convention on Climate Change and the Convention on Biological Diversity (Rio de Janeiro, 1992), the Rio Declaration on Environment and Development (UN Conference on Environment and Development, 1992), the Vienna Declaration and Programme of Action (World Conference on Human Rights, 1993) and a number of UN General Assembly resolutions relating to the protection of the global climate for present and future generations adopted since 1990.

Sexual Orientation and Gender Identity

Sexual orientation and gender identity rights relate to the expression of sexual orientation and gender identity based on the right to respect for private life and the right not to be discriminated against on the ground of "other status" as defined in various human rights conventions, such as article 17 and 26 in the United Nations International Covenant on Civil and Political Rights and article 8 and article 14 in the European Convention on Human Rights.

Through the way many because of their religious beliefs claim that they support human rights in general while denying that LGBT rights are human rights, LGBT rights stand prominent in the very defense of the universal principle of the human rights. If human rights are understood in a way that makes it possible to exclude the basic rights of certain groups only because of certain religious and cultural prejudices, we find that the principle of universality is taken right out of the human rights, and human rights are transformed to a set of rules only reflecting certain historically values.

Homosexuality is illegal in 76 countries, and is punishable by execution in seven countries. The criminalization of private, consensual, adult sexual relations, especially in countries where corporal or capital punishment is involved, is one of the primary concerns of LGBT human rights advocates.

Other issues include: government recognition of same-sex relationships, LGBT adoption, sexual orientation and military service, immigration equality, anti-discrimination laws, hate crime laws regarding violence against LGBT people, sodomy laws, anti-lesbianism laws, and equal age of consent for same-sex activity.

A global charter for sexual orientation and gender identity rights has been proposed in the form of the 'Yogyakarta Principles', a set of 29 principles whose authors say they apply International Human Rights Law statutes and precedent to situations relevant to LGBT people's experience. The principles were presented at a United Nations event in New York on November 7, 2007, co-sponsored by Argentina, Brazil and Uruguay.

The principles have been acknowledged with influencing the French proposed UN declaration on sexual orientation and gender identity, which focuses on ending violence, criminalization and capital punishment and does not include dialogue about same-sex marriage or right to start a family. The proposal was supported by 67 of the then 192 member countries of the United Nations, including all EU member states and the United States. An alternative statement opposing the proposal was initiated by Syria and signed by 57 member nations, including all 27 nations of the Arab League as well as Iran and North Korea.

Trade

Although both the Universal Declaration of Human Rights and the International Covenant on Economic, Social and Cultural Rights emphasize the importance of a right to work, neither of these documents explicitly mention trade as a mechanism for ensuring this fundamental right. And yet trade plays a key role in providing jobs.

Some experts argue that trade is inherent to human nature and that when governments inhibit international trade they directly inhibit the right to work and the other indirect benefits, like the right to education, that increased work and investment help accrue. Others have argued that the ability to trade does not affect everyone equally—often groups like the rural poor, indigenous groups and women are less likely to access the benefits of increased trade.

On the other hand, others think that it is no longer primarily individuals but companies that trade, and therefore it cannot be guaranteed as a human right. Additionally, trying to fit too many concepts under the umbrella of what qualifies as a human right has the potential to dilute their importance. Finally, it is difficult to define a right to trade as either "fair" or "just" in that the current trade regime produces winners and losers but its reform is likely to produce (different) winners and losers.

Water

In November 2002, the United Nations Committee on Economic, Social and Cultural Rights issued a non-binding comment affirming that access to water was a human right:

> the human right to water is indispensable for leading a life in human dignity. It is a prerequisite for the realization of other human rights.(United Nations Committee on Economic, Social and Cultural Rights),

This principle was reaffirmed at the 3rd and 4th World Water Councils in 2003 and 2006. This marks a departure from the conclusions of the 2nd World Water Forum in The Hague in 2000, which stated that water was a commodity to be bought and sold, not a right. There are calls from many NGOs and politicians to enshrine access to water as a binding human right, and not as a commodity. According to the United Nations, nearly 900 million people lack access to clean water and more than 2.6 billion people lack access to basic sanitation. On July 28, 2010, the UN declared water and sanitation as human rights. By declaring safe and clean drinking water and sanitation as a human right, the U.N. General Assembly made a step towards the Millennium Development Goal to ensure environmental sustainability, which in part aims to "halve, by 2015, the proportion of the population without sustainable access to safe drinking water and basic sanitation".

Reproductive Rights

Reproductive rights are rights relating to reproduction and reproductive health. The World Health Organisation defines reproductive rights as follows:

> Reproductive rights rest on the recognition of the basic right of all couples and individuals to decide freely and responsibly the number, spacing and timing of their children and to have the information and means to do so, and the right to attain the highest standard of sexual and reproductive health. They also include the right of all to make decisions concerning reproduction free of discrimination, coercion and violence.(World Health Organisation)

Reproductive rights were first established as a subset of human rights at the United Nations 1968 International Conference on Human Rights. The sixteenth article of the resulting Proclamation of Teheran states, "Parents have a basic human right to determine freely and responsibly the number and the spacing of their children."

Reproductive rights may include some or all of the following rights: the right to legal or safe abortion, the right to control one's reproductive functions, the right to quality reproductive healthcare, and the right to education and access in order to make reproductive choices free from coercion, discrimination, and violence.

Reproductive rights may also be understood to include education about contraception and sexually transmitted infections, and freedom from coerced sterilization and contraception, protection from gender-based practices such as female genital cutting (FGC) and male genital mutilation (MGM).

Information and Communication Technologies

In October 2009, Finland's Ministry of Transport and Communications announced that every person in Finland would have the legal right to Internet access. Since July 2010, the government has legally obligated telecommunications companies to offer broadband Internet access to every permanent residence and office. The connection must be "reasonably priced" and have a downstream rate of at least 1 Mbit/s. In March 2010, the BBC, having commissioned an opinion poll, reported that "almost four in five people around the world believe that access to the internet is a fundamental right." The poll, conducted by the polling company GlobeScan for the BBC World Service, collated the answers of 27,973 adult citizens across 26 countries to find that 79% of adults either strongly agreed or somewhat agreed with the statement: "access to the internet should be a fundamental right of all people".

Relationship with Other Topics

Human rights and the Environment

There are two basic conceptions of environmental human rights in the current human rights system. The first is that the right to a healthy or adequate environment is itself a human right (as seen in both Article 24 of the African Charter on Human and Peoples' Rights, and Article 11 of the San Salvador Protocol to the American Convention on Human Rights). The second conception is the idea that environmental human rights can be derived from other human rights, usually – the right to life, the right to health, the right to private family life and the right to property (among many others). This second theory enjoys much more widespread use in human rights courts around the world, as those rights are contained in many human rights documents.

The onset of various environmental issues, especially climate change, has created potential conflicts between different human rights. Human rights ultimately require a working ecosystem and healthy environment, but the granting of certain rights to individuals may damage these. Such as the conflict between right to decide number of offspring and the common need for a healthy environment, as noted in the tragedy of the commons. In the area of environmental rights, the responsibilities of multinational corporations, so far relatively unaddressed by human rights legislation, is of paramount consideration. Environmental Rights revolve largely around the idea of a right to a livable environment both for the present and the future generations.

National Security

With the exception of non-derogable human rights (international conventions class the right to life, the right to be free from slavery, the right to be free from torture and the right to be free from retroactive application of penal laws as non-derogable), the UN recognises that human rights can be limited or even pushed aside during times of national emergency – although the emergency must be actual, affect the whole population and the threat must be to the very existence of the nation. The declaration of emergency must also be a last resort and a temporary measure.

Rights that cannot be derogated for reasons of national security in any circumstances are known as peremptory norms or jus cogens. Such United Nations Charter obligations are binding on all states and cannot be modified by treaty.

Examples of national security being used to justify human rights violations include the Japanese American internment during World War II, Stalin's Great Purge, and the modern-day abuses of terror suspects rights by some countries, often in the name of the War on Terror.

Relativism and Universalism

The UDHR enshrines universal rights that apply to all humans equally, whichever geographical location, state, race or culture they belong to. However, in academia there is a dispute between scholars that advocate moral relativism and scholars that advocate moral universalism. Relativists do not argue against human rights, but concede that human rights are social constructed and are shaped by cultural and environmental contexts. Universalists argue that human rights have always existed, and apply to all people regardless of culture, race, sex, or religion.

More specifically, proponents of cultural relativism argue for acceptance of different cultures, which may have practices conflicting with human rights. Relativists caution that universalism could be used as a form of cultural, economic or political imperialism. The White Man's Burden is used as an example of imperialism and the destruction of local cultures justified by the desire to spread Eurocentric values. In particular, the concept of human rights is often claimed to be fundamentally rooted in a politically liberal outlook which, although generally accepted in Europe, Japan or North America, is not necessarily taken as standard elsewhere.

Opponents of relativism argue that some practices exist that violate the norms of all human cultures. A common example is female genital mutilation, which occurs in different cultures in Africa, Asia and South America. It is not mandated by any religion, but has become a tradition in many cultures. It is considered a violation of women's and girl's rights by much of the international community, and is outlawed in some countries.

The former Prime Ministers of Singapore, Lee Kuan Yew, and of Malaysia, Mahathir bin Mohamad both claimed in the 1990s that Asian values were significantly different from Western values and included a sense of loyalty and foregoing personal freedoms for the sake of social stability and prosperity, and therefore authoritarian government is more appropriate in Asia than democracy. Lee Kuan Yew argued that:

> What Asians value may not necessarily be what Americans or Europeans value. Westerners value the freedoms and liberties of the individual. As an Asian of Chinese cultural background, my values are for a government which is honest, effective, and efficient. (Lee Kuan Yew).

In response, critics have pointed out that cultural relativism could be used as a justification for authoritarianism. An example is in 1981, when the Iranian representative to the United Nations, Said Rajaie-Khorassani, articulated the position of his country regarding the Universal Declaration of Human Rights by saying that the UDHR was "a secular understanding of the Judeo-Christian tradition", which could not be implemented by Muslims without trespassing the Islamic law.

Defenders of moral universalism argue that relativistic arguments neglect the fact that modern human rights are new to all cultures, dating back no further than the UDHR in 1948. They argue that the UDHR was drafted by people from many different cultures and traditions, including a US Roman Catholic, a Chinese Confucian philosopher, a French zionist and a representative from the Arab League, amongst others, and drew upon advice from thinkers such as Mahatma Gandhi. Michael Ignatieff has argued that cultural relativism is almost exclusively an argument used by those who wield power in cultures which commit human rights abuses, and that those whose human rights are compromised are the powerless.

Although the argument between universalism and relativism is far from complete, it is an academic discussion in that all international human rights instruments adhere to the principle that human rights are universally applicable. The 2005 World Summit reaffirmed the international community's adherence to this principle:

> The universal nature of human rights and freedoms is beyond question. (2005 World Summit, paragraph 121).

References

Abouharb, R. and D. Cingranelli (2007). "Human Rights and Structural Adjustment". New York: Cambridge University Press.

Barsh, R. (1993). "Measuring Human Rights: Problems of Methodology and Purpose." Human Rights Quarterly 15: 87-121.

Chauhan, O.P. (2004). *Human Rights: Promotion and Protection.* Anmol Publications PVT. LTD.

Forsythe, David P. (2000). *Human Rights in International Relations.* Cambridge: Cambridge University Press. International Progress Organization.

Gerald M. Steinberg, Anne Herzberg and Jordan Berman (2012). *Best Practices for Human Rights and Humanitarian NGO Fact-Finding.* Martinus Nijhoff Publishers.

2

The International Bill of Human Rights

The International Bill of Human Rights consists of the Universal Declaration of Human Rights, the International Covenant on Economic, Social and Cultural Rights, and the International Covenant on Civil and Political Rights and its two Optional Protocols.

Human rights had already found expression in the Covenant of the League of Nations, which led, inter alia, to the creation of the International Labour Organisation. At the 1945 San Francisco Conference, held to draft the Charter of the United Nations, a proposal to embody a "Declaration on the Essential Rights of Man" was put forward but was not examined because it required more detailed consideration than was possible at the time. The Charter clearly speaks of "promoting and encouraging respect for human rights and for fundamental freedoms for all without distinction as to race, sex, language or religion" (Art. 1, para. 3). The idea of promulgating an "international bill of rights" was also considered by many as basically implicit in the Charter.

The Preparatory Commission of the United Nations, which met immediately after the closing session of the San Francisco Conference, recommended that the Economic and Social Council should, at its first session, establish a commission for the promotion of human rights as envisaged in Article 68 of the Charter. Accordingly, the Council established the Commission on Human Rights early in 1946.

At its first session, in 1946, the General Assembly considered a draft Declaration on Fundamental Human Rights and Freedoms and transmitted it to the Economic and Social Council "for reference to the Commission on Human Rights for consideration . . . in its preparation of an international bill of rights" (resolution 43 (I)). The Commission, at its first session early in 1947, authorized its officers to formulate what it termed "a preliminary draft International Bill of Human Rights". Later the work was taken over by a formal drafting committee, consisting of members of the Commission from eight States, selected with due regard for geographical distribution.

Towards the Universal Declaration

In the beginning, different views were expressed about the form the bill of rights should take. The Drafting Committee decided to prepare two documents: one in the form of a declaration, which would set forth general principles or standards of human rights; the other in the form of a convention, which would define specific rights and their limitations. Accordingly, the Committee transmitted to the Commission on Human Rights draft articles of an international declaration and an international convention on human rights. At its second session, in December 1947, the Commission decided to apply the term "International Bill of Human Rights" to the series of documents in preparation and established three working groups: one on the declaration, one on the convention (which it renamed "covenant") and one on implementation. The Commission revised the draft declaration at its third session, in May/June 1948, taking into consideration comments received from Governments. It did not have time, however, to consider the covenant or the question of implementation. The declaration was therefore submitted through the Economic and Social Council to the General Assembly, meeting in Paris.

By its resolution 217 A (III) of 10 December 1948, the General Assembly adopted the Universal Declaration of Human Rights as the first of these projected instruments.

Towards the International Covenants

On the same day that it adopted the Universal Declaration, the General Assembly requested the Commission on Human Rights to prepare, as a matter of priority, a draft covenant on human rights and draft measures of implementation. The Commission examined the text of the draft covenant in 1949 and the following year it revised the first 18 articles, on the basis of comments received from Governments. In 1950, the General Assembly declared that "the enjoyment of civic and political freedoms and of economic, social and cultural rights are interconnected and interdependent" (resolution 421 (V), sect. E).

The Assembly thus decided to include in the covenant on human rights economic, social and cultural rights and an explicit recognition of the equality of men and women in related rights, as set forth in the Charter. In 1951, the Commission drafted 14 articles on economic, social and cultural rights on the basis of proposals made by Governments and suggestions by specialized agencies. It also formulated 10 articles on measures for implementation of those rights under which States parties to the covenant would submit periodic reports. After a long debate at its sixth session, in 1951/1952, the General Assembly requested the Commission "to draft two Covenants on Human Rights, . . . one to contain civil and political rights and the other to contain economic, social and cultural rights" (resolution 543 (VI), para. 1). The Assembly specified that the two covenants should contain as many similar provisions as possible. It also decided to include an article providing that "all peoples shall have the right of self-determination" (resolution 545 (VI)).

The Commission completed preparation of the two drafts at its ninth and tenth sessions, in 1953 and 1954. The General Assembly reviewed those texts at its ninth session, in 1954, and decided to give the drafts the widest possible publicity in order that Governments might study them thoroughly and that public opinion might express itself freely. It recommended that its Third Committee start an article-by-article discussion of the texts at its tenth session, in 1955. Although the article-by-article discussion began as scheduled, it was not until 1966 that the preparation of the two covenants was completed.

The International Covenant on Economic, Social and Cultural Rights and the International Covenant on Civil and Political Rights were adopted by the General Assembly by its resolution 2200 A (XXI) of 16 December 1966. The first Optional Protocol to the International Covenant on Civil and Political Rights, adopted by the same resolution, provided international machinery for dealing with communications from individuals claiming to be victims of violations of any of the rights set forth in the Covenant.

UNIVERSAL DECLARATION OF HUMAN RIGHTS

The Universal Declaration of Human Rights (UDHR) is a declaration adopted by the United Nations General Assembly on 10 December 1948 at Palais de Chaillot, Paris. The Declaration arose directly from the experience of the Second World War and represents the first global expression of rights to which all human beings are inherently entitled. It consists of 30 articles which have been elaborated in subsequent international treaties, regional human rights instruments, national constitutions and laws. The International Bill of Human Rights consists of the Universal Declaration of Human Rights, the International Covenant on Economic, Social and Cultural Rights, and the International Covenant on Civil and Political Rights and its two Optional Protocols. In 1966 the General Assembly adopted the two detailed Covenants, which complete the International Bill of Human Rights; and in 1976, after the Covenants had been ratified by a sufficient number of individual nations, the Bill took on the force of international law.

Precursors

During the Second World War the allies adopted the Four Freedoms: freedom of speech, freedom of religion, freedom from fear, and freedom from want, as their basic war aims. The United Nations Charter "reaffirmed faith in fundamental human rights, and dignity and worth of the human person" and committed all member states to promote "universal respect for, and observance of, human rights and fundamental freedoms for all without distinction as to race, sex, language, or religion".

When the atrocities committed by Nazi Germany became apparent after the Second World War, the consensus within the world community was that the United Nations Charter did not sufficiently define the rights it referenced. A universal declaration that specified the rights of individuals was necessary to give effect to the Charter's provisions on human rights.

Drafting of UDHR

Canadian John Peters Humphrey was called upon by the United Nations Secretary-General to work on the project and became the Declaration's principal drafter. At the time Humphrey was newly appointed as Director of the Division of Human Rights within the United Nations Secretariat. The Commission on Human Rights, a standing body of the United Nations, was constituted to undertake the work of preparing what was initially conceived as an International Bill of Rights. The membership of the Commission was designed to be broadly representative of the global community with representatives of the following countries serving: Australia, Belgium, Byelorussian Soviet Socialist Republic, Chile, China, Egypt, France, India, Iran, Lebanon, Panama, Philippines, United Kingdom, United States, Union of Soviet Socialist Republics, Uruguay and Yugoslavia. Well known members of the Commission included Eleanor Roosevelt of the United States, who was the Chairperson, Jacques Maritain, René Cassin and Stéphane Hessel of France, Charles Malik of Lebanon, and P. C. Chang of the Republic of China, among others. Humphrey provided the initial draft which became the working text of the Commission.

According to Globalizing Family Values, the Declaration's pro-family phrases were the result of the Christian Democratic movement's influence on Cassin and Malik.

The Final Draft of UDHR

Preamble

Whereas recognition of the inherent dignity and of the equal and inalienable rights of all members of the human family is the foundation of freedom, justice and peace in the world,

Whereas disregard and contempt for human rights have resulted in barbarous acts which have outraged the conscience of mankind, and the advent of a world in which human beings shall enjoy freedom of speech and belief and freedom from fear and want has been proclaimed as the highest aspiration of the common people,

Whereas it is essential, if man is not to be compelled to have recourse, as a last resort, to rebellion against tyranny and oppression, that human rights should be potected by the rule of law,

Whereas it is essential to promote the development of friendly relations between nations,

Whereas the peoples of the United Nations have in the Charter reaffirmed their faith in fundamental human rights, in the dignity and worth of the human person and in the equal rights of men and women and have determined to pomote social progress and better standards of life in larger freedom,

Whereas Member States have pledged themselves to achieve, in co-operation with the United Nations, the promotion of universal respect for and observance of human rights and fundamental freedoms,

Whereas common understanding of these rights and freedoms is of the greatest importance for the full realization of this pledge,

Now, therefore,

The General Assembly Proclaims this Universal Declaration of Human Rights as a common standard of achievement for all peoples and all nations, to the end that every individual and every organ of society, keeping this Declaration constantly in mind, shall strive by teaching and education to promote respect for these rights and freedoms and by pogressive measures, national and international, to secure their universal and effective recognition and observance, both among the peoples of Member States themselves and among the peoples of territories under their jurisdiction.

Article 1

All human beings are born free and equal in dignity and rights. They are endowed with reason and conscience and should act towards one another in a spirit of brotherhood.

Article 2

Everyone is entitled to all the rights and freeedoms set forth in this Declaration, without distinction of any kind, such as race, color, sex, language, religion, political or other opinion, national or social origin, birth or other status.

Furthermore, no distinction shall be made on the basis of the political, jurisdictional or international status of the country or.territory to which a person belongs, whether it be independent, trust, non-self-governing or under any other limitation of sovereignty.

Article 3

Everyone has the right to life, liberty, and the security of person.

Article 4

No one shall be held in slavery or servitude; slavery and the slave trade shall be prohibited in all their forms.

Article 5

No one shall be subjected to torture or to cruel, inhuman or degrading treatment or punishment.

Article 6

Everyone has the right to recognition everywhere as a person before the law.

Article 7

All are equal before the law and are entitled without any discrimination to equal protection of the law. All are entitled to equal protection against any discrimination in violation of this Declaration and against any incitement to such discrimination.

Article 8

Everyone has the right to an effective remedy by the competent national tribunals for acts violating the fundamental rights granted him by the constitution or by law.

Article 9

No one shall be subjected to arbitrary arrest, detention or exile. Article 10.Everyone is entitled in full equality to a fair, and public, hearing by an independent and impartial tribunal, in the determination of his rights and obligations and of any criminal charge against him.

Article 11

1. Everyone charged with a penal offence has the right to be presumed innocent until proved guilty according to law in a public trial at which he has had all the guarantees necessary for his defence.
2. No one shall be held guilty of any penal offence on account of any act or omission which did not constitute a penal offence, under national or international law, at the time when it was committed. Nor shall a heavier penalty be imposed than the one that was applicable at the time the penal offence was committed.

Article 12

No one shall be subjected to arbitrary interference with his privacy, family, home or correspondence, not to attacks upon his honour and reputation. Everyone has the right to the protection of the law against such interference or attacks.

Article 13

1. Everyone has the right ot freedom of movement and residence within the borders of each State.

2. Everyone has the right to leave any country, including his own, and to return to his country.

Article 14

1. Everyone has the right to seek and to enjoy in other countries asylum from persecution.
2. This right may not be invoked in the case of prosecutions genuinely arising from non-political crimes or from acts contrary to the purposes and principles of the United Nations.

Article 15

1. Everyone has the right to a nationality.
2. No one shall be arbitrarily deprived of his nationality nor denied the right to change his nationality.

Article 16

1. Men and women of full age, without any limitation due to race, nationality or religion, have the right to marry and to found a family. They are entitled to equal rights as to marriage, during marriage, and at its dissolution.
2. Marriage shall be entered into only with the free and full consent of the intending spouses.
3. The family is the natural and fundamental group unit of society and is entitled to protection by society and the State.

Article 17

1. Everyone has the right to own property alone as well as in association with others.
2. No one shall be arbitrarily deprived of his property.

Article 18

Everyone has the right to freedom of thought, conscience and religion; this right includes the freedom to change his religion or belief, and freedom, either alone or in community with others and in public or private, to manifest his religion or belief in teaching, practice, worship and observance.

Article 19

Everyone has the right to freedom of opinion and expression; this right includes freedom to hold opinions without interference and seek, receive and impart information and ideas through any media and regardless of frontiers.

Article 20

1. Everyone has the right to freedom of peaceful assembly and association.
2. No one may be compelled to belong to an association.

Article 21

1. Everyone has the right to take part in the government of his country, directly or through freely chosen representatives.
2. Everyone has the right of equal access to public service in his country.
3. The will of the people shall be the basis of the authority of government; this will shall be expressed in periodic and genuine elections which shall be by universal and equal sufferage and shall be held by secret vote or by equivalent free voting procedures.

Article 22

Everyone, as a member of society, has the right to social security and is entitled to realization, through national effort and international cooperation and in accordance with the organization and resources of each State, of the economic, social and cultural rights indispensable for his dignity and the free development of his personality.

Article 23

1. Everyone has the right to work, to free choice of employment, to just and favourable conditions of work and protection against unemployment.
2. Everyone, without any discrimination, has the right to equal pay for equal work.
3. Everyone who works has the right to just and favourable remuneration ensuring for himself and his family an existence worthy of human dignity, and supplemented, if necessary, by other means of social protection.
4. Everyone has the right to form and to join trade unions for the protection of his interests.

Article 24

Everyone has the right to rest and leisure, including reasonable limitation of working hours and periodic holidays with pay.

Article 25

1. Everyone has the right to a standard of living adequate for the health and well-being of himself and of his family, including food, clothing, housing and medical care and necessary social services, and the right to security on the event of unemployment, sickness, disability, widowhood, old age or other lack of livelihood in circumstances beyond his control.
2. Motherhood and childhood are entitled to special care and assistance. All children, whether born in or out of wedlock, shall enjoy the same social protection.

Article 26

1. Everyone has the right to education. Education shall be free, at least in the elementary and fundamental stages. Elementary education shall be compulsory. Technical and professional.education shall be made generally available an higher education shall be equally accessible to all on the basis of merit.
2. Education shall be directed to the full development of the human personality and to the strengthening of respect for human rights and fundamental freedoms. It shall promote understanding, tolerance and friendship among all nations, racial or religious groups and shall further the activities of the United Nations for the maintenance of peace.
3. Parents have a prior right to choose the kind of education that shall be given to their children.

Article 27

1. Everyone has the right freely to participate in the cultural life of the community, to enjoy the arts and to share in scientific advancement and its benefits.
2. Everyone has the right to the protection of the moral and material interests resulting from any scientific, literary or artistic production of which he is the author.

Article 28

Everyone is entitled to a social and international order in which the rights and freedoms set forth in this Declaration can be fully realized.

Article 29

1. Everyone has duties to the community in which alone the free and full development of his personality is possible.
2. In the exercise of his rights and freedoms, everyone shall be subject only to such limitations as are determined by law solely for the purpose of securing due recognition and respect for the rights and freedoms of others and of meeting the just requirements of.morality, public order and the general welfare in a democratic society.
3. These rights and freedoms may in no case be exercised contrary to the purposes and principles of the United Nations.

Article 30

Nothing in this Declaration may be interpreted as implying for any State, group or person any right to engage in any activity or to perform any act aimed at the destuction of any of the rights and freedoms set forth herein.

Adoption of UDHR

The Universal Declaration was adopted by the General Assembly on 10 December 1948 by a vote of 48 in favour, 0 against, with eight abstentions: the USSR, Ukrainian SSR, Byelorussian SSR, People's Federal Republic of Yugoslavia, People's Republic of Poland, Union of South Africa, Czechoslovakia and the Kingdom of Saudi Arabia. South Africa's opposition had been clear throughout the process. Roosevelt attributed the abstention of the Soviet bloc nations to Article 13, which provided the right of citizens to leave their countries.

The following countries voted in favour of the Declaration:

Afghanistan	Republic of China	Ethiopia
Argentina	Colombia	France
Australia	Costa Rica	Guatemala
Belgium	Cuba	Haiti
Bolivia	Denmark	India
Brazil	Dominican Republic	Iran
Burma	Ecuador	Iraq
Canada	El Salvador	Lebanon
Chile	Egypt	Liberia

Pakistan	Nicaragua	Syria
Romania	Norway	Thailand
Greece	Panama	Turkey
Iceland	Paraguay	United Kingdom
Luxembourg	Peru	United States
Mexico	Philippines	Uruguay
Netherlands	Sweden	Venezuela
New Zealand		

Despite the central role played by Canadian John Humphrey, the Canadian Government at first abstained from voting on the Declaration's draft, but later voted in favour of the final draft in the General Assembly.

Structure of UDHR

The underlying structure of the Universal Declaration was introduced in its second draft which was prepared by René Cassin. Cassin worked from a first draft prepared by John Peters Humphrey. The structure was influenced by the Code Napoleon, including a preamble and introductory general principles. Cassin compared the Declaration to the portico of a Greek temple, with a foundation, steps, four columns and a pediment. Articles 1 and 2 are the foundation blocks, with their principles of dignity, liberty, equality and brotherhood. The seven paragraphs of the preamble, setting out the reasons for the Declaration, represent the steps. The main body of the Declaration forms the four columns. The first column (articles 3–11) constitutes rights of the individual, such as the right to life and the prohibition of slavery. The second column (articles 12–17) constitutes the rights of the individual in civil and political society. The third column (articles 18–21) is concerned with spiritual, public and political freedoms such as freedom of religion and freedom of association. The fourth column (articles 22–27) sets out social, economic and cultural rights. In Cassin's model, the last three articles of the Declaration provide the pediment which binds the structure together. These articles are concerned with the duty of the individual to society and the prohibition of use of rights in contravention of the purposes of the United Nations Organisation.

The International Human Rights Day

The adoption of the Universal Declaration is a significant international commemoration marked each year on 10 December and is known as Human Rights Day or International Human Rights Day. The commemoration is observed by individuals, community and religious groups, human rights organisations, parliaments, governments and the United Nations. Decadal commemorations are often accompanied by campaigns to promote awareness of the Declaration and human rights. 2008 marked the 60th anniversary of the Declaration and was accompanied by year-long activities around the theme "Dignity and justice for all of us".

Importance and influence of the Declaration

Conceived as "a common standard of achievement for all peoples and all nations", the Universal Declaration of Human Rights has become just that: a yardstick by which to measure the degree of respect for, and compliance with, international human rights standards. Since 1948 it has been and rightly continues to be the most important and far-reaching of all United Nations declarations, and a fundamental source of inspiration for national and international efforts to promote and protect human rights and fundamental freedoms. It has set the direction for all subsequent work in the field of human rights and has provided the basic philosophy for many legally binding international instruments designed to protect the rights and freedoms which it proclaims.

In the Proclamation of Teheran, adopted by the International Conference on Human Rights held in Iran in 1968, the Conference agreed that "the Universal Declaration of Human Rights states a common understanding of the peoples of the world concerning the inalienable and inviolable rights of all members of the human family and constitutes an obligation for the members of the international community". The Conference affirmed its faith in the principles set forth in the Declaration, and urged all peoples and Governments "to dedicate themselves to [those] principles . . . and to redouble their efforts to provide for all human beings a life consonant with freedom and dignity and conducive to physical, mental, social and spiritual welfare". In recent years, there has been a growing tendency for United Nations organs, in preparing international instruments in the filed of human rights, to refer not only to the Universal Declaration, but also to other parts of the International Bill of Human Rights.

THE INTERNATIONAL COVENANT ON CIVIL AND POLITICAL RIGHTS

Preamble

The States Parties to the present Covenant,

Considering that, in accordance with the principles proclaimed in the Charter of the United Nations, recognition of the inherent dignity and of the equal and inalienable rights of all members of the human family is the foundation of freedom, justice and peace in the world,

Recognizing that these rights derive from the inherent dignity of the human person,

Recognizing that, in accordance with the Universal Declaration of Human Rights, the ideal of free human beings enjoying civil and political freedom and freedom from fear and want can only be achieved if conditions are created whereby everyone may enjoy his civil and political rights, as well as his economic, social and cultural rights,

Considering the obligation of States under the Charter of the United Nations to promote universal respect for, and observance of, human rights and freedoms,

Realizing that the individual, having duties to other individuals and to the community to which he belongs, is under a responsibility to strive for the promotion and observance of the rights recognized in the present Covenant,

Agree upon the following articles:

Part I

Article 1. General Comment on its Implementation

1. All peoples have the right of self-determination. By virtue of that right they freely determine their political status and freely pursue their economic, social and cultural development.
2. All peoples may, for their own ends, freely dispose of their natural wealth and resources without prejudice to any obligations arising out of international economic cooperation, based upon the principle of mutual benefit, and international law. In no case may a people be deprived of its own means of subsistence.
3. The States Parties to the present Covenant, including those having responsibility for the administration of Non-Self-Governing and Trust

Territories, shall promote the realization of the right of self-determination, and shall respect that right, in conformity with the provisions of the Charter of the United Nations.

Part II

Article 2 General Comment on its Implementation

1. Each State Party to the present Covenant undertakes to respect and to ensure to all individuals within its territory and subject to its jurisdiction the rights recognized in the present Covenant, without distinction of any kind, such as race, colour, sex, language, religion, political or other opinion, national or social origin, property, birth or other status.
2. Where not already provided for by existing legislative or other measures, each State Party to the present Covenant undertakes to take the necessary steps, in accordance with its constitutional processes and with the provisions of the present Covenant, to adopt such laws or other measures as may be necessary to give effect to the rights recognized in the present Covenant.
3. Each State Party to the present Covenant undertakes:
   (a) To ensure that any person whose rights or freedoms as herein recognized are violated shall have an effective remedy, notwithstanding that the violation has been committed by persons acting in an official capacity;
   (b) To ensure that any person claiming such a remedy shall have his right thereto determined by competent judicial, administrative or legislative authorities, or by any other competent authority provided for by the legal system of the State, and to develop the possibilities of judicial remedy;
   (c) To ensure that the competent authorities shall enforce such remedies when granted.

Article 3 General Comment on its Implementation

The States Parties to the present Covenant undertake to ensure the equal right of men and women to the enjoyment of all civil and political rights set forth in the present Covenant. General comment on its implementation

Article 4 General Comment on its Implementation

1. In time of public emergency which threatens the life of the nation and

the existence of which is officially proclaimed, the States Parties to the present Covenant may take measures derogating from their obligations under the present Covenant to the extent strictly required by the exigencies of the situation, provided that such measures are not inconsistent with their other obligations under international law and do not involve discrimination solely on the ground of race, colour, sex, language, religion or social origin.

2. No derogation from articles 6, 7, 8 (paragraphs I and 2), 11, 15, 16 and 18 may be made under this provision.

3. Any State Party to the present Covenant availing itself of the right of derogation shall immediately inform the other States Parties to the present Covenant, through the intermediary of the Secretary-General of the United Nations, of the provisions from which it has derogated and of the reasons by which it was actuated. A further communication shall be made, through the same intermediary, on the date on which it terminates such derogation.

Article 5

1. Nothing in the present Covenant may be interpreted as implying for any State, group or person any right to engage in any activity or perform any act aimed at the destruction of any of the rights and freedoms recognized herein or at their limitation to a greater extent than is provided for in the present Covenant.

2. There shall be no restriction upon or derogation from any of the fundamental human rights recognized or existing in any State Party to the present Covenant pursuant to law, conventions, regulations or custom on the pretext that the present Covenant does not recognize such rights or that it recognizes them to a lesser extent.

Part III

Article 6 General comment on its implementation

1. Every human being has the inherent right to life. This right shall be protected by law. No one shall be arbitrarily deprived of his life.

2. In countries which have not abolished the death penalty, sentence of death may be imposed only for the most serious crimes in accordance with the law in force at the time of the commission of the crime and not contrary to the provisions of the present Covenant and to the

Convention on the Prevention and Punishment of the Crime of Genocide. This penalty can only be carried out pursuant to a final judgement rendered by a competent court.

3. When deprivation of life constitutes the crime of genocide, it is understood that nothing in this article shall authorize any State Party to the present Covenant to derogate in any way from any obligation assumed under the provisions of the Convention on the Prevention and Punishment of the Crime of Genocide.
4. Anyone sentenced to death shall have the right to seek pardon or commutation of the sentence. Amnesty, pardon or commutation of the sentence of death may be granted in all cases.
5. Sentence of death shall not be imposed for crimes committed by persons below eighteen years of age and shall not be carried out on pregnant women.
6. Nothing in this article shall be invoked to delay or to prevent the abolition of capital punishment by any State Party to the present Covenant.

Article 7 General comment on its implementation

No one shall be subjected to torture or to cruel, inhuman or degrading treatment or punishment. In particular, no one shall be subjected without his free consent to medical or scientific experimentation.

Article 8

1. No one shall be held in slavery; slavery and the slave-trade in all their forms shall be prohibited.
2. No one shall be held in servitude.
3.

(a) No one shall be required to perform forced or compulsory labour;

(b) Paragraph 3 (a) shall not be held to preclude, in countries where imprisonment with hard labour may be imposed as a punishment for a crime, the performance of hard labour in pursuance of a sentence to such punishment by a competent court;

(c) For the purpose of this paragraph the term "forced or compulsory labour" shall not include:

(i) Any work or service, not referred to in subparagraph (b), normally required of a person who is under detention in consequence of a lawful order of a court, or of a person during conditional release from such detention;

(ii) Any service of a military character and, in countries where conscientious objection is recognized, any national service required by law of conscientious objectors;

(iii) Any service exacted in cases of emergency or calamity threatening the life or well-being of the community;

(iv) Any work or service which forms part of normal civil obligations.

Article 9 General Comment on its Implementation

1. Everyone has the right to liberty and security of person. No one shall be subjected to arbitrary arrest or detention. No one shall be deprived of his liberty except on such grounds and in accordance with such procedure as are established by law.
2. Anyone who is arrested shall be informed, at the time of arrest, of the reasons for his arrest and shall be promptly informed of any charges against him.
3. Anyone arrested or detained on a criminal charge shall be brought promptly before a judge or other officer authorized by law to exercise judicial power and shall be entitled to trial within a reasonable time or to release. It shall not be the general rule that persons awaiting trial shall be detained in custody, but release may be subject to guarantees to appear for trial, at any other stage of the judicial proceedings, and, should occasion arise, for execution of the judgement.
4. Anyone who is deprived of his liberty by arrest or detention shall be entitled to take proceedings before a court, in order that court may decide without delay on the lawfulness of his detention and order his release if the detention is not lawful.
5. Anyone who has been the victim of unlawful arrest or detention shall have an enforceable right to compensation.

Article 10 General comment on its implementation

1. All persons deprived of their liberty shall be treated with humanity and with respect for the inherent dignity of the human person.

2.

(a) Accused persons shall, save in exceptional circumstances, be segregated from convicted persons and shall be subject to separate treatment appropriate to their status as unconvicted persons;

(b) Accused juvenile persons shall be separated from adults and brought as speedily as possible for adjudication. 3. The penitentiary system shall comprise treatment of prisoners the essential aim of which shall be their reformation and social rehabilitation. Juvenile offenders shall be segregated from adults and be accorded treatment appropriate to their age and legal status.

Article 11

No one shall be imprisoned merely on the ground of inability to fulfil a contractual obligation.

Article 12 General Comment on its Implementation

1. Everyone lawfully within the territory of a State shall, within that territory, have the right to liberty of movement and freedom to choose his residence.
2. Everyone shall be free to leave any country, including his own.
3. The above-mentioned rights shall not be subject to any restrictions except those which are provided by law, are necessary to protect national security, public order (ordre public), public health or morals or the rights and freedoms of others, and are consistent with the other rights recognized in the present Covenant.
4. No one shall be arbitrarily deprived of the right to enter his own country.

Article 13

An alien lawfully in the territory of a State Party to the present Covenant may be expelled therefrom only in pursuance of a decision reached in accordance with law and shall, except where compelling reasons of national security otherwise require, be allowed to submit the reasons against his expulsion and to have his case reviewed by, and be represented for the purpose before, the competent authority or a person or persons especially designated by the competent authority.

Article 14 General comment on its implementation

1. All persons shall be equal before the courts and tribunals. In the determination of any criminal charge against him, or of his rights and obligations in a suit at law, everyone shall be entitled to a fair and public hearing by a competent, independent and impartial tribunal established by law. The press and the public may be excluded from all or part of a trial for reasons of morals, public order (ordre public) or national security in a democratic society, or when the interest of the private lives of the parties so requires, or to the extent strictly necessary in the opinion of the court in special circumstances where publicity would prejudice the interests of justice; but any judgement rendered in a criminal case or in a suit at law shall be made public except where the interest of juvenile persons otherwise requires or the proceedings concern matrimonial disputes or the guardianship of children.
2. Everyone charged with a criminal offence shall have the right to be presumed innocent until proved guilty according to law.
3. In the determination of any criminal charge against him, everyone shall be entitled to the following minimum guarantees, in full equality:
   (a) To be informed promptly and in detail in a language which he understands of the nature and cause of the charge against him;
   (b) To have adequate time and facilities for the preparation of his defence and to communicate with counsel of his own choosing;
   (c) To be tried without undue delay;
   (d) To be tried in his presence, and to defend himself in person or through legal assistance of his own choosing; to be informed, if he does not have legal assistance, of this right; and to have legal assistance assigned to him, in any case where the interests of justice so require, and without payment by him in any such case if he does not have sufficient means to pay for it;
   (e) To examine, or have examined, the witnesses against him and to obtain the attendance and examination of witnesses on his behalf under the same conditions as witnesses against him;
   (f) To have the free assistance of an interpreter if he cannot understand or speak the language used in court;

(g) Not to be compelled to testify against himself or to confess guilt.

4. In the case of juvenile persons, the procedure shall be such as will take account of their age and the desirability of promoting their rehabilitation.
5. Everyone convicted of a crime shall have the right to his conviction and sentence being reviewed by a higher tribunal according to law.
6. When a person has by a final decision been convicted of a criminal offence and when subsequently his conviction has been reversed or he has been pardoned on the ground that a new or newly discovered fact shows conclusively that there has been a miscarriage of justice, the person who has suffered punishment as a result of such conviction shall be compensated according to law, unless it is proved that the non-disclosure of the unknown fact in time is wholly or partly attributable to him.
7. No one shall be liable to be tried or punished again for an offence for which he has already been finally convicted or acquitted in accordance with the law and penal procedure of each country.

Article 15

1. No one shall be held guilty of any criminal offence on account of any act or omission which did not constitute a criminal offence, under national or international law, at the time when it was committed. Nor shall a heavier penalty be imposed than the one that was applicable at the time when the criminal offence was committed. If, subsequent to the commission of the offence, provision is made by law for the imposition of the lighter penalty, the offender shall benefit thereby.
2. Nothing in this article shall prejudice the trial and punishment of any person for any act or omission which, at the time when it was committed, was criminal according to the general principles of law recognized by the community of nations.

Article 16

Everyone shall have the right to recognition everywhere as a person before the law.

Article 17 General comment on its implementation

1. No one shall be subjected to arbitrary or unlawful interference with

his privacy, family, home or correspondence, nor to unlawful attacks on his honour and reputation.

2. Everyone has the right to the protection of the law against such interference or attacks.

Article 18 General Comment on its Implementation

1. Everyone shall have the right to freedom of thought, conscience and religion. This right shall include freedom to have or to adopt a religion or belief of his choice, and freedom, either individually or in community with others and in public or private, to manifest his religion or belief in worship, observance, practice and teaching.
2. No one shall be subject to coercion which would impair his freedom to have or to adopt a religion or belief of his choice.
3. Freedom to manifest one's religion or beliefs may be subject only to such limitations as are prescribed by law and are necessary to protect public safety, order, health, or morals or the fundamental rights and freedoms of others. 4. The States Parties to the present Covenant undertake to have respect for the liberty of parents and, when applicable, legal guardians to ensure the religious and moral education of their children in conformity with their own convictions.

Article 19 General Comment on its Implementation

1. Everyone shall have the right to hold opinions without interference.
2. Everyone shall have the right to freedom of expression; this right shall include freedom to seek, receive and impart information and ideas of all kinds, regardless of frontiers, either orally, in writing or in print, in the form of art, or through any other media of his choice.
3. The exercise of the rights provided for in paragraph 2 of this article carries with it special duties and responsibilities. It may therefore be subject to certain restrictions, but these shall only be such as are provided by law and are necessary:
   (a) For respect of the rights or reputations of others;
   (b) For the protection of national security or of public order (ordre public), or of public health or morals.

Article 20 General Comment on its Implementation

1. Any propaganda for war shall be prohibited by law.

2. Any advocacy of national, racial or religious hatred that constitutes incitement to discrimination, hostility or violence shall be prohibited by law.

Article 21

The right of peaceful assembly shall be recognized. No restrictions may be placed on the exercise of this right other than those imposed in conformity with the law and which are necessary in a democratic society in the interests of national security or public safety, public order (ordre public), the protection of public health or morals or the protection of the rights and freedoms of others.

Article 22

1. Everyone shall have the right to freedom of association with others, including the right to form and join trade unions for the protection of his interests.
2. No restrictions may be placed on the exercise of this right other than those which are prescribed by law and which are necessary in a democratic society in the interests of national security or public safety, public order (ordre public), the protection of public health or morals or the protection of the rights and freedoms of others. This article shall not prevent the imposition of lawful restrictions on members of the armed forces and of the police in their exercise of this right.
3. Nothing in this article shall authorize States Parties to the International Labour Organisation Convention of 1948 concerning Freedom of Association and Protection of the Right to Organize to take legislative measures which would prejudice, or to apply the law in such a manner as to prejudice, the guarantees provided for in that Convention.

Article 23 General comment on its implementation

1. The family is the natural and fundamental group unit of society and is entitled to protection by society and the State.
2. The right of men and women of marriageable age to marry and to found a family shall be recognized.
3. No marriage shall be entered into without the free and full consent of the intending spouses.
4. States Parties to the present Covenant shall take appropriate steps to ensure equality of rights and responsibilities of spouses as to marriage,

during marriage and at its dissolution. In the case of dissolution, provision shall be made for the necessary protection of any children.

Article 24 General comment on its implementation

1. Every child shall have, without any discrimination as to race, colour, sex, language, religion, national or social origin, property or birth, the right to such measures of protection as are required by his status as a minor, on the part of his family, society and the State.
2. Every child shall be registered immediately after birth and shall have a name.
3. Every child has the right to acquire a nationality.

Article 25 General comment on its implementation

Every citizen shall have the right and the opportunity, without any of the distinctions mentioned in article 2 and without unreasonable restrictions:

(a) To take part in the conduct of public affairs, directly or through freely chosen representatives;

(b) To vote and to be elected at genuine periodic elections which shall be by universal and equal suffrage and shall be held by secret ballot, guaranteeing the free expression of the will of the electors;

(c) To have access, on general terms of equality, to public service in his country.

Article 26

All persons are equal before the law and are entitled without any discrimination to the equal protection of the law. In this respect, the law shall prohibit any discrimination and guarantee to all persons equal and effective protection against discrimination on any ground such as race, colour, sex, language, religion, political or other opinion, national or social origin, property, birth or other status.

Article 27 General comment on its implementation

In those States in which ethnic, religious or linguistic minorities exist, persons belonging to such minorities shall not be denied the right, in community with the other members of their group, to enjoy their own culture, to profess and practise their own religion, or to use their own language.

Part IV

Article 28

1. There shall be established a Human Rights Committee (hereafter referred to in the present Covenant as the Committee). It shall consist of eighteen members and shall carry out the functions hereinafter provided.
2. The Committee shall be composed of nationals of the States Parties to the present Covenant who shall be persons of high moral character and recognized competence in the field of human rights, consideration being given to the usefulness of the participation of some persons having legal experience.
3. The members of the Committee shall be elected and shall serve in their personal capacity.

Article 29

1. The members of the Committee shall be elected by secret ballot from a list of persons possessing the qualifications prescribed in article 28 and nominated for the purpose by the States Parties to the present Covenant.
2. Each State Party to the present Covenant may nominate not more than two persons. These persons shall be nationals of the nominating State.
3. A person shall be eligible for renomination.

Article 30

1. The initial election shall be held no later than six months after the date of the entry into force of the present Covenant.
2. At least four months before the date of each election to the Committee, other than an election to fill a vacancy declared in accordance with article 34, the Secretary-General of the United Nations shall address a written invitation to the States Parties to the present Covenant to submit their nominations for membership of the Committee within three months.
3. The Secretary-General of the United Nations shall prepare a list in alphabetical order of all the persons thus nominated, with an indication of the States Parties which have nominated them, and shall submit it to the States Parties to the present Covenant no later than one month before the date of each election.

4. Elections of the members of the Committee shall be held at a meeting of the States Parties to the present Covenant convened by the Secretary General of the United Nations at the Headquarters of the United Nations. At that meeting, for which two thirds of the States Parties to the present Covenant shall constitute a quorum, the persons elected to the Committee shall be those nominees who obtain the largest number of votes and an absolute majority of the votes of the representatives of States Parties present and voting.

Article 31

1. The Committee may not include more than one national of the same State.
2. In the election of the Committee, consideration shall be given to equitable geographical distribution of membership and to the representation of the different forms of civilization and of the principal legal systems.

Article 32

1. The members of the Committee shall be elected for a term of four years. They shall be eligible for re-election if renominated. However, the terms of nine of the members elected at the first election shall expire at the end of two years; immediately after the first election, the names of these nine members shall be chosen by lot by the Chairman of the meeting referred to in article 30, paragraph 4.
2. Elections at the expiry of office shall be held in accordance with the preceding articles of this part of the present Covenant.

Article 33

1. If, in the unanimous opinion of the other members, a member of the Committee has ceased to carry out his functions for any cause other than absence of a temporary character, the Chairman of the Committee shall notify the Secretary-General of the United Nations, who shall then declare the seat of that member to be vacant.
2. In the event of the death or the resignation of a member of the Committee, the Chairman shall immediately notify the Secretary-General of the United Nations, who shall declare the seat vacant from the date of death or the date on which the resignation takes effect.

Article 34

1. When a vacancy is declared in accordance with article 33 and if the term of office of the member to be replaced does not expire within six months of the declaration of the vacancy, the Secretary-General of the United Nations shall notify each of the States Parties to the present Covenant, which may within two months submit nominations in accordance with article 29 for the purpose of filling the vacancy.
2. The Secretary-General of the United Nations shall prepare a list in alphabetical order of the persons thus nominated and shall submit it to the States Parties to the present Covenant. The election to fill the vacancy shall then take place in accordance with the relevant provisions of this part of the present Covenant.
3. A member of the Committee elected to fill a vacancy declared in accordance with article 33 shall hold office for the remainder of the term of the member who vacated the seat on the Committee under the provisions of that article.

Article 35

The members of the Committee shall, with the approval of the General Assembly of the United Nations, receive emoluments from United Nations resources on such terms and conditions as the General Assembly may decide, having regard to the importance of the Committee's responsibilities.

Article 36

The Secretary-General of the United Nations shall provide the necessary staff and facilities for the effective performance of the functions of the Committee under the present Covenant.

Article 37

1. The Secretary-General of the United Nations shall convene the initial meeting of the Committee at the Headquarters of the United Nations.
2. After its initial meeting, the Committee shall meet at such times as shall be provided in its rules of procedure.
3. The Committee shall normally meet at the Headquarters of the United Nations or at the United Nations Office at Geneva.

Article 38

Every member of the Committee shall, before taking up his duties, make a solemn declaration in open committee that he will perform his functions impartially and conscientiously.

Article 39

1. The Committee shall elect its officers for a term of two years. They may be re-elected.
2. The Committee shall establish its own rules of procedure, but these rules shall provide, inter alia, that:
   (a) Twelve members shall constitute a quorum;
   (b) Decisions of the Committee shall be made by a majority vote of the members present.

Article 40

1. The States Parties to the present Covenant undertake to submit reports on the measures they have adopted which give effect to the rights recognized herein and on the progress made in the enjoyment of those rights:
   (a) Within one year of the entry into force of the present Covenant for the States Parties concerned;
   (b) Thereafter whenever the Committee so requests.
2. All reports shall be submitted to the Secretary-General of the United Nations, who shall transmit them to the Committee for consideration. Reports shall indicate the factors and difficulties, if any, affecting the implementation of the present Covenant.
3. The Secretary-General of the United Nations may, after consultation with the Committee, transmit to the specialized agencies concerned copies of such parts of the reports as may fall within their field of competence.
4. The Committee shall study the reports submitted by the States Parties to the present Covenant. It shall transmit its reports, and such general comments as it may consider appropriate, to the States Parties. The Committee may also transmit to the Economic and Social Council these comments along with the copies of the reports it has received from States Parties to the present Covenant.
5. The States Parties to the present Covenant may submit to the Committee observations on any comments that may be made in accordance with paragraph 4 of this article.

Article 41 General comment on its implementation

1. A State Party to the present Covenant may at any time declare under this article that it recognizes the competence of the Committee to receive and consider communications to the effect that a State Party claims that another State Party is not fulfilling its obligations under the present Covenant. Communications under this article may be received and considered only if submitted by a State Party which has made a declaration recognizing in regard to itself the competence of the Committee. No communication shall be received by the Committee if it concerns a State Party which has not made such a declaration. Communications received under this article shall be dealt with in accordance with the following procedure:

    (a) If a State Party to the present Covenant considers that another State Party is not giving effect to the provisions of the present Covenant, it may, by written communication, bring the matter to the attention of that State Party. Within three months after the receipt of the communication the receiving State shall afford the State which sent the communication an explanation, or any other statement in writing clarifying the matter which should include, to the extent possible and pertinent, reference to domestic procedures and remedies taken, pending, or available in the matter;

    (b) If the matter is not adjusted to the satisfaction of both States Parties concerned within six months after the receipt by the receiving State of the initial communication, either State shall have the right to refer the matter to the Committee, by notice given to the Committee and to the other State;

    (c) The Committee shall deal with a matter referred to it only after it has ascertained that all available domestic remedies have been invoked and exhausted in the matter, in conformity with the generally recognized principles of international law. This shall not be the rule where the application of the remedies is unreasonably prolonged;

    (d) The Committee shall hold closed meetings when examining communications under this article;

(e) Subject to the provisions of subparagraph ©, the Committee shall make available its good offices to the States Parties concerned with a view to a friendly solution of the matter on the basis of respect for human rights and fundamental freedoms as recognized in the present Covenant;

(f) In any matter referred to it, the Committee may call upon the States Parties concerned, referred to in subparagraph (b), to supply any relevant information;

(g) The States Parties concerned, referred to in subparagraph (b), shall have the right to be represented when the matter is being considered in the Committee and to make submissions orally and/or in writing;

(h) The Committee shall, within twelve months after the date of receipt of notice under subparagraph (b), submit a report:

(i) If a solution within the terms of subparagraph (e) is reached, the Committee shall confine its report to a brief statement of the facts and of the solution reached;

(ii) If a solution within the terms of subparagraph (e) is not reached, the Committee shall confine its report to a brief statement of the facts; the written submissions and record of the oral submissions made by the States Parties concerned shall be attached to the report. In every matter, the report shall be communicated to the States Parties concerned.

2. The provisions of this article shall come into force when ten States Parties to the present Covenant have made declarations under paragraph I of this article. Such declarations shall be deposited by the States Parties with the Secretary-General of the United Nations, who shall transmit copies thereof to the other States Parties. A declaration may be withdrawn at any time by notification to the Secretary-General. Such a withdrawal shall not prejudice the consideration of any matter which is the subject of a communication already transmitted under this article; no further communication by any State Party shall be received after the notification of withdrawal of the declaration has been received by the Secretary-General, unless the State Party concerned has made a new declaration.

Article 42

1.

   (a) If a matter referred to the Committee in accordance with article 41 is not resolved to the satisfaction of the States Parties concerned, the Committee may, with the prior consent of the States Parties concerned, appoint an ad hoc Conciliation Commission (hereinafter referred to as the Commission). The good offices of the Commission shall be made available to the States Parties concerned with a view to an amicable solution of the matter on the basis of respect for the present Covenant;

   (b) The Commission shall consist of five persons acceptable to the States Parties concerned. If the States Parties concerned fail to reach agreement within three months on all or part of the composition of the Commission, the members of the Commission concerning whom no agreement has been reached shall be elected by secret ballot by a two-thirds majority vote of the Committee from among its members.

2. The members of the Commission shall serve in their personal capacity. They shall not be nationals of the States Parties concerned, or of a State not Party to the present Covenant, or of a State Party which has not made a declaration under article 41.

3. The Commission shall elect its own Chairman and adopt its own rules of procedure.

4. The meetings of the Commission shall normally be held at the Headquarters of the United Nations or at the United Nations Office at Geneva. However, they may be held at such other convenient places as the Commission may determine in consultation with the Secretary-General of the United Nations and the States Parties concerned.

5. The secretariat provided in accordance with article 36 shall also service the commissions appointed under this article.

6. The information received and collated by the Committee shall be made available to the Commission and the Commission may call upon the States Parties concerned to supply any other relevant information. 7. When the Commission has fully considered the matter, but in any event not later than twelve months after having been seized of the matter, it

shall submit to the Chairman of the Committee a report for communication to the States Parties concerned:

(a) If the Commission is unable to complete its consideration of the matter within twelve months, it shall confine its report to a brief statement of the status of its consideration of the matter;

(b) If an amicable solution to the matter on tie basis of respect for human rights as recognized in the present Covenant is reached, the Commission shall confine its report to a brief statement of the facts and of the solution reached;

(c) If a solution within the terms of subparagraph (b) is not reached, the Commission's report shall embody its findings on all questions of fact relevant to the issues between the States Parties concerned, and its views on the possibilities of an amicable solution of the matter. This report shall also contain the written submissions and a record of the oral submissions made by the States Parties concerned;

(d) If the Commission's report is submitted under subparagraph ©, the States Parties concerned shall, within three months of the receipt of the report, notify the Chairman of the Committee whether or not they accept the contents of the report of the Commission.

8. The provisions of this article are without prejudice to the responsibilities of the Committee under article 41.

9. The States Parties concerned shall share equally all the expenses of the members of the Commission in accordance with estimates to be provided by the Secretary-General of the United Nations.

10. The Secretary-General of the United Nations shall be empowered to pay the expenses of the members of the Commission, if necessary, before reimbursement by the States Parties concerned, in accordance with paragraph 9 of this article.

Article 43

The members of the Committee, and of the ad hoc conciliation commissions which may be appointed under article 42, shall be entitled to the facilities, privileges and immunities of experts on mission for the United Nations as laid down in the relevant sections of the Convention on the Privileges and Immunities of the United Nations.

Article 44

The provisions for the implementation of the present Covenant shall apply without prejudice to the procedures prescribed in the field of human rights by or under the constituent instruments and the conventions of the United Nations and of the specialized agencies and shall not prevent the States Parties to the present Covenant from having recourse to other procedures for settling a dispute in accordance with general or special international agreements in force between them.

Article 45

The Committee shall submit to the General Assembly of the United Nations, through the Economic and Social Council, an annual report on its activities.

Part V

Article 46

Nothing in the present Covenant shall be interpreted as impairing the provisions of the Charter of the United Nations and of the constitutions of the specialized agencies which define the respective responsibilities of the various organs of the United Nations and of the specialized agencies in regard to the matters dealt with in the present Covenant.

Article 47

Nothing in the present Covenant shall be interpreted as impairing the inherent right of all peoples to enjoy and utilize fully and freely their natural wealth and resources.

Part VI

Article 48

1. The present Covenant is open for signature by any State Member of the United Nations or member of any of its specialized agencies, by any State Party to the Statute of the International Court of Justice, and by any other State which has been invited by the General Assembly of the United Nations to become a Party to the present Covenant.
2. The present Covenant is subject to ratification. Instruments of ratification shall be deposited with the Secretary-General of the United Nations.
3. The present Covenant shall be open to accession by any State referred to in paragraph 1 of this article.

4. Accession shall be effected by the deposit of an instrument of accession with the Secretary-General of the United Nations.
5. The Secretary-General of the United Nations shall inform all States which have signed this Covenant or acceded to it of the deposit of each instrument of ratification or accession.

Article 49

1. The present Covenant shall enter into force three months after the date of the deposit with the Secretary-General of the United Nations of the thirty-fifth instrument of ratification or instrument of accession.
2. For each State ratifying the present Covenant or acceding to it after the deposit of the thirty-fifth instrument of ratification or instrument of accession, the present Covenant shall enter into force three months after the date of the deposit of its own instrument of ratification or instrument of accession.

Article 50

The provisions of the present Covenant shall extend to all parts of federal States without any limitations or exceptions.

Article 51

1. Any State Party to the present Covenant may propose an amendment and file it with the Secretary-General of the United Nations. The Secretary-General of the United Nations shall thereupon communicate any proposed amendments to the States Parties to the present Covenant with a request that they notify him whether they favour a conference of States Parties for the purpose of considering and voting upon the proposals. In the event that at least one third of the States Parties favours such a conference, the Secretary-General shall convene the conference under the auspices of the United Nations. Any amendment adopted by a majority of the States Parties present and voting at the conference shall be submitted to the General Assembly of the United Nations for approval.
2. Amendments shall come into force when they have been approved by the General Assembly of the United Nations and accepted by a two-thirds majority of the States Parties to the present Covenant in accordance with their respective constitutional processes.

3. When amendments come into force, they shall be binding on those States Parties which have accepted them, other States Parties still being bound by the provisions of the present Covenant and any earlier amendment which they have accepted.

Article 52

Irrespective of the notifications made under article 48, paragraph 5, the Secretary-General of the United Nations shall inform all States referred to in paragraph I of the same article of the following particulars:

(a) Signatures, ratifications and accessions under article 48;

(b) The date of the entry into force of the present Covenant under article 49 and the date of the entry into force of any amendments under article 51.

Article 53

1. The present Covenant, of which the Chinese, English, French, Russian and Spanish texts are equally authentic, shall be deposited in the archives of the United Nations.
2. The Secretary-General of the United Nations shall transmit certified copies of the present Covenant to all States referred to in article 48.

THE INTERNATIONAL COVENANT ON ECONOMIC, SOCIAL AND CULTURAL RIGHTS

Preamble

The States Parties to the present Covenant,

Considering that, in accordance with the principles proclaimed in the Charter of the United Nations, recognition of the inherent dignity and of the equal and inalienable rights of all members of the human family is the foundation of freedom, justice and peace in the world,

Recognizing that these rights derive from the inherent dignity of the human person,

Recognizing that, in accordance with the Universal Declaration of Human Rights, the ideal of free human beings enjoying freedom from fear and want can only be achieved if conditions are created whereby everyone may enjoy his economic, social and cultural rights, as well as his civil and political rights,

Considering the obligation of States under the Charter of the United Nations to promote universal respect for, and observance of, human rights and freedoms,

Realizing that the individual, having duties to other individuals and to the community to which he belongs, is under a responsibility to strive for the promotion and observance of the rights recognized in the present Covenant,

Agree upon the following articles:

Part I

Article 1

1. All peoples have the right of self-determination. By virtue of that right they freely determine their political status and freely pursue their economic, social and cultural development.
2. All peoples may, for their own ends, freely dispose of their natural wealth and resources without prejudice to any obligations arising out of international economic co-operation, based upon the principle of mutual benefit, and international law. In no case may a people be deprived of its own means of subsistence.
3. The States Parties to the present Covenant, including those having responsibility for the administration of Non-Self-Governing and Trust Territories, shall promote the realization of the right of self-determination, and shall respect that right, in conformity with the provisions of the Charter of the United Nations.

Part II

Article 2

1. Each State Party to the present Covenant undertakes to take steps, individually and through international assistance and co-operation, especially economic and technical, to the maximum of its available resources, with a view to achieving progressively the full realization of the rights recognized in the present Covenant by all appropriate means, including particularly the adoption of legislative measures.
2. The States Parties to the present Covenant undertake to guarantee that the rights enunciated in the present Covenant will be exercised without discrimination of any kind as to race, colour, sex, language, religion,

political or other opinion, national or social origin, property, birth or other status.

3. Developing countries, with due regard to human rights and their national economy, may determine to what extent they would guarantee the economic rights recognized in the present Covenant to non-nationals.

Article 3

The States Parties to the present Covenant undertake to ensure the equal right of men and women to the enjoyment of all economic, social and cultural rights set forth in the present Covenant.

Article 4

The States Parties to the present Covenant recognize that, in the enjoyment of those rights provided by the State in conformity with the present Covenant, the State may subject such rights only to such limitations as are determined by law only in so far as this may be compatible with the nature of these rights and solely for the purpose of promoting the general welfare in a democratic society.

Article 5

1. Nothing in the present Covenant may be interpreted as implying for any State, group or person any right to engage in any activity or to perform any act aimed at the destruction of any of the rights or freedoms recognized herein, or at their limitation to a greater extent than is provided for in the present Covenant.
2. No restriction upon or derogation from any of the fundamental human rights recognized or existing in any country in virtue of law, conventions, regulations or custom shall be admitted on the pretext that the present Covenant does not recognize such rights or that it recognizes them to a lesser extent.

Part III

Article 6

1. The States Parties to the present Covenant recognize the right to work, which includes the right of everyone to the opportunity to gain his living by work which he freely chooses or accepts, and will take appropriate steps to safeguard this right.

2. The steps to be taken by a State Party to the present Covenant to achieve the full realization of this right shall include technical and vocational guidance and training programmes, policies and techniques to achieve steady economic, social and cultural development and full and productive employment under conditions safeguarding fundamental political and economic freedoms to the individual.

Article 7

The States Parties to the present Covenant recognize the right of everyone to the enjoyment of just and favourable conditions of work which ensure, in particular:

(a) Remuneration which provides all workers, as a minimum, with:

  (i) Fair wages and equal remuneration for work of equal value without distinction of any kind, in particular women being guaranteed conditions of work not inferior to those enjoyed by men, with equal pay for equal work;

  (ii) A decent living for themselves and their families in accordance with the provisions of the present Covenant;

(b) Safe and healthy working conditions;

(c) Equal opportunity for everyone to be promoted in his employment to an appropriate higher level, subject to no considerations other than those of seniority and competence;

(d) Rest, leisure and reasonable limitation of working hours and periodic holidays with pay, as well as remuneration for public holidays

Article 8

1. The States Parties to the present Covenant undertake to ensure:

  (a) The right of everyone to form trade unions and join the trade union of his choice, subject only to the rules of the organization concerned, for the promotion and protection of his economic and social interests. No restrictions may be placed on the exercise of this right other than those prescribed by law and which are necessary in a democratic society in the interests of national security or public order or for the protection of the rights and freedoms of others;

(b) The right of trade unions to establish national federations or confederations and the right of the latter to form or join international trade-union organizations;

(c) The right of trade unions to function freely subject to no limitations other than those prescribed by law and which are necessary in a democratic society in the interests of national security or public order or for the protection of the rights and freedoms of others;

(d) The right to strike, provided that it is exercised in conformity with the laws of the particular country.

2. This article shall not prevent the imposition of lawful restrictions on the exercise of these rights by members of the armed forces or of the police or of the administration of the State.

3. Nothing in this article shall authorize States Parties to the International Labour Organisation Convention of 1948 concerning Freedom of Association and Protection of the Right to Organize to take legislative measures which would prejudice, or apply the law in such a manner as would prejudice, the guarantees provided for in that Convention.

Article 9

The States Parties to the present Covenant recognize the right of everyone to social security, including social insurance.

Article 10

The States Parties to the present Covenant recognize that:

1. The widest possible protection and assistance should be accorded to the family, which is the natural and fundamental group unit of society, particularly for its establishment and while it is responsible for the care and education of dependent children. Marriage must be entered into with the free consent of the intending spouses.

2. Special protection should be accorded to mothers during a reasonable period before and after childbirth. During such period working mothers should be accorded paid leave or leave with adequate social security benefits.

3. Special measures of protection and assistance should be taken on behalf of all children and young persons without any discrimination for

reasons of parentage or other conditions. Children and young persons should be protected from economic and social exploitation. Their employment in work harmful to their morals or health or dangerous to life or likely to hamper their normal development should be punishable by law. States should also set age limits below which the paid employment of child labour should be prohibited and punishable by law.

Article 11

1. The States Parties to the present Covenant recognize the right of everyone to an adequate standard of living for himself and his family, including adequate food, clothing and housing, and to the continuous improvement of living conditions. The States Parties will take appropriate steps to ensure the realization of this right, recognizing to this effect the essential importance of international co-operation based on free consent.
2. The States Parties to the present Covenant, recognizing the fundamental right of everyone to be free from hunger, shall take, individually and through international co-operation, the measures, including specific programmes, which are needed:
   (a) To improve methods of production, conservation and distribution of food by making full use of technical and scientific knowledge, by disseminating knowledge of the principles of nutrition and by developing or reforming agrarian systems in such a way as to achieve the most efficient development and utilization of natural resources;
   (b) Taking into account the problems of both food-importing and food-exporting countries, to ensure an equitable distribution of world food supplies in relation to need.

Article 12

1. The States Parties to the present Covenant recognize the right of everyone to the enjoyment of the highest attainable standard of physical and mental health.
2. The steps to be taken by the States Parties to the present Covenant to achieve the full realization of this right shall include those necessary for:

(a) The provision for the reduction of the stillbirth-rate and of infant mortality and for the healthy development of the child;

(b) The improvement of all aspects of environmental and industrial hygiene;

(c) The prevention, treatment and control of epidemic, endemic, occupational and other diseases;

(d) The creation of conditions which would assure to all medical service and medical attention in the event of sickness.

Article 13

1. The States Parties to the present Covenant recognize the right of everyone to education. They agree that education shall be directed to the full development of the human personality and the sense of its dignity, and shall strengthen the respect for human rights and fundamental freedoms. They further agree that education shall enable all persons to participate effectively in a free society, promote understanding, tolerance and friendship among all nations and all racial, ethnic or religious groups, and further the activities of the United Nations for the maintenance of peace.

2. The States Parties to the present Covenant recognize that, with a view to achieving the full realization of this right:

   (a) Primary education shall be compulsory and available free to all;

   (b) Secondary education in its different forms, including technical and vocational secondary education, shall be made generally available and accessible to all by every appropriate means, and in particular by the progressive introduction of free education;

   (c) Higher education shall be made equally accessible to all, on the basis of capacity, by every appropriate means, and in particular by the progressive introduction of free education;

   (d) Fundamental education shall be encouraged or intensified as far as possible for those persons who have not received or completed the whole period of their primary education;

   (e) The development of a system of schools at all levels shall be actively pursued, an adequate fellowship system shall be established, and the material conditions of teaching staff shall be continuously improved.

3. The States Parties to the present Covenant undertake to have respect for the liberty of parents and, when applicable, legal guardians to choose for their children schools, other than those established by the public authorities, which conform to such minimum educational standards as may be laid down or approved by the State and to ensure the religious and moral education of their children in conformity with their own convictions.

4. No part of this article shall be construed so as to interfere with the liberty of individuals and bodies to establish and direct educational institutions, subject always to the observance of the principles set forth in paragraph I of this article and to the requirement that the education given in such institutions shall conform to such minimum standards as may be laid down by the State.

Article 14

Each State Party to the present Covenant which, at the time of becoming a Party, has not been able to secure in its metropolitan territory or other territories under its jurisdiction compulsory primary education, free of charge, undertakes, within two years, to work out and adopt a detailed plan of action for the progressive implementation, within a reasonable number of years, to be fixed in the plan, of the principle of compulsory education free of charge for all.

Article 15

1. The States Parties to the present Covenant recognize the right of everyone:
   (a) To take part in cultural life;
   (b) To enjoy the benefits of scientific progress and its applications;
   (c) To benefit from the protection of the moral and material interests resulting from any scientific, literary or artistic production of which he is the author.

2. The steps to be taken by the States Parties to the present Covenant to achieve the full realization of this right shall include those necessary for the conservation, the development and the diffusion of science and culture.

3. The States Parties to the present Covenant undertake to respect the freedom indispensable for scientific research and creative activity.

4. The States Parties to the present Covenant recognize the benefits to be derived from the encouragement and development of international contacts and co-operation in the scientific and cultural fields.

Part IV

Article 16

1. The States Parties to the present Covenant undertake to submit in conformity with this part of the Covenant reports on the measures which they have adopted and the progress made in achieving the observance of the rights recognized herein.

2.

   (a) All reports shall be submitted to the Secretary-General of the United Nations, who shall transmit copies to the Economic and Social Council for consideration in accordance with the provisions of the present Covenant;

   (b) The Secretary-General of the United Nations shall also transmit to the specialized agencies copies of the reports, or any relevant parts therefrom, from States Parties to the present Covenant which are also members of these specialized agencies in so far as these reports, or parts therefrom, relate to any matters which fall within the responsibilities of the said agencies in accordance with their constitutional instruments.

Article 17

1. The States Parties to the present Covenant shall furnish their reports in stages, in accordance with a programme to be established by the Economic and Social Council within one year of the entry into force of the present Covenant after consultation with the States Parties and the specialized agencies concerned.
2. Reports may indicate factors and difficulties affecting the degree of fulfilment of obligations under the present Covenant.
3. Where relevant information has previously been furnished to the United Nations or to any specialized agency by any State Party to the present Covenant, it will not be necessary to reproduce that information, but a precise reference to the information so furnished will suffice.

Article 18

Pursuant to its responsibilities under the Charter of the United Nations in the field of human rights and fundamental freedoms, the Economic and Social Council may make arrangements with the specialized agencies in respect of their reporting to it on the progress made in achieving the observance of the provisions of the present Covenant falling within the scope of their activities. These reports may include particulars of decisions and recommendations on such implementation adopted by their competent organs.

Article 19

The Economic and Social Council may transmit to the Commission on Human Rights for study and general recommendation or, as appropriate, for information the reports concerning human rights submitted by States in accordance with articles 16 and 17, and those concerning human rights submitted by the specialized agencies in accordance with article 18.

Article 20

The States Parties to the present Covenant and the specialized agencies concerned may submit comments to the Economic and Social Council on any general recommendation under article 19 or reference to such general recommendation in any report of the Commission on Human Rights or any documentation referred to therein.

Article 21

The Economic and Social Council may submit from time to time to the General Assembly reports with recommendations of a general nature and a summary of the information received from the States Parties to the present Covenant and the specialized agencies on the measures taken and the progress made in achieving general observance of the rights recognized in the present Covenant.

Article 22

The Economic and Social Council may bring to the attention of other organs of the United Nations, their subsidiary organs and specialized agencies concerned with furnishing technical assistance any matters arising out of the reports referred to in this part of the present Covenant which may assist such bodies in deciding, each within its field of competence, on the advisability of international measures likely to contribute to the effective progressive implementation of the present Covenant.

Article 23

The States Parties to the present Covenant agree that international action for the achievement of the rights recognized in the present Covenant includes such methods as the conclusion of conventions, the adoption of recommendations, the furnishing of technical assistance and the holding of regional meetings and technical meetings for the purpose of consultation and study organized in conjunction with the Governments concerned.

Article 24

Nothing in the present Covenant shall be interpreted as impairing the provisions of the Charter of the United Nations and of the constitutions of the specialized agencies which define the respective responsibilities of the various organs of the United Nations and of the specialized agencies in regard to the matters dealt with in the present Covenant.

Article 25

Nothing in the present Covenant shall be interpreted as impairing the inherent right of all peoples to enjoy and utilize fully and freely their natural wealth and resources.

Part V

Article 26

1. The present Covenant is open for signature by any State Member of the United Nations or member of any of its specialized agencies, by any State Party to the Statute of the International Court of Justice, and by any other State which has been invited by the General Assembly of the United Nations to become a party to the present Covenant.
2. The present Covenant is subject to ratification. Instruments of ratification shall be deposited with the Secretary-General of the United Nations.
3. The present Covenant shall be open to accession by any State referred to in paragraph 1 of this article.
4. Accession shall be effected by the deposit of an instrument of accession with the Secretary-General of the United Nations.

5. The Secretary-General of the United Nations shall inform all States which have signed the present Covenant or acceded to it of the deposit of each instrument of ratification or accession.

Article 27

1. The present Covenant shall enter into force three months after the date of the deposit with the Secretary-General of the United Nations of the thirty-fifth instrument of ratification or instrument of accession.
2. For each State ratifying the present Covenant or acceding to it after the deposit of the thirty-fifth instrument of ratification or instrument of accession, the present Covenant shall enter into force three months after the date of the deposit of its own instrument of ratification or instrument of accession.

Article 28

The provisions of the present Covenant shall extend to all parts of federal States without any limitations or exceptions.

Article 29

1. Any State Party to the present Covenant may propose an amendment and file it with the Secretary-General of the United Nations. The Secretary-General shall thereupon communicate any proposed amendments to the States Parties to the present Covenant with a request that they notify him whether they favour a conference of States Parties for the purpose of considering and voting upon the proposals. In the event that at least one third of the States Parties favours such a conference, the Secretary-General shall convene the conference under the auspices of the United Nations. Any amendment adopted by a majority of the States Parties present and voting at the conference shall be submitted to the General Assembly of the United Nations for approval.
2. Amendments shall come into force when they have been approved by the General Assembly of the United Nations and accepted by a two-thirds majority of the States Parties to the present Covenant in accordance with their respective constitutional processes.
3. When amendments come into force they shall be binding on those States Parties which have accepted them, other States Parties still being

bound by the provisions of the present Covenant and any earlier amendment which they have accepted.

Article 30

Irrespective of the notifications made under article 26, paragraph 5, the Secretary-General of the United Nations shall inform all States referred to in paragraph I of the same article of the following particulars:

(a) Signatures, ratifications and accessions under article 26;-

(b) The date of the entry into force of the present Covenant under article 27 and the date of the entry into force of any amendments under article 29.

Article 31

1. The present Covenant, of which the Chinese, English, French, Russian and Spanish texts are equally authentic, shall be deposited in the archives of the United Nations.
2. The Secretary-General of the United Nations shall transmit certified copies of the present Covenant to all States referred to in article 26.

CONDITIONS

The Universal Declaration of Human Rights affirms that the exercise of a person's rights and freedoms may be subject to certain limitations, which must be determined by law, solely for the purpose of securing due recognition of the rights and freedoms of others and of meeting the just requirements of morality, public order and the general welfare in a democratic society. Rights may not be exercised contrary to the purposes and principles of the United Nations, or if they are aimed at destroying any of the rights set forth in the Declaration (arts. 29 and 30).

The International Covenant on Economic, Social and Cultural Rights states that the rights provided for therein may be limited by law, but only in so far as it is compatible with the nature of the rights and solely to promote the general welfare in a democratic society (art. 4).

Unlike the Universal Declaration and the Covenant on Economic, Social and Cultural Rights, the International Covenant on Civil and Political Rights contains no general provision applicable to all the rights provided for in the Covenant authorizing restrictions on their exercise. However, several articles in the Covenant provide that the rights being dealt with shall not be subject to any restrictions except those which are prescribed by law and are necessary to protect national security, public order, or the rights and freedoms of others.

Certain rights, therefore, may never be suspended or limited, even in emergency situations. These are the rights to life, to freedom from torture, to freedom from enslavement or servitude, to protection from imprisonment for debt, to freedom from retroactive penal laws, to recognition as a person before the law, and to freedom of thought, conscience and religion.

The Covenant on Civil and Political Rights allows a State to limit or suspend the enjoyment of certain rights in cases of officially proclaimed public emergencies which threaten the life of the nation. Such limitations or suspensions are permitted only "to the extent strictly required by the exigencies of the situation" and may never involve discrimination solely on the ground of race, colour, sex, language, religion or social origin (art. 4). The limitations or suspensions must also be reported to the United Nations.

First Optional Protocol

The first Optional Protocol to the International Covenant on Civil and Political Rights enables the Human Rights Committee, set up under that Covenant, to receive and consider communications from individuals claiming to be victims of violations of any of the rights set forth in the Covenant.

Under article I of the Optional Protocol, a State party to the Covenant that becomes a party to the Protocol recognizes the competence of the Human Rights Committee to receive and consider communications from individuals subject to its jurisdiction who claim to be victims of a violation by that State of any of the rights set forth in the Covenant. Individuals who make such a claim, and who have exhausted all available domestic remedies, are entitled to submit a written communication to the Committee (art. 2).

Such communications as are determined to be admissible by the Committee (in addition to article 2, articles 3 and 5 (2) lay down conditions for admissibility) are brought to the attention of the State party alleged to be violating a provision of the Covenant. Within six months, that State must submit to the Committee written explanations or statements clarifying the matter and indicating the remedy, if any, that it may have applied (art. 4).

The Human Rights Committee considers the admissible communications, at closed meetings, in the light of all written information made available to it by the individual and the State party concerned. It then forwards its views to the State party and to the individual (art. 5).

A summary of the Committee's activities under the Optional Protocol is included in the report which it submits annually to the General Assembly through the Economic and Social Council (art. 6).

Second Optional Protocol

The Second Optional Protocol to the International Covenant on Civil and Political Rights, aiming at the abolition of the death penalty, was adopted by the General Assembly by its resolution 44/128 of 15 December 1989. Under its article 1, no one within the jurisdiction of a State party to the Protocol may be executed.

Under article 3 of the Protocol, States parties must include in the reports which they submit to the Human Rights Committee information on measures taken to give effect to the Protocol.

Article 5 of the Second Optional Protocol provides that, with respect to any State party to the first Optional Protocol, the competence of the Human Rights Committee to receive and consider communications from individuals subject to that State's jurisdiction shall extend to the provisions of the Second Optional Protocol, unless the State party concerned has made a statement to the contrary at the moment of ratification or accession.

Under article 6, the provisions of the Second Optional Protocol apply as additional provisions to the Covenant.

Entry into force of the Covenants and the Optional Protocols

The International Covenant on Economic, Social and Cultural Rights entered into force on 3 January 1976, three months after the date of deposit with the Secretary-General of the thirty-fifth instrument of ratification or accession, as provided in article 27. As at 30 September 1995, the Covenant had been ratified or acceded to by 132 States:

Afghanistan, Albania, Algeria, Angola, Argentina, Armenia, Australia, Austria, Azerbaijan, Barbados, Belarus, Belgium, Benin, Bolivia, Bosnia and Herzegovina, Brazil, Bulgaria, Burundi, Cambodia, Cameroon, Canada, Cape Verde, Central African Republic, Chad, Chile, Colombia, Congo, Costa Rica, Côte d'Ivoire, Croatia, Cyprus, Czech Republic, Democratic People's Republic of Korea, Denmark, Dominica, Dominican Republic, Ecuador,

Egypt, El Salvador, Equatorial Guinea, Estonia, Ethiopia, Finland, France, Gabon, Gambia, Georgia, Germany, Greece, Grenada, Guatemala, Guinea, Guinea-Bissau, Guyana, Haiti, Hungary, Iceland, India, Iran (Islamic Republic of), Iraq, Ireland, Israel, Italy, Jamaica, Japan, Jordan, Kenya, Kyrgyzstan, Latvia, Lebanon, Lesotho, Libyan Arab Jamahiriya, Lithuania, Luxembourg, Madagascar, Malawi, Mali, Malta, Mauritius, Mexico, Mongolia, Morocco, Mozambique, Namibia, Nepal, Netherlands, New Zealand, Nicaragua, Niger, Nigeria, Norway, Panama, Paraguay, Peru, Philippines, Poland, Portugal, Republic of Korea, Republic of Moldova, Romania, Russian Federation, Rwanda, Saint Vincent and the Grenadines, San Marino, Senegal, Seychelles, Slovakia, Slovenia, Somalia, Spain, Sri Lanka, Sudan, Suriname, Sweden, Switzerland, Syrian Arab Republic, The former Yugoslav Republic of Macedonia, Togo, Trinidad and Tobago, Tunisia, Ukraine, United Kingdom, United Republic of Tanzania, United States of America, Uruguay, Venezuela, Viet Nam, Yemen, Yugoslavia, Zaire, Zambia and Zimbabwe.

The International Covenant on Civil and Political Rights entered into force on 23 March 1976, three months after the date of deposit with the Secretary-General of the thirty-fifth instrument of ratification or accession, as provided in article 49. As at 30 September 1995, the Covenant had been ratified or acceded to by 132 States:

Afghanistan, Albania, Algeria, Angola, Argentina, Armenia, Australia, Austria, Azerbaijan, Barbados, Belarus, Belgium, Benin, Bolivia, Bosnia and Herzegovina, Brazil, Bulgaria, Burundi, Cambodia, Cameroon, Canada, Cape Verde, Central African Republic, Chad, Chile, Colombia, Congo, Costa Rica, Côte d'Ivoire, Croatia, Cyprus, Czech Republic, Democratic People's Republic of Korea, Denmark, Dominica, Dominican Republic, Ecuador, Egypt, El Salvador, Equatorial Guinea, Estonia, Ethiopia, Finland, France, Gabon, Gambia, Georgia, Germany, Grenada, Guatemala, Guinea, Guyana, Haiti, Hungary, Iceland, India, Iran (Islamic Republic of), Iraq, Ireland, Israel, Italy, Jamaica, Japan, Jordan, Kenya, Kyrgyzstan, Latvia, Lebanon, Lesotho, Libyan Arab Jamahiriya, Lithuania, Luxembourg, Madagascar, Malawi, Mali, Malta, Mauritius, Mexico, Mongolia, Morocco, Mozambique, Namibia, Nepal, Netherlands, New Zealand, Nicaragua, Niger, Nigeria, Norway, Panama, Paraguay, Peru, Philippines, Poland, Portugal, Republic of Korea, Republic of Moldova, Romania, Russian Federation, Rwanda, Saint Vincent and the Grenadines, San Marino, Senegal, Seychelles,

Slovakia, Slovenia, Somalia, Spain, Sri Lanka, Sudan, Suriname, Sweden, Switzerland, Syrian Arab Republic, The former Yugoslav Republic of Macedonia, Togo, Trinidad and Tobago, Tunisia, Uganda, Ukraine, United Kingdom, United Republic of Tanzania, United States of America, Uruguay, Uzbekistan, Venezuela, Viet Nam, Yemen, Yugoslavia, Zaire, Zambia and Zimbabwe.

As at the same date, 44 States parties to the International Covenant on Civil and Political Rights had made the declaration under its article 41, recognizing the competence of the Human Rights Committee "to receive and consider communications to the effect that a State Party claims that another State Party is not fulfilling its obligations" under the Covenant. The provisions of article 41 entered into force on 28 March 1979 in accordance with paragraph 2 of that article.

The first Optional Protocol to the International Covenant on Civil and Political Rights entered into force simultaneously with the Covenant, having received the minimum 10 ratifications or accessions required. As at 30 September 1995, 85 States parties to the Covenant had also become parties to the first Optional Protocol:

Algeria, Angola, Argentina, Armenia, Australia, Austria, Barbados, Belarus, Belgium, Benin, Bolivia, Bosnia and Herzegovina, Bulgaria, Cameroon, Canada, Central African Republic, Chad, Chile, Colombia, Congo, Costa Rica, Cyprus, Czech Republic, Denmark, Dominican Republic, Ecuador, El Salvador, Equatorial Guinea, Estonia, Finland, France, Gambia, Georgia, Germany, Guinea, Guyana, Hungary, Iceland, Ireland, Italy, Jamaica, Kyrgyzstan, Latvia, Libyan Arab Jamahiriya, Lithuania, Luxembourg, Madagascar, Malta, Mauritius, Mongolia, Namibia, Nepal, Netherlands, New Zealand, Nicaragua, Niger, Norway, Panama, Paraguay, Peru, Philippines, Poland, Portugal, Republic of Korea, Romania, Russian Federation, Saint Vincent and the Grenadines, San Marino, Senegal, Seychelles, Slovakia, Slovenia, Somalia, Spain, Suriname, Sweden, The former Yugoslav Republic of Macedonia, Togo, Trinidad and Tobago, Ukraine, Uruguay, Uzbekistan, Venezuela, Zaire and Zambia.

The Second Optional Protocol to the International Covenant on Civil and Political Rights, aiming at the abolition of the death penalty, entered into force on 11 July 1991, having received the minimum 10 ratifications or accessions required. As at 30 September 1995, the Protocol had been ratified or acceded to by 28 States:

Australia, Austria, Denmark, Ecuador, Finland, Germany, Hungary, Iceland, Ireland, Italy, Luxembourg, Malta, Mozambique, Namibia, Netherlands, New Zealand, Norway, Panama, Portugal, Romania, Seychelles, Slovenia, Spain, Sweden, Switzerland, The former Yugoslav Republic of Macedonia, Uruguay and Venezuela.

Worldwide Influence of the International Bill of Human Rights

From 1948, when the Universal Declaration of Human Rights was adopted and proclaimed, until 1976, when the International Covenants on Human Rights entered into force, the Declaration was the only completed portion of the International Bill of Human Rights. The Declaration, and at a later stage the Covenants, exercised a profound influence on the thoughts and actions of individuals and their Governments in all parts of the world.

The International Conference on Human Rights, which met at Teheran from 22 April to 13 May 1968 to review the progress made in the 20 years since the adoption of the Universal Declaration and to formulate a programme for the future, solemnly declared in the Proclamation of Teheran:

1. It is imperative that the members of the international community fulfil their solemn obligations to promote and encourage respect for human rights and fundamental freedoms for all without distinctions of any kind such as race, colour, sex, language, religion, political or other opinions;
2. The Universal Declaration of Human Rights states a common understanding, of the peoples of the world concerning the inalienable and inviolable rights of all members of the human family and constitutes an obligation for the members of the international community;
3. The International Covenant on Civil and Political Rights, the International Covenant on Economic, Social and Cultural Rights, the Declaration on the Granting of Independence to Colonial Countries and Peoples, the International Convention on the Elimination of All Forms of Racial Discrimination as well as other conventions and declarations in the field of human rights adopted under the auspices of the United Nations, the specialized agencies and the regional intergovernmental organizations, have created new standards and obligations to which States should conform;

. . .

Thus, for more than 25 years, the Universal Declaration on Human Rights stood alone as an international "standard of achievement for all peoples and all nations". It became known and was accepted as authoritative both in States which became parties to one or both of the Covenants and in those which did not ratify or accede to either. Its provisions were cited as the basis and justification for many important decisions taken by United Nations bodies; they inspired the preparation of a number of international human rights instruments, both within and outside the United Nations system; they exercised a significant influence on a number of multilateral and bilateral treaties; and they had a strong impact as the basis for the preparation of many new national constitutions and national laws.

The Universal Declaration came to be recognized as a historic document articulating a common definition of human dignity and values. The Declaration is a yardstick by which to measure the degree of respect for, and compliance with, international human rights standards everywhere on earth.

The coming into force of the Covenants, by which States parties accepted a legal as well as a moral obligation to promote and protect human rights and fundamental freedoms, did not in any way diminish the widespread influence of the Universal Declaration. On the contrary, the very existence of the Covenants, and the fact that they contain the measures of implementation required to ensure the realization of the rights and freedoms set out in the Declaration, gives greater strength to the Declaration.

Moreover, the Universal Declaration is truly universal in scope, as it preserves its validity for every member of the human family, everywhere, regardless of whether or not Governments have formally accepted its principles or ratified the Covenants. On the other hand, the Covenants, by their nature as multilateral conventions, are legally binding only on those States which have accepted them by ratification or accession.

In many important resolutions and decisions adopted by United Nations bodies, including the General Assembly and the Security Council, the Universal Declaration of Human Rights and one or both Covenants have been cited as the basis for action.

Nearly all the international human rights instruments adopted by United Nations bodies since 1948 elaborate principles set out in the Universal Declaration of Human Rights. The International Covenant on Economic,

Social and Cultural Rights states in its preamble that it developed out of recognition of the fact that

> in accordance with the Universal Declaration of Human Rights, the ideal of free human beings enjoyin freedom from fear and want can only be achieved if conditions are created whereby everyone may enjoy his economic, social and cultural rights, as well as his civil and political rights.

A similar statement is made in the preamble to the International Covenant on Civil and Political Rights.

The Declaration on the Protection of All Persons from Being Subjected to Torture and Other Cruel, Inhuman or Degrading Treatment or Punishment, adopted by the General Assembly in 1975 (resolution 3452 (XXX)), spells out the meaning of article 5 of the Universal Declaration of Human Rights and article 7 of the International Covenant on Civil and Political Rights, both of which provide that no one may be subjected to torture or to cruel, inhuman or degrading treatment or punishment. This prohibition was further reinforced by the adoption in 1984 of the Convention against Torture and Other Cruel, Inhuman or Degrading Treatment or Punishment (General Assembly resolution 39/46). Similarly, the Declaration on the Elimination of All Forms of Intolerance and of Discrimination Based on Religion or Belief, proclaimed by the General Assembly in 1981 (resolution 36/55); clearly defines the nature and scope of the principles of non discrimination and equality before the law and the right to freedom of thought, conscience, religion and belief contained in the Universal Declaration and the International Covenants.

A similar situation prevails as regards international human rights instruments adopted outside the United Nations system. For example, the preamble to the Convention for the Protection of Human Rights and Fundamental Freedoms, adopted by the Council of Europe at Rome in 1950, concludes with the following words:

> Being resolved, as the Governments of European countries which are like-minded and have a common heritage of political traditions, ideals, freedom and the rule of law, to take the first steps for the collective enforcement of certain of the rights stated in the Universal Declaration;

Article II of the Charter of the Organization of African Unity, adopted at Addis Ababa in 1963, provides that one of the purposes of the Organization is "to promote international cooperation, having due regard to the Charter of the United Nations and the Universal Declaration of Human Rights". The American Convention on Human Rights, signed at San José, Costa Rica, in 1969, states in its preamble that the principles to which it gives effect are those set forth in the Charter of the Organization of American States, in the American Declaration of the Rights and Duties of Man, and in the Universal Declaration of Human Rights.

Judges of the International Court of Justice have occasionally invoked principles contained in the International Bill of Human Rights as a basis for their decisions.

National and local tribunals have frequently cited principles set out in the International Bill of Human Rights in their decisions. Moreover, in recent years, national constitutional and legislative texts have increasingly provided measures of legal protection for those principles; indeed, many recent national and local laws are clearly modelled on provisions set forth in the Universal Declaration of Human Rights and the International Covenants, which remain a beacon for all present and future efforts in the field of human rights, both nationally and internationally.

Finally, the World Conference on Human Rights, held at Vienna in June 1993, adopted by acclamation the Vienna Declaration and Programme of Action, in which it welcomed the progress made in the codification of human rights instruments and urged the universal ratification of human rights treaties. In addition, all States were encouraged to avoid, as far as possible, the resort to reservations (part 1, para. 26).

Thus the International Bill of Human Rights represents a milestone in the history of human rights, a veritable Magna Carta marking mankind's arrival at a vitally important phase: the conscious acquisition of human dignity and worth.

References

Brownlie, Ian (2003). *Principles of Public International Law*. OUP.

Doebbler, Curtis (2006). *Introduction to international human rights law.*. Cd Publishing.

Glendon, Mary Ann (2001). *A world made new : Eleanor Roosevelt and the Universal Declaration of Human Rights*. New York: Random House.

Shaw, Malcom (2008). *International Law*. Leiden: Cambridge University Press.

Ishay, Micheline R. (2008). *The history of human rights : from ancient times to the globalization era*. Berkeley, Calif.: University of California Press.

3

Human Rights Bodies

The Office of the High Commissioner for Human Rights (OHCHR) works to offer the best expertise and support to the different human rights monitoring mechanisms in the United Nations system : UN Charter-based bodies, including the Human Rights Council, and bodies created under the international human rights treaties and made up of independent experts mandated to monitor State parties' compliance with their treaty obligations. Most of these bodies receive secretariat support from the Human Rights Council and Treaties Division of the Office of the High Commissioner for Human Rights (OHCHR).

Charter-based bodies

Charter bodies include the former Commission on Human Rights, the Human Rights Council , and Special Procedures. The Human Rights Council, which replaced the Commission on Human Rights, held its first meeting on 19 June 2006. This intergovernmental body, which meets in Geneva 10 weeks a year, is composed of 47 elected United Nations Member States who serve for an initial period of 3 years, and cannot be elected for more than two consecutive terms. The Human Rights Council is a forum empowered to prevent abuses, inequity and discrimination, protect the most vulnerable, and expose perpetrators.

The Human Rights Council is a separate entity from OHCHR. This distinction originates from the separate mandates they were given by the General Assembly. Nevertheless, OHCHR provides substantive support for the meetings of the Human Rights Council, and follow-up to the Council's deliberations.

Special Procedures is the general name given to the mechanisms established by the Commission on Human Rights and assumed by the Human Rights Council to address either specific country situations or thematic issues in all parts of the world. Special Procedures are either an individual –a special rapporteur or representative, or independent expert—or a working group. They are prominent, independent experts working on a voluntary basis, appointed by the Human Rights Council.

Special Procedures' mandates usually call on mandate-holders to examine, monitor, advise and publicly report on human rights situations in specific countries or territories, known as country mandates, or on major phenomena of human rights violations worldwide, known as thematic mandates. There are 30 thematic mandates and 8 country mandates. All report to the Human Rights Council on their findings and recommendations. They are sometimes the only mechanism that will alert the international community on certain human rights issues.

OHCHR supports the work of rapporteurs, representatives and working groups through its Special Procedures Division (SPD) which services 27 thematic mandates; and the Research and Right to Development Division (RRDD) which aims to improve the integration of human rights standards and principles, including the rights to development; while the Field Operations and Technical Cooperation Division (FOTCD) supports the work of country-mandates.

The United Nations Human Rights Council

The United Nations Human Rights Council (UNHRC) is an inter-governmental body within the United Nations System. The UNHRC is the successor to the United Nations Commission on Human Rights (UNCHR, herein CHR), and is a subsidiary body of the United Nations General Assembly. The council works closely with the Office of the High Commissioner for Human Rights (OHCHR) and engages the United Nations' Special procedures.

The General Assembly established the UNHRC by adopting a resolution (A/RES/60/251) on 15 March 2006, in order to replace the previous CHR, which had been heavily criticised for allowing countries with poor human rights records to be members.

The UN Secretary General Ban Ki Moon and former High Commissioner for Human Rights Mary Robinson criticized the council for acting according to political considerations as opposed to human rights. Specifically, Secretaries General Kofi Annan and Ban Ki Moon, the council's president Doru Costea, the European Union, Canada and the United States have accused the council of focusing disproportionately on the Israeli–Palestinian conflict. The United States boycotted the Council during the George W. Bush administration, but reversed its position on it during the Obama administration.

Beginning in 2009, however, commentators began to argue that the HRC was becoming increasingly relevant as the Council addressed country situations in Burma, Guinea, North Korea, Côte d'Ivoire, Kyrgyzstan, Syria, Libya, Iran, and Sri Lanka, and addressed important thematic human rights issues such as Freedom of Association and Assembly, Freedom of Expression, Discrimination Against Women and Freedom of Religion and the rights of LGBT people.

On 18 June 2007, one year after holding its first meeting, the UNHRC adopted its Institution-building package, which provides elements to guide it in its future work. Among the elements was the Universal Periodic Review. The Universal Periodic Review assesses the human rights situations in all 193 UN Member States. Another element is an Advisory Committee, which serves as the UNHRC's think tank, and provides it with expertise and advice on thematic human rights issues, that is, issues which pertain to all parts of the world. Another element is a Complaint procedure, which allows individuals and organizations to bring complaints about human rights violations to the attention of the Council.

Structure of Human Rights Council

The members of the General Assembly elect the members who occupy the UNHRC's forty-seven seats. The General Assembly takes into account the candidate States' contribution to the promotion and protection of human rights, as well as their voluntary pledges and commitments in this regard. The term of each seat is three years, and no member may occupy a seat for more than two consecutive terms. The seats are distributed among the UN's regional groups as follows: 13 for Africa, 13 for Asia, six for Eastern Europe, eight for Latin America and the Caribbean (GRULAC), and seven for the Western European and Others Group (WEOG). The previous CHR had a membership of 53 elected by the Economic and Social Council (ECOSOC) through a majority of those present and voting.

The General Assembly can suspend the rights and privileges of any Council member that it decides has persistently committed gross and systematic violations of human rights during its term of membership. The suspension process requires a two-thirds majority vote by the General Assembly. The resolution establishing the UNHRC states that "members elected to the Council shall uphold the highest standards in the promotion and protection of human rights."

Sessions

The UNHRC holds regular sessions three times a year, in March, June and September. The UNHRC can decide at any time to hold a special session to address human rights violations and emergencies, at the request of one-third of the member states. To date there have been 19 Special Sessions.

Members

The United Nations Commission on Human Rights was a functional commission within the overall framework of the United Nations from 1946 until it was replaced by the UN Human Rights Council in 2006. It was a subsidiary body of the UN Economic and Social Council (ECOSOC), which elected members through the mechanism of the United Nations Regional Groups.

2007 Group

- *African States:* Algeria, Morocco, South Africa and Tunisia.
- *Asian States*: Bahrain, India, Indonesia and Philippines.
- *Eastern European States*: Czech Republic and Poland.
- *Latin American & Caribbean States*: Argentina and Ecuador.
- *Western European & Other States:* Finland and the Netherlands.

2008 Group

- *African States:* Gabon, Ghana, Mali and Zambia.
- *Asian States:* Japan, Pakistan, South Korea and Sri Lanka.
- *Eastern European States:* Romania and the Ukraine.
- *Latin American & Caribbean States:* Brazil, Guatemala and Peru.
- *Western European & Other States:* France and the United Kingdom.

2009 Group

- *African States:* Cameroon, Djibouti, Mauritius, Nigeria and Senegal.
- *Asian States:* Bangladesh, China, Jordan, Malaysia and Saudi Arabia.
- *Eastern European States:* Azerbaijan and the Russian Federation.
- *Latin American & Caribbean States*: Cuba, Mexico and Uruguay.
- *Western European & Other States:* Canada, Germany, Switzerland and Turkey.

2010 Group

The replacement for the 2007 Group, was duly elected by the General Assembly on 17 May 2007, known as the 2010 Group, the year when their terms expire. In this election, Angola and Egypt were elected to the council, whereas Belarus was rejected.

- *African States*: Angola, Egypt, Madagascar and South Africa, .
- *Asian States*: India, Indonesia, Philippines and Qatar.
- *Eastern European States*: Slovenia and Bosnia & Herzegovina.
- *Latin American & Caribbean States:* Nicaragua and Bolivia.
- *Western European & Other States*: Netherlands and Italy.

2011 Group

The replacement for the 2008 Group, was duly elected by the General Assembly on 21 May 2008, known as the 2011 Group, the year when their terms expire.

- *African States*: Burkina Faso, Gabon, Ghana and Zambia.
- *Asian States*: Bahrain, Japan, Pakistan and South Korea.
- *Eastern European States*: Slovakia and Ukraine.
- *Latin American & Caribbean States*: Argentina, Brazil and Chile.
- *Western European & Other States*: France and United Kingdom.

2012 Group

The replacement for the 2009 Group, was duly elected by the General Assembly on 12 May 2009, known as the 2012 Group, the year when their terms expire.

- *African States*: Cameroon, Djibouti, Mauritius, Nigeria and Senegal.
- *Asian States*: Bangladesh, China, Jordan, Kyrgystan and Saudi Arabia.

- *Eastern European States*: Hungary and the Russian Federation.
- *Latin American & Caribbean States*: Cuba, Mexico and Uruguay.
- *Western European & Other States*: United States, Belgium, Norway and Turkey.

2013 Group

The replacement for the 2010 Group, was duly elected by the General Assembly on 13 May 2010, known as the 2013 Group, the year when their terms expire.

- *African States:* Angola, Libyan Arab Jamahiriya, Mauritania and Uganda.
- *Asian States:* Malaysia, Maldives, Qatar and Thailand.
- *Eastern European States:* Poland and Republic of Moldova .
- *Latin American & Caribbean State*s: Ecuador, Guatemala and Peru.
- *Western European & Other States:* Spain and Switzerland.

2014 Group

The replacement for the 2011 Group, was duly elected by the General Assembly on 20 May 2011, known as the 2014 Group, the year when their terms expire.

- *African States*: Benin, Botswana, Burkina Faso and Congo.
- *Asian States:* India, Indonesia, Kuwait and Philippine.
- *Eastern European States:* Czech Republic and Romania.
- *Latin American & Caribbean States:* Chile, Costa Rica and Peru.
- *Western European & Other States*: Austria and Italy.

Presidents

- Mr. Luis Alfonso de Alba (Mexico) 19 June 2006 to 18 June 2007.
- Mr. Doru Romulus Costea (Romania) 19 June 2007 to 18 June 2008.
- Mr. Martin Ihoeghian Uhomoibhi (Nigeria) 19 June 2008 to 18 June 2009.
- Mr. Alex Van Meeuwen (Belgium) 19 June 2009 to 18 June 2010.
- Mr. Sihasak Phuangketkeow (Thailand) 19 June 2010 to 18 June 2011.
- Laura Dupuy Lasserre (Uruguay) 19 June 2011 to current.

Subsidiary Bodies That Directly Report to the HRC

Universal Periodic Review Working Group

A key component of the Council consists in a periodic review of all 193 UN member states, called the Universal Periodic Review (UPR).

The new mechanism is based on reports coming from different sources, one of them being contributions from NGOs. Each country's situation will be examined during a three-hour debate.

- *First session (7–18 April 2008)*: Tunisia, Morocco, Algeria, South Africa, Bahrain, Indonesia, India, Philippines, Ecuador, Brazil, Argentina, Finland, United Kingdom, Netherlands, Poland, Czech Republic.
- *Second session (5–16 May 2008)*: Gabon, Ghana, Peru, Guatemala, Benin, Republic of Korea, Switzerland, Pakistan, Zambia, Japan, Ukraine, Sri Lanka, France, Tonga, Romania, and Mali.
- *Third session (1–12 December 2008)*: Botswana, Bahamas, Burundi, Luxembourg, Barbados, Montenegro, United Arab Emirates, Israel, Liechtenstein, Serbia, Turkmenistan, Burkina Faso, Cape Verde, Colombia, Uzbekistan, and Tuvalu.
- *Fourth session (2–13 February 2009):* Germany, Djibouti, Canada, Bangladesh, Russian Federation, Azerbaijan, Cameroon, Cuba, Saudi Arabia, Senegal, China, Nigeria, Mexico, Mauritius, Jordan, Malaysia.
- *Fifth session (4–15 May 2009):* Central African Republic, Monaco, Belize, Chad, Congo, Malta, New Zealand, Afghanistan, Chile, Vietnam, Uruguay, Yemen, Vanuatu, Former Yugoslav Republic of Macedonia, Comoros, Slovakia.
- *Sixth session (30 November – 11 December 2009)*: Côte d'Ivoire, Democratic Republic of the Congo, Equatorial Guinea, Eritrea, Ethiopia, Bhutan, Brunei Darussalam, Cambodia, Democratic People's Republic of Korea, Costa Rica, Dominica, Dominican Republic, Norway, Portugal, Albania.
- The second half of the complete UPR cycle will take place until 2011, after which the status of the Human Rights Council will be reviewed by the General Assembly. The Universal Periodic Review is an evolving process; the Council, after the conclusion of the first review cycle, may review the modalities and the periodicity of this mechanism, based on best practices and lessons learned.

June 2006: In applying General Assembly Resolution 60/251 dated 15 March 2006, the Human Rights Council adopted a non-official document relating to the procedure of universal periodic review (UPR). This document was elaborated by the Intergovernmental Working Group, open to all, mandated to develop the follow-up terms and conditions of the UPR procedure and give full effect to Decision 1/103 of the Human Rights Council.

The following terms and procedures were set out:

Reviews are to occur over a four-year period (48 countries per year). Accordingly, the 192 countries that are members of the United Nations shall normally all have such a "review" between 2008 and 2011;

- The order of review should follow the principles of universality and equal treatment;
- All Member States of the Council will be reviewed while they sit at the Council and the initial members of the Council will be first;
- The selection of the countries to be reviewed must respect the principle of equitable geographical allocation;
- The first Member States and the first observatory States to be examined will be selected randomly in each regional group in order to guarantee full compliance with the equitable geographical allocation. Reviews shall then be conducted alphabetically.

Similar mechanisms exist in other organizations: International Atomic Energy Agency, Council of Europe, International Monetary Fund, Organization of American States, International Labour Bureau and the World Trade Organization.

Except for the tri-annual reports on development of human rights policies, that Member States have to submit to the Secretary General since 1956, the Human Rights Council UPR procedure constitutes a first in the area. It marks the end of the discrimination that had plagued the work of the Human Rights Commission and had caused it to be harshly criticised. Finally, this mechanism demonstrates and confirms the universal nature of human rights.

Advisory Committee

The Sub-Commission on the Promotion and Protection of Human Rights was the main subsidiary body of the CHR. The Sub-Commission was composed of 26 elected human rights experts whose mandate was to conduct studies on discriminatory practices and to make recommendations to ensure that racial, national, religious, and linguistic minorities are protected by law.

In 2006 the newly-created UNHRC assumed responsibility for the Sub-Commission on the Promotion and Protection of Human Rights, previously the main subsidiary body of the CHR, composed of 26 elected human rights experts whose mandate was to conduct studies on discriminatory practices and to make recommendations to ensure that racial, national, religious, and linguistic minorities are protected by law. The Sub-Commission's mandate was extended for one year (to June 2007), but it met for the final time in August 2006. At its final meeting, the Sub-Commission recommended the creation of a Human Rights Consultative Committee to provide advice to the UNHRC, and in September 2007, the UNHRC decided to create an Advisory Committee to provide expert advice. The Advisory Committee has eighteen members. Those members are distributed as follows: five from African states; five from Asian states; three from Latin American and Caribbean States; three from Western European and other states; and two members from Eastern European states.

Complaint procedure

On 18 June 2007, the UNHRC adopted Resolution 5/1 to establish a Complaint procedure. The Complaint procedure's purpose is to address consistent patterns of gross and reliably attested violations of all human rights and all fundamental freedoms occurring in any part of the world and under any circumstances. Two working groups make up the Complaint procedure: the Working Group on Communications (WGC) and the Working Group on Situations (WGS).

The WGC consists of five independent and highly qualified experts, and is geographically representative of the five regions represented by the Human Rights Council (Africa, Asia, Latin America and the Caribbean, Eastern Europe, and Western Europe and Others). The Advisory Committee designates the WGC's experts from among its members. The experts serve for three years with the possibility of one renewal. The experts determine whether a complaint deserves investigation. If a complaint deserves investigation, the WGC passes the complaint to the WGS.

The WGS comprises five members appointed by the regional groups from among the States member of the Council for the period of one year (mandate renewable once). It meets twice a year for a period of five working days in order to examine the communications transferred to it by the Working Group on Communications, including the replies of States thereon, as well as the situations which the Council is already seized of under the complaint procedure. The Working Group on Situations, on the basis of the information and recommendations provided by the Working Group on Communications, presents the Council with a report on consistent patterns of gross and reliably attested violations of human rights and fundamental freedoms and makes recommendations to the Council on the course of action to take.

Other Subsidiary Bodies

In addition to the UPR, the Complaints Procedure and the Advisory Committee, the HRC's other subsidiary bodies include:

- Expert Mechanism on the Rights of Indigenous Peoples, which replaced the CHR's Working Group on Indigenous Populations
- Forum on Minority Issues, established to provide a platform for promoting dialogue and cooperation on issues pertaining to national or ethnic, religious and linguistic minorities
- Social Forum, established as a space for dialogue between the representatives of Member States, civil society, including grass-roots organizations, and intergovernmental organizations on issues linked with the national and international environment needed for the promotion of the enjoyment of all human rights by all

Special Procedures

"Special procedures" is the general name given to the mechanisms established by the Human Rights Council to address either specific country situations or thematic issues in all parts of the world. Special procedures can be either individuals (called "Special Rapporteurs" or "Independent Experts") who are independent experts in a particular area of human rights, or working groups usually composed of five members (one from each UN region).

Special procedures are categorized according to thematic mandates - which focus on major phenomena of human rights abuses worldwide - and country mandates - which report on human rights situations in specific countries or territories. Currently there are 36 thematic and 10 country special procedures mandates. Country mandates must be renewed yearly by the HRC, thematic mandates must be renewed every three years. The Office of the United Nations High Commissioner for Human Rights provides staffing and logistical support to aid each mandate-holder in carrying out their work.

The mandates of the special procedures are established and defined by the resolution creating them. Various activities can be undertaken by special procedures, including responding to individual complaints, conducting studies, providing advice on technical cooperation, and engaging in promotional activities. Generally the special procedures report to the Human Rights Council at least once a year on their findings.

Special Procedure Mandate Holders

Mandate-holders of the special procedures serve in their personal capacity, and do not receive pay for their work. The independent status of the mandate-holders is crucial in order to be able to fulfill their functions in all impartiality.

Applicants for Special Procedures mandates are reviewed by a Consultative Group of five countries, one from each region. Following interviews by the Consultative Group, the Group provides a shortlist of candidates to the HRC President. Following consultations with the leadership of each regional grouping, the President presents a single candidate to be approved by the Member states of the HRC at the session following a new mandate's creation or on the expiration of the term of an existing mandate holder.

Mandate holders are generally appointed serve for three year terms, renewable for a second three year term.

The following is a list of thematic special procedures mandate holders:

Thematic Mandate Holders

Special Rapporteurs:

- Adequate Housing, Ms. Raquel Rolnik (Brazil)
- Cultural Rights, Ms. Farida Shaheed (Pakistan)
- Education, Mr. Kishore Singh (India)
- Extrajudicial, Summary or Arbitrary Executions, Mr. Christof Heyns (South Africa)
- Extreme Poverty, Maria Magdalenan Sepulveda (Chile)

- Freedom of Assembly and Association, Mr. Maina Kiai (Kenya)
- Freedom of Opinion and Expression, Mr. Frank La Rue (Guatemala)
- Freedom of Religion or Belief, Mr. Heiner Bielefeldt(Germany)
- Hazardous Substances and Waste, Mr. Calin Georgescu (Romania)
- Health, Mr. Anand Grover (India)
- Human Rights Defenders, Ms. Margaret Sekaggya (Uganda)
- Human Rights While Countering Terrorism, Mr. Ben Emmerson (United Kingdom of Great Britain and Northern Ireland)
- Independence of Judges and Lawyers, Ms. Gabriela Knaul (Brazil)
- Indigenous people, James Anaya (United States)
- Internally Displaced Persons, Mr. Chaloka Beyani (Zambia)
- Migrants, Mr. François Crepeau (Canada)
- Racism, Mr. Mutuma Ruteere (Kenya)
- Right to Food, Olivier de Schutter (Belgium)
- Sale of Children, Child Prostitution and Child Pornography, Najat M'jid Maala (Morocco)
- Slavery, Gulnara Shahinian (Armenia)
- Torture, Mr. Juan Mendez (Argentina)
- Trafficking in Persons, Ms. Joy Ngozi Ezeilo (Nigeria)
- Truth, Justice, Reparation and Guarantees of non-Recurrence, Mr. Pablo de Greiff (Colombia)
- Violence Against Women, Ms. Rashida Manjoo (South Africa)
- Water, Ms. Catarina de Albuquerque (Portugal)

Independent Experts:

- Democratic and Equitable International Order, Mr. Alfred de Zayas (USA)
- Environment (TBD)
- Foreign Debt, Cephas Lumina (Zambia)
- International Solidarity, Ms. Virginia Dandan (Philippines)
- Minority Issues, Ms. Rita Izsak (Hungary)

Working Groups:

- Arbitrary Detention, Mr. El Hadji Malick Sow (Senegal), Ms. Shaheen Sardar Ali(Pakistan), Mr. Roberto Garreton (Chile), Mr. Vladimir Tochilovsky (Ukraine), Mr. Mads Andenas (Norway)
- Discrimination Against Women in Law and Practice, Ms. Kamala Chandrakirana (Indonesia), Ms. Emna Aouij, (Tunisia), Ms. Mercedes Barquet (Mexico), Ms. Frances Raday (Israel/United Kingdom), Ms. Eleonora Zielinska (Poland)
- Enforced or Involuntary Disappearances, Mr. Olivier de Frouville (France), Mr. Ariel Dulitzky (Argentina/United States of America), Ms. Jazminka Dzumhur (Bosnia and Herzegovina), Mr. Jeremy Sarkin (South Africa), Mr. Osman el-Hajje (Lebanon)
- Human Rights and Transnational Corporations, Ms. Margaret Jungk(USA)Mr. Michael K. Addo (Ghana), Ms. Alexandra Guaqueta (Colombia/USA), Mr. Puvan J. Selvanathan (Malaysia), Mr. Pavel Sulyandziga (Russian Federation)
- Mercenaries, Ms. Faiza Patel (Pakistan), Ms. Patricia Arias (Chile), Ms. Elzbieta Karska (Poland), Mr. Anton Katz (South Africa), Mr. Gabor Rona(USA/Hungary)
- Peoples of African Descent, Ms. Mirjana Najcevska (The Former Yugoslav Republic of Macedonia), Ms. Monorama Biswas(Bangladesh), Ms. Mireille Fanon-Mendes-France (France), Ms. Maya Sahli (Algeria) and Ms. Verene Shepherd (Jamaica)

Country Specific Mandate Holders

Special Rapporteurs:

- Cambodia, Mr. Surya Prasad Subedi (Nepal);
- Democratic People's Republic of Korea, Mr. Marzuki Darusman (Indonesia);
- "Disputed Palestinian Territories", Mr. Richard Falk (United States);
- The Islamic Republic of Iran, Mr. Ahmed Shaheed (Maldives);
- Myanmar, Mr. Thomas Ojea Quintana (Argentina);
- Syria, Mr. Paulo Sergio Pinheiro (Brazil - to begin once Commission of Inquiry Ends)

Independent Experts:

- Côte d'Ivoire, Mr. Doudou Diene (Senegal);
- Haiti, Mr. Michel Forst (France);
- Somalia, Mr. Shamsul Bari (Bangladesh);
- Sudan, Mr. Mashood Baderin (Nigeria)

Special Rapporteur on Freedom of Expression

An amendment to the duties of the Special Rapporteur on Freedom of Expression, passed by the Human Rights Council on 28 March 2008, has given rise to sharp criticism from western countries and human rights NGO's. The additional duty is phrased thus: (d) To report on instances in which the abuse of the right of freedom of expression constitutes an act of racial or religious discrimination, taking into account articles 19 (3) and 20 of the International Covenant on Civil and Political Rights, and general comment No. 15 of the Committee on the Elimination of All Forms of Racial Discrimination, which stipulates that the prohibition of the dissemination of all ideas based upon racial superiority or hatred is compatible with the freedom of opinion and expression (quoted from p. 67 in the official draft record of the council). The amendment was proposed by Egypt and Pakistan and passed by 27 votes to 15 against, with three abstentions with the support of other members of the Organisation of the Islamic Conference, China, Russia and Cuba. As a result of the amendment over 20 of the original 53 co-sponsors of the main resolution – to renew the mandate of the Special Rapporteur – withdrew their support, although the resolution was carried by 32 votes to 0, with 15 abstentions. Inter alia the delegates from India and Canada protested that the Special Rapporteur now has as his/her duty to report not only infringements of the rights to freedom of expression, but in some cases also employment of the rights, which "turns the special rapporteur's mandate on its head".

Outside the UN, the amendment was criticised by organizations including Reporters Without Borders, Index on Censorship, Human Rights Watch and the International Humanist and Ethical Union, all of whom share the view that the amendment threatens freedom of expression.

In terms of the finally cast votes, this was far from the most controversial of the 36 resolutions adapted by the 7'th session of the Council. The highest dissents concerned combating defamation of religions, with 21 votes for, 10 against, and 14 abstentions (resolution 19, pp. 91–97), and the continued severe condemnation of and appointment of a Special Rapporteur for North Korea, with votes 22–7 and 18 abstentions (resolution 15, pp. 78–80). There were also varying degrees of dissent for most of the various reports criticising Israel; while on the other hand a large number of resolutions were taken unanimously without voting, including the rather severe criticism of Myanmar (resolutions 31 and 32)., and the somewhat less severe on Sudan (resolution 16).

Specific Issues

Israel

As of 2010, Israel had been condemned in 32 resolutions by the Council since its creation in 2006. The 32 resolutions comprised 48.1% of all country-specific resolutions passed by the Council. By April 2007, the Council had passed nine resolutions condemning Israel, the only country which it had specifically condemned. Toward Sudan, a country with human rights abuses as documented by the Council's working groups, it has expressed "deep concern.".

The council voted on 30 June 2006 to make a review of alleged human rights abuses by Israel a permanent feature of every council session. The Council's special rapporteur on the Israeli-Palestinian conflict is its only expert mandate with no year of expiry. The resolution, which was sponsored by Organisation of the Islamic Conference, passed by a vote of 29 to 12 with five abstentions. Human Rights Watch urged it to look at international human rights and humanitarian law violations committed by Palestinian armed groups as well. Human Rights Watch called on the Council to avoid the selectivity that discredited its predecessor and urged it to hold special sessions on other urgent situations, such as that in Darfur.

The Special Rapporteur on the question of Palestine to the previous UNCHR, the current UNHRC and the General Assembly was, between 2001 and 2008, John Dugard. Bayefski quotes him as saying that his mandate is to "investigate human rights violations by Israel only, not by Palestinians". Dugard was replaced in 2008 with Richard Falk, who has compared Israel's treatment of Palestinians with the Nazis' treatment of Jews during the Holocaust. Like his predecessor, Falk's mandate only covers Israel's human rights record. The Palestinian Authority has informally asked Falk to resign, among other reasons due to viewing him as "a partisan of Hamas." Falk disputes this and has called the reasons given "essentially untrue" In July 2011, Richard Falk posted a cartoon some critics has described as anti-Semitic onto his blog. The cartoon depicted a bloodthirsty dog with the word "USA" on it wearing a kippah, or Jewish headcovering. In response, Falk was heavily criticized by world leaders in the United States and certain Europen countries. The United States called Falk's behavior "shameful and outrageous" and "an embarrassment to the United Nations", and officially called on him to resign. US Rep. Ileana Ros-Lehtinen, chairwoman of the US House of Representatives Foreign Affairs Committee called on Falk to resign as well. The Anti-Defamation League described the cartoon as a "message of hatred".

The UN Human Rights Council was castigated by Israeli Prime Minister Binyamin Netanyahu for facilitating an event featuring a Hamas politician. The Hamas parliamentarian had spoken at an NGO event in the UN Geneva building. Israel's ambassador to the UN, Ron Prosor, denounced the speech stating that Hamas was an internationally recognized terrorist organization that targeted civilians. "Inviting a Hamas terrorist to lecture to the world about human rights is like asking Charles Manson to run the murder investigation unit at the NYPD", he said.

UN Secretaries General

In 2006, UN Secretary-General Kofi Annan argued that the Commission should not have a "disproportionate focus on violations by Israel. Not that Israel should be given a free pass. Absolutely not. But the Council should give the same attention to grave violations committed by other states as well."

On 20 June 2007, Secretary-General Ban Ki-moon issued a statement that read: "The Secretary-General is disappointed at the council's decision to single out only one specific regional item given the range and scope of allegations of human rights violations throughout the world."

United States and UNHRC President

The Council's charter preserves the watchdog's right to appoint special investigators for countries whose human rights records are of particular concern, something many developing states have long opposed. A Council meeting in Geneva in 2007 caused controversy after Cuba and Belarus, both accused of abuses, were removed from a list of nine special mandates. The list, which included North Korea, Cambodia and Sudan, had been carried forward from the defunct Commission. Commenting on Cuba and Belarus, the UN statement said that Ban noted "that not having a Special Rapporteur assigned to a particular country does not absolve that country from its obligations under the Universal Declaration of Human Rights."

The United States said a day before the UN statement that the Council deal raised serious questions about whether the new body could be unbiased. Alejandro Wolff, deputy US permanent representative at the United Nations, accused the council of "a pathological obsession with Israel" and also denounced its action on Cuba and Belarus. "I think the record is starting to speak for itself," he told journalists.

The UNHRC President Doru Costea responded: "I agree with him. The functioning of the Council must be constantly improved." He added that the Council must examine the behaviour of all parties involved in complex disputes and not place just one state under the magnifying glass.

Netherlands

Speaking at the IDC's Herzliya Conference in Israel in January 2008, Dutch Foreign Minister Maxime Verhagen criticized the actions of the Human Rights Council actions against Israel. "At the United Nations, censuring Israel has become something of a habit, while Hamas's terror is referred to in coded language or not at all. The Netherlands believes the record should be set straight, both in New York and at the Human Rights Council in Geneva," Verhagen said.

2006 Lebanon conflict

At its Second Special Session in August 2006, the Council announced the establishment of a High-Level Commission of Inquiry charged with probing allegations that Israel systematically targeted and killed Lebanese civilians during the 2006 Israel-Lebanon conflict. The resolution was passed by a vote of 27 in favour to 11 against, with 8 abstentions. Before and after the vote several member states and NGOs objected that by targeting the resolution solely at Israel and failing to address Hezbollah attacks on Israeli civilians, the Council risked damaging its credibility. The members of the Commission of Inquiry, as announced on 1 September 2006, were Clemente Baena Soares of Brazil, Mohamed Chande Othman of Tanzania, and Stelios Perrakis of Greece. The Commission noted that its report on the conflict would be incomplete without fully investigating both sides, but that "the Commission is not entitled, even if it had wished, to construe [its charter] as equally authorizing the investigation of the actions by Hezbollah in Israel," as the Council had explicitly prohibited it from investigating the actions of Hezbollah.

January 2008 decree

The Council released a statement calling on Israel to stop its military operations in the Gaza Strip and to open the Strip's borders to allow the entry of food, fuel and medicine. The Council adopted the resolution by a vote of 30 to 1. 15 states abstained.

"Unfortunately, neither this resolution nor the current session addressed the role of both parties. It was regretful that the current draft resolution did not condemn the rocket attacks on Israeli civilians," said Canada's representative Terry Cormier, the lone voter against.

The United States and Israel boycotted the session. US ambassador Warren Tichenor said the Council's unbalanced approach had "squandered its credibility" by failing to address continued rocket attacks against Israel. "Today's actions do nothing to help the Palestinian people, in whose name the supporters of this session claim to act," he said in a statement. "Supporters of a Palestinian state must avoid the kind of inflammatory rhetoric and actions that this session represents, which only stoke tensions and erode the chances for peace," he added. "We believe that this council should deplore the fact that innocent civilians on both sides are suffering," Slovenian Ambassador Andrej Logar said on behalf of the seven EU states on the council.

At a press conference in Geneva on Wednesday, UN Secretary General Ban Ki-moon responded when asked about its special session on Gaza, that "I appreciate that the council is looking in depth into this particular situation. And it is rightly doing so. I would also appreciate it if the council will be looking with the same level of attention and urgency at all other matters around the world. There are still many areas where human rights are abused and not properly protected," he said.

Gaza report

On 3 April 2009, South African Judge Richard Goldstone was named as the head of the independent United Nations Fact-Finding Mission to investigate international human rights and humanitarian law violations related to the Gaza War. The Mission was established by Resolution S-9/1 of the United Nations Human Rights Council.

On 15 September 2009, the UN Fact-Finding mission released its report. The report found that there was evidence "indicating serious violations of international human rights and humanitarian law were committed by Israel during the Gaza conflict, and that Israel committed actions amounting to war crimes, and possibly crimes against humanity." The mission also found that there was evidence that "Palestinian armed groups committed war crimes, as well as possibly crimes against humanity, in their repeated launching of rockets and mortars into Southern Israel." The mission called for referring either side in the conflict to the UN Security Council for prosecution at the International Criminal Court if they refuse to launch fully independent investigations by December 2009.

Goldstone has since partially retracted the reports conclusions that Israel committed war crimes, as new evidence has shed light upon the decision making by Israeli commanders. He said, "I regret that our fact-finding mission did not have such evidence explaining the circumstances in which we said civilians in Gaza were targeted, because it probably would have influenced our findings about intentionality and war crimes."

Goldstone acknowledged that Israel has "to a significant degree" implemented the reports recommendations that "each party to investigate [the incidents] transparently and in good faith," but "Hamas has done nothing." The Palestinian Authority has also implemented the reports recommendations by investigating "assassinations, torture and illegal detentions, perpetrated by Fatah in the West Bank," but Goldstone noted that "most of those allegations were confirmed by this inquiry."

March 2011 controversy

At the UNHRC's opening session in February 2011, U.S. Secretary of State Hillary Clinton criticized the council's "structural bias" against the State of Israel: "The structural bias against Israel – including a standing agenda item for Israel, whereas all other countries are treated under a common item – is wrong. And it undermines the important work we are trying to do together."

An editorial in the Jerusalem Post subsequently revealed that the UNHRC was "poised to adopt six resolutions ... condemning Israel," noting that it was the highest number of resolutions ever to be adopted against Israel in a single session. Human rights activist and Hudson Institute senior fellow Anne Bayefsky accused the UNHRC of failing to remove antisemitic propaganda distributed by the IHH during one of its sessions. The material in question was an illustration depicting Israel as a sinister Nazi octopus seizing control of a ship.

Chair of the United States House Committee on Foreign Affairs Rep. Ileana Ros-Lehtinen (R) said she will propose legislation making U.S. funding for the U.N. contingent on extensive reform. Her bill will also call for the U.S. to withdraw from the UNHRC, as "Israel is the only country on the council's permanent agenda, while abuses by rogue regimes like Cuba, China, and Syria are ignored."

The hosting of a Hamas member controversy

In March 2012, the UN Human Rights Council was criticised for facilitating an event featuring a Hamas politician. The Hamas parliamentarian had spoken at an NGO event in the UN Geneva building. Israeli Prime Minister Binyamin Netanyahu castigated the UNHRC's decision stating, "He represents an organization that indiscriminately targets children and grown-ups, and women and men. Innocents – is their special favorite target." Israel's ambassador to the UN, Ron Prosor, denounced the speech stating that Hamas was an internationally recognized terrorist organization that targeted civilians. "Inviting a Hamas terrorist to lecture to the world about human rights is like asking Charles Manson to run the murder investigation unit at the NYPD", he said.

March 2012 Criticism

The United States urged the United Nations Human Rights Council in Geneva to stop its anti-Israel bias. It took particular exception to the council's Agenda Item 7, under which at every session, Israel's human rights record is debated. No other country has a dedicated agenda item. The US Ambassador to the UNHRC Eileen Chamberlain Donahoe said that the United States was deeply troubled by the "Council's biased and disproportionate focus on Israel." She said that the hypocrisy was further exposed in the Golan Heights resolution that was advocated by the Syrian regime at a time when it was murdering its own citizens.

"Defamation of religion"

From 1999, the CHR and the UNHRC adopted resolutions in opposition to the "defamation of religion."

Climate Change

The Human Rights Council has adopted the Resolution 10/4 about human rights and climate change.

Syrian candidacy

In July 2012, Syria announced that it would seek a seat on the United Nations Human Rights Council. President Bashar al-Assad of Syria has been accused by human rights organizations of slaughtering thousands of civilians, with estimates of 14,000 civilians being killed as of July 2012 during the uprising against his dictatorship. According to the NGO UN Watch, Syria's candidacy would be virtually assured of victory due to the prevailing system of elections. Syria would be responsible for promoting human rights if elected. In response, the United States and European Union drafted a resolution to oppose this move.

Sudan & Ethiopian candidacy

In July 2012, it was reported that Sudan and Ethiopia were nominated for a seat on the council, despite being accused by human rights organizations of grave human rights violations. The NGO UN Watch condemned the move to nominate Sudan, and pointed out that President Omar Al-Bashir of Sudan was indicted for genocide by the International Criminal Court. According to UN Watch, Sudan is virtually assured of securing the seat. A joint letter of 18 African and international civil society organizations urged foreign ministers of the African Union to reverse its endorsement of Ethiopia and Sudan for a seat, accusing them of serious human rights violations and listing examples of such violations, and stating that they shouldn't be rewarded with a seat.

Bloc voting

Human rights groups say the council is being controlled by some Middle East and African nations, supported by China, Russia and Cuba, which protect each other from criticism. This drew criticism from the UN Secretary General Ban Ki-moon at the ineffectiveness of the council, saying it had fallen short of its obligations. He urged countries to 'drop rhetoric' and rise above "partisan posturing and regional divides" and get on with defending people around the world. This follows criticism since the council was set up, where Israel has been condemned on most occasions and other incidences in the world such as Darfur, Tibet, North Korea and Zimbabwe have not been discussed at the council. Ban Ki-Moon also appealed for the United States to fully join the council and play a more active role. The UNHRC was criticized in 2009 for adopting a resolution submitted by Sri Lanka praising its conduct in Vanni that year, ignoring pleas for an international war crimes investigation.

Position of the United States

In regard to the United Nations Human Rights Council, the position of the United States is: "human rights have been a cornerstone of American values since the country's birth and the United States is committed to support the work of the UN Commission in promoting the principles embodied in the Universal Declaration of Human Rights. U.S. President George W. Bush declared that the United States would not seek a seat on the Council, saying it would be more effective from the outside. He did pledge, however, to support the Council financially. State Department spokesman Sean McCormack said, "We will work closely with partners in the international community to encourage the council to address serious cases of human rights abuse in countries such as Iran, Cuba, Zimbabwe, Burma, Sudan, and North Korea."

The U.S. State Department said on 5 March 2007 that, for the second year in a row, the United States has decided not to seek a seat on the Human Rights Council, asserting the body had lost its credibility with repeated attacks on Israel and a failure to confront other rights abusers. Spokesman Sean McCormack said the council has had a "singular focus" on Israel, while countries such as Cuba, Myanmar and North Korea have been spared scrutiny. He said that though the United States will have only an observer role, it will continue to shine a spotlight on human rights issues. The most senior Republican member of the Foreign Affairs Committee of the U.S. House of Representatives, Ileana Ros-Lehtinen, supported the administration decision. "Rather than standing as a strong defender of fundamental human rights, the Human Rights Council has faltered as a weak voice subject to gross political manipulation," she said.

Upon passage of UNHRC's June 2007 institution building package, the U.S. restated its condemnation of bias in the institution's agenda. Spokesman Sean McCormack again criticised the Commission for focusing on Israel in light of many more pressing human rights issues around the world, such as Sudan or Myanmar, and went on to criticise the termination of Special Rapporteurs to Cuba and Belarus, as well as procedural irregularities that prevented member-states from voting on the issues; a similar critique was issued by the Canadian representative. On September 2007, The US Senate voted to cut off funding to the council.

The United States joined with Australia, Canada, Israel, and three other countries in opposing the UNHRC's draft resolution on working rules citing continuing misplaced focus on Israel at the expense of action against countries with poor human-rights records. The resolution passed 154–7 in a rare vote forced by Israel including the support of France, the United Kingdom, and China, although it is usually approved through consensus. United States Ambassador to the United Nations, Zalmay Khalilzad, spoke about the "council's relentless focus during the year on a single country – Israel," contrasting that with failure "to address serious human rights violations taking place in other countries such as Zimbabwe, DPRK (North Korea), Iran, Belarus and Cuba." Khalilzad said that aside from condemnation of the crackdown of the Burmese anti-government protests, the council's past year was "very bad" and it "had failed to fulfill our hopes."

On 6 June 2008, Human Rights Tribune announced that the United States had withdrawn entirely from the UNHRC, and had withdrawn its observer status.

On 31 March 2009 the administration of Barack Obama announced that it would reverse the country's previous position and would join the UNHRC; New Zealand has indicated its willingness not to seek election to the council to make room for the United States to run unopposed along with Belgium and Norway for the WEOG seats.

Position of Sri Lanka

Sri Lanka has come under increasing scrutiny with a draft resolution tabled by the US on reconciliation and accountability in Sri Lanka. The draft resolution, currently being reviewed notes "with concern that the LLRC report does not adequately address serious allegations of violations of international law,

1. Calls on the Government of Sri Lanka to implement the constructive recommendations in the LLRC report and take all necessary additional steps to fulfill its relevant legal obligations and commitment to initiate credible and independent actions to ensure justice, equity, accountability and reconciliation for all Sri Lankans,

2. Requests that the Government of Sri Lanka present a comprehensive action plan as expeditiously as possible detailing the steps the Government has taken and will take to implement the LLRC recommendations and also to address alleged violations of international law,
3. Encourages the Office of the High Commissioner for Human Rights and relevant special procedures to provide, and the Government of Sri Lanka to accept, advice and technical assistance on implementing those steps and requests the Office of the High Commissioner for Human Rights to present a report to the Council on the provision of such assistance at its twenty-second session."

Sri Lankan Ambassador in Geneva, Ms. Tamara Kunanayakam pointed out that 80 per cent of the UNHRC's funding requirements are supplied by powerful nations such as the United States and its allies. Also, key positions in the UNHCR are mostly held by those who have served in the foreign services of such countries. Sri Lanka's position is that this fact is significantly detrimental to the impartiality of the UNHRC activities, especially when dealing with the developing world. As a result, Sri Lanka, along with Cuba and Pakistan, will co-sponsor a resolution seeking transparency in funding and staffing the UNHRC, during its 19th session starting in February 2012. China, Russia and Algeria have agreed to back this resolution.

The Universal Periodic Review (UPR)

The Universal Periodic Review (UPR) is a new and unique mechanism of the Human Rights Council (HRC) aiming at improving the human rights situation on the ground of each of the 193 United Nations (UN) Member States.

Under this mechanism, the human rights situation of all UN Member States is reviewed every 4,5 years. 42 States are reviewed each year during three Working Group sessions dedicated to 14 States each. These three sessions are usually held in January/February, May/June and October/ November.

The result of each review is reflected in an "outcome report" listing therecommendations the State under review (SuR) will have to implement before the next review.

The UPR is a full-circle process comprising 3 key stages:

1) Review of the human rights situation of the SuR;
2) Implementation between two reviews (4,5 years) by the SuR of the recommendations received and the voluntary pledges made;
3) Reporting at the next review on the implementation of those recommendations and pledges and on the human rights situation in the country since the previous review.

Principles and Objectives

HRC Resolution 5/1 of 18 June 2007 and HRC decision 6/102 of 27 September 2007 elaborated the UPR's operation. HRC resolution 5/1 provides that the UPR should:

- Promote the universality, interdependence, indivisibility and interrelatedness of all human rights
- Be a cooperative mechanism based on objective and reliable information and on interactive dialogue
- Ensure universal coverage and equal treatment of all States
- Be an intergovernmental process, UN Member-driven and action oriented
- Fully involve the country under review
- Complement and not duplicate other human rights mechanisms, thus representing an added value
- Be conducted in an objective, transparent, non-selective, constructive, non-confrontational and non-politicized manner
- Not be overly burdensome to the concerned State or to the agenda of the HRC
- Not be overly long; it should be realistic and not absorb a disproportionate amount of time or human and financial resources
- Not diminish the HRC's capacity to respond to urgent human rights situations
- Fully integrate a gender perspective
- Take into account the level of development and specificities of countries
- Ensure the participation of all relevant stakeholders, including non-governmental organizations (NGOs) and national human rights institutions (NHRIs).

The objectives of the UPR are:

- The improvement of the human rights situation on the ground
- The fulfilment of the State's human rights obligations and commitments and assessment of positive developments and challenges faced by the State
- The enhancement of the State's capacity and of technical assistance, in consultation with, and with the consent of, the State concerned
- The sharing of best practice among States and other stakeholders
- Support for cooperation in the promotion and protection of human rights
- The encouragement of full cooperation and engagement with the HRC, other human rights bodies and the Office of the UN High Commissioner for Human Rights (OHCHR).

Procedure

UPR Cycle

The UPR currently operates on a four-year cycle. Forty-eight States are reviewed each year during three sessions of the HRC's Working Group on the UPR, with 16 States reviewed at each session. The HRC determined the order of review for the first UPR cycle (2008-2011) on 21 September 2007 through the drawing of lots. This process was instructed by the resolution 5/1 requirements that: all 47 member States of the HRC be reviewed during their term of membership; that initial members of the HRC, especially those elected for one or two-year terms, should be reviewed first; that a mix of HRC member and observer States should be reviewed at each Working Group session; and that equitable geographic distribution should be respected in the selection of countries for review.

Basis of Country Reviews

The basis of country reviews is: (a) the Charter of the UN; (b) the Universal Declaration of Human Rights; (c) human rights instruments to which a State is party; and (d) voluntary pledges and commitments made by the State, including those undertaken when presenting their candidature for election to the HRC. Country reviews also take into account applicable international humanitarian law.

Documentation upon which country reviews are based

Country reviews are based on three documents:

- A 20-page national report prepared by the State under review
- A ten-page compilation of UN information (including Special Procedures reports, human rights treaty body reports, and other relevant UN documentation) prepared by OHCHR; and
- A ten-page summary of information received from stakeholders (including NHRIs, NGOs, and other civil society actors) also prepared by OHCHR. Strict technical guidelines govern the form and content of stakeholder submissions (which are restricted to five pages).

In decision 6/102, the HRC provided guidelines for the preparation of information under the UPR. It specifies that States, in preparing national reports, should address/provide:

- A description of the methodology and the broad consultation process followed for the preparation of information provided under the UPR
- Background of the country under review and framework (particularly normative and institutional framework) for the promotion and protection of human rights: constitution, legislation, policy measures, national jurisprudence, human rights infrastructure including NHRIs, and scope of international obligations identified in the "basis of review" in resolution 5/1
- Promotion and protection of human rights on the ground: implementation of international human rights obligations identified in the "basis of review" in resolution 5/1, national legislation and voluntary commitments, NHRI activities, public awareness of human rights, cooperation with human rights mechanisms
- Identification of achievements, best practices, challenges and constraints
- Key national priorities, initiatives and commitments that the State concerned intends to undertake to overcome those challenges and constraints and improve its human rights situation
- Expectations of the State concerned in terms of capacity-building and requests, if any, for technical assistance; and
- In future UPR cycles, presentation by the State concerned of its work on follow-up to the previous review.

Working Group on the UPR

The Working Group on the UPR, which is composed of the HRC's 47 Member States and chaired by the HRC President, conducts country reviews. The Working Group, which met in Geneva for the first time in April 2008, allocates three hours to each review, one hour of which is given to the State under review to discuss its domestic human rights framework, measures taken to promote and protect human rights in country, human rights issues of particular national pertinence, and steps taken to address and redress violations. It is also an opportunity for the State to present voluntary human rights pledges and commitments. A two-hour interactive dialogue follows the State's presentation, during which HRC member States question the State and make recommendations towards the improvement of its human rights situation and performance.

Issues addressed during country reviews have included:

- Accountability and impunity
- Asylum seekers, refugees and internally displaced persons
- Counter-terrorism measures
- Death penalty
- Detention, including arbitrary detention and prison conditions
- Development
- Due process protections
- Education
- Elections
- Employment
- Enforced disappearances
- Environment
- Extrajudicial executions
- Freedom of association
- Freedom of opinion and expression, including media freedom
- Freedom of movement
- Freedom of religion and belief
- Gender equality
- Health

- Housing
- Human rights defenders
- Human rights education and training
- Human trafficking
- Indigenous peoples
- International humanitarian law, including the protection of civilians in armed conflict
- Judiciaries and justice systems
- Migrant workers
- Minorities
- National human rights mechanisms, including the establishment of NHRIs
- Non-discrimination, including on the bases of ethnicity, race, sex, and sexual orientation and gender identity
- Persons with disabilities
- Police and military
- Ratification of/accession to international human rights instruments
- Torture and other cruel, inhuman and degrading treatment or punishment
- Violence against women.

Each review is facilitated by a group of three States, known as a "troika", which serve as rapporteurs. The troika is first responsible for receiving questions from UN member States in advance of the country review, clustering them, and transmitting them to the UPR Secretariat (OHCHR), which in turn transmits them to the State under review. The second role of the troika is to prepare an outcome document on the review, which includes a summary of the review proceedings, recommendations presented by States, conclusions, and voluntary commitments presented by the State under review. The outcome document is prepared with the assistance of the UPR secretariat and with the full involvement of the State under review. A different troika is formed for each review. The selection of troika members is also confirmed through the drawing of lots.

Thirty minutes is allocated to the adoption of the outcome document at a later stage in the same Working Group session, during which the State under review is given a preliminary opportunity to indicate whether it supports the recommendations presented to it by States (known as 'UPR outcomes') as well as the conclusions reflected in the outcome document. Once adopted, the outcome document is transferred to the HRC for discussion and adoption in plenary. In the intervening period between the Working Group and plenary sessions, the reviewed State is expected to confirm which UPR outcomes it accepts and does not accept.

HRC plenary session

The UPR is a standing item on the HRC's agenda (item 6). At each HRC session, time is allocated to the consideration and adoption of the outcome documents transferred from the Working Group on the UPR. An hour is allocated to the adoption of each document, during which the reviewed State is offered the opportunity to present replies to questions or issues not sufficiently addressed during the interactive dialogue at the Working Group. HRC member and observer States are also given the opportunity to express their views on the outcome of the review before the HRC takes action on it. 'A' status NHRIs and NGOs in consultative relationship with the UN Economic and Social Council (ECOSOC) have the opportunity to make 'general comments' before the adoption of the outcome report.

Follow-up to UPR outcomes

States bear the primary responsibility for implementing UPR outcomes. However, other stakeholders, including NHRIs and NGOs, also have a role in outcome implementation. The State's progress in implementing UPR outcomes will be examined in subsequent reviews.

State non-cooperation with the UPR

After exhausting all efforts to encourage a State to cooperate with the UPR mechanism, the HRC will address, as appropriate, cases of persistent non-cooperation with the mechanism. At June 2011, the HRC had not taken any such action.

Stakeholder UPR contribution opportunities

The rules governing the participation of NHRIs and NGOs at the HRC, and therefore in the UPR mechanism, are prescribed by resolution 5/1, which states that their participation shall be based on the 'practices observed by the [CHR], while ensuring the most effective contribution of these entities'.

While the UPR is an intergovernmental process, there are a number of contribution opportunities available to non-governmental stakeholders. These include:

- Participating in national consultations toward the preparation of a State's national report. States are encouraged to undertake broad national consultation processes towards the preparation of their national reports
- The submission of information toward State reviews. Submissions may be incorporated into the OHCHR-prepared summary of stakeholders' information discussed above
- Attending the review of the State at the Working Group on the UPR. Stakeholders may attend Working Group sessions, but cannot partake in the interactive dialogue
- Attending the HRC session at which the outcome report on a State is adopted. 'A' status NHRIs and ECOSOC-accredited NGOs may make 'general comments' before the adoption of the outcome report
- Submitting written statements under HRC agenda item 6 (UPR). Adhering to HRC convention, 'A' status NHRIs and ECOSOC-accredited NGOs can submit written statements under any HRC agenda item
- As appropriate, working on follow-up to UPR outcomes.

HRC review process

In resolution 60/251, the General Assembly required the HRC to review and report on its work and functioning after its first five years. In October 2009, the HRC established the open-ended intergovernmental working group on the review of the work and functioning of the HRC (composed of the HRC's 47 member States) to lead its review process. Chaired by the then HRC President (Ambassador Sihasak Phuangketkeow of Thailand), the Working Group met for two substantive sessions. The first Working Group session took place on 25-29 October 2010; the second session was held on 7, 17-18, and 23-24 February 2011.

On 25 March 2011, the HRC adopted as resolution 16/21 the outcome of its review of the work and functioning of the HRC. While it is yet to be confirmed by the General Assembly, the resolution provides that the second cycle of the UPR will commence in June 2012. It also proposes a number of changes to the UPR's operation. These include:

- Changing the periodicity of the UPR cycle to four-and-a-half years, implying that 42 States (rather than the current 48 States) will be reviewed each year
- Extending the duration of country reviews from the present three hours. The modalities for this extension were expected to be agreed on at the HRC's 17th session (30 May - 17 June 2011)
- Clustering recommendations contained in UPR outcome documents thematically, with the full involvement and consent of the State under review and the States that made the recommendations
- Requiring the State under review to clearly communicate to the HRC, in a written format preferably prior to the HRC plenary session at which the outcome document on its review will be adopted, its positions on all received recommendations
- Encouraging States to provide the HRC, on a voluntary basis, with a midterm update on their follow-up to accepted UPR outcomes
- Dedicating a separate section of future summaries of stakeholders' information to 'A' status NHRIs
- Allowing 'A' status NHRIs to intervene immediately after their State during the adoption of the outcome of the review of that State by the HRC plenary.

United Nations Commission on Human Rights

The United Nations Commission on Human Rights (UNCHR) was a functional commission within the overall framework of the United Nations from 1946 until it was replaced by the United Nations Human Rights Council in 2006. It was a subsidiary body of the UN Economic and Social Council (ECOSOC), and was also assisted in its work by the Office of the United Nations High Commissioner for Human Rights (UNHCHR). It was the UN's principal mechanism and international forum concerned with the promotion and protection of human rights.

On 15 March 2006, the UN General Assembly voted overwhelmingly to replace UNCHR with the UN Human Rights Council.

The UNCHR was established on 10 December 1946 at the first meeting of ECOSOC, and was one of the first two "Functional Commissions" set up within the early UN structure (the other being the Commission on the Status of Women). It was a body created under the terms of the United

Nations Charter (specifically, under Article 68) to which all UN member states are signatories.

The body went through two distinct phases. From 1947 to 1967, it followed the policy of absenteeism, which meant that the Commission would concentrate on promoting human rights and helping states elaborate treaties, but not on investigating or condemning violators. It was a period of strict observance of the sovereignty principle.

In 1967, the Commission adopted interventionism as its policy. The context of the decade was of decolonization of Africa and Asia, and many countries of the continent pressed for a more active UN policy on human rights issues, especially in light of massive violations in apartheid South Africa. The new policy meant that the Commission would also investigate and produce reports on violations.

To allow better fulfillment of this new policy, other changes took place. In the 1970s, the possibility of geographically-oriented workgroups was created. These groups would specialize their activities on the investigation of violations on a given region or even a single country, as was the case with Chile. With the 1980s came the creation of theme-oriented workgroups, which would specialize in specific types of abuses.

None of these measures, however, were able to make the Commission as effective as desired, mainly because of the presence of human rights violators and the politicization of the body. During the following years until its extinction, the UNCHR became increasingly discredited among activists and governments alike.The Commission held its final meeting in Geneva on March 27, 2006 and was replaced by the United Nations Human Rights Council in the same year.

Mandate

The Commission on Human Rights was intended to examine, monitor and publicly report on human rights situations in specific countries or territories (known as country mechanisms or mandates) as well as on major phenomena of human rights violations worldwide (known as thematic mechanisms or mandates).

Structure

At the time it was extinguished, the Commission consisted of representatives drawn from 53 member states, elected by the members of ECOSOC. There were no permanent members; each year (usually in May) approximately a third of the seats of the Commission would come up for election, and the representatives were appointed for a three-year term.

Seats on the Commission were apportioned by region, using the mechanism of the United Nations Regional Groups. During its last year of service in 2005, the representation by region was as follows:

- 15 from the African Group:

  Burkina Faso, Republic of the Congo, Egypt, Eritrea, Ethiopia, Gabon, Guinea, Kenya, Mauritania, Nigeria, South Africa, Sudan, Swaziland, Togo, Zimbabwe
- 12 from the Asian Group:

  Bhutan, People's Republic of China, India, Indonesia, Japan, Malaysia, Nepal, Pakistan, Qatar, Republic of Korea, Saudi Arabia, Sri Lanka
- 5 from the Eastern European Group:

  Armenia, Hungary, Romania, Russian Federation, Ukraine
- 11 from the Latin American and Caribbean Group:

  Argentina, Brazil, Costa Rica, Cuba, Dominican Republic, Ecuador, Guatemala, Honduras, Mexico, Paraguay, Peru
- 10 from the Western European and Others Group:

  Australia, Canada, Finland, France, Germany, Ireland, Italy, Netherlands, United Kingdom, United States of America

The Commission would meet each year in regular session for six weeks during March and April in Geneva, Switzerland. In January 2004, Australia was elected as chair of the 60th Session. In January 2005, Indonesia was elected chair of the 61st Session. Peru was elected chair of the 62nd Session in January 2006. The Commission held its final meeting in Geneva on March 27, 2006.

Sub-Commission on the Promotion and Protection of Human Rights

In 1999 the Economic and Social Council changed its title from the Sub-Commission on Prevention of Discrimination and Protection of Minorities to the Sub-Commission on the Promotion and Protection of Human Rights".

The Sub-Commission on the Promotion and Protection of Human Rights was the main subsidiary body of the Commission on Human Rights. It was composed of twenty-six experts whose responsibility was to undertake studies, particularly in light of the Universal Declaration of Human Rights, and make recommendations to the Commission concerning the prevention of discrimination of any kind relating to human rights and fundamental freedoms and the protection of racial, national, religious and linguistic minorities. Membership was selected with regard to equitable geographical distribution.

The Sub-Commission established seven Working Groups that investigate specific human rights concerns, including:

- Minorities
- Transnational corporations
- Administration of justice
- Anti-terrorism
- Contemporary Forms of Slavery
- Indigenous Populations
- Communication
- Social Forum

The United Nations Human Rights Council assumed responsibility for the Sub-Commission when it replaced the Commission on Human Rights in 2006.

Special procedures

The Commission on Human Rights established 30 special procedures, or mechanisms, to address specific country situations or thematic issues such as freedom of expression and opinion, torture, the right to food, and the right to education.

Individuals with expertise in particular areas of human rights were appointed by the chair of the Commission to serve as Special Rapporteurs for a maximum of six years. They are unpaid, independent experts who receive personnel and logistical support from the Office of the High Commissioner for Human Rights for their work. Their main activities are to examine, monitor, advise and publicly report on human rights situations in specific countries or territories. They are able to write to governments about reported violations and conduct fact-finding visits to countries that invite them.

The special mechanisms are categorised according to:

- Thematic Mandates.
- Country Mandates.

Special procedures also include working groups made up of up to five experts who monitor and investigate specific human rights concerns. Three groups were established by the Commission:

- Working Group on Arbitrary Detention
- Working Group on Enforced or Involuntary Disappearances
- Working Group on the use of mercenaries as a means of impeding the exercise of the right of peoples to self-determination
- The special procedures are now under the direction of the United Nations Human Rights Council.

Human Rights Council Complaint Procedure

On 18 June 2007, the Human Rights Council adopted the President text entitled "UN Human Rights Council: Institution Building" (resolution 5/1) by which a new Complaint Procedure is being established to address consistent patterns of gross and reliably attested violations of all human rights and all fundamental freedoms occurring in any part of the world and under any circumstances.

The new Complaint Procedure is established in compliance with the mandate entrusted to the Human Rights Council by General Assembly resolution 60/251 of 15 March 2006, in which the Council was requested to review and, where necessary, improve and rationalize, within one year after the holding of its first session, all mandates, mechanisms, functions and responsibilities of the former Commission on Human Rights, including the 1503 procedure, in order to maintain a system of special procedures, expert advice and a complaint procedure.

Accordingly, ECOSOC resolution 1503 (XLVIII) of 27 May 1970 as revised by resolution 2000/3 of 19 June 2000, served as a working basis for the establishment of a new Complaint Procedure and was improved where necessary to ensure that the complaint procedure be impartial, objective, efficient, victims-oriented and conducted in a timely manner.

Review of the 1503 procedure

In compliance with the mandate entrusted to it by the General Assembly, the Council decided on 30 June 2006 to establish the Working Group on the implementation of operative paragraph 6 of General Assembly resolution 60/251 (decision 1/104), to formulate concrete recommendations on the issue of reviewing and when necessary, improving and rationalizing all mandates, mechanisms, functions and responsibilities of the former Commission on Human Rights, including the 1503 procedure.

The Working Group held three formal open-ended sessions from 13 to 24 November 2006, 5 to 16 February 2007 and 10 to 27 April 2007. The segment on the complaint procedure was chaired by the Permanent Representative of Switzerland , who was appointed by the President of the Council to facilitate the consultations on this mechanism. Discussions in the Working Group and various rounds of informal consultations were conducted on the basis of an initial and subsequently revised framework for discussions prepared by the Facilitator. Following the last session of the Working Group, a final proposal (A/HRC/5/15) was submitted by the Facilitator to the President, taking into account to the greatest extent possible, the positions expressed during several months of consultations, with a view to facilitating the drafting of the section on the Complaint Procedure of a final document on institution building of the Council to be adopted in June 2007.

How does the complaint procedure work?

Pursuant to Council resolution 5/1, the Complaint Procedure is being established to address consistent patterns of gross and reliably attested violations of all human rights and all fundamental freedoms occurring in any part of the world and under any circumstances.

It retains its confidential nature, with a view to enhancing cooperation with the State concerned. The procedure, inter alia, is to be victims-oriented and conducted in a timely manner.

Two distinct working groups - the Working Group on Communications and the Working Group on Situations - are established with the mandate to examine the communications and to bring to the attention of the Council consistent patterns of gross and reliably attested violations of human rights and fundamental freedoms.

Manifestly ill-founded and anonymous communications are screened out by the Chairperson of the Working Group on Communications, together with the Secretariat, based on the admissibility criteria. Communications not rejected in the initial screening are transmitted to the State concerned to obtain its views on the allegations of violations.

The Working Group on Communications (WGC) is designated by the Human Rights Council Advisory Committee from among its members for a period of three years (mandate renewable once). It consists of five independent and highly qualified experts and is geographically representative of the five regional groups. The Working Group meets twice a year for a period of five working days to assess the admissibility and the merits of a communication, including whether the communication alone or in combination with other communications, appears to reveal a consistent pattern of gross and reliably attested violations of human rights and fundamental freedoms. All admissible communications and recommendations thereon are transmitted to the Working Group on Situations.

The Working Group on Situations (WGS) comprises five members appointed by the regional groups from among the States member of the Council for the period of one year (mandate renewable once). It meets twice a year for a period of five working days in order to examine the communications transferred to it by the Working Group on Communications, including the replies of States thereon, as well as the situations which the Council is already seized of under the complaint procedure. The Working Group on Situations, on the basis of the information and recommendations provided by the Working Group on Communications, presents the Council with a report on consistent patterns of gross and reliably attested violations of human rights and fundamental freedoms and makes recommendations to the Council on the course of action to take.

Subsequently, it is the turn of the Council to take a decision concerning each situation thus brought to its attention.

What are the criteria for a communication to be accepted for examination?

A communication related to a violation of human rights and fundamental freedoms is admissible, unless:

- It has manifestly political motivations and its object is not consistent with the UN Charter, the Universal Declaration of Human Rights and other applicable instruments in the field of human rights law;
- It does not contain a factual description of the alleged violations, including the rights which are alleged to be violated;

- Its language is abusive. However, such communication may be considered if it meets the other criteria for admissibility after deletion of the abusive language;
- It is not submitted by a person or a group of persons claiming to be the victim of violations of human rights and fundamental freedoms or by any person or group of persons, including NGOs acting in good faith in accordance with the principles of human rights, not resorting to politically motivated stands contrary to the provisions of the UN Charter and claiming to have direct and reliable knowledge of those violations. Nonetheless, reliably attested communications shall not be inadmissible solely because the knowledge of the individual author is second hand, provided they are accompanied by clear evidence;
- It is exclusively based on reports disseminated by mass media;
- It refers to a case that appears to reveal a consistent pattern of gross and reliably attested violations of human rights already being dealt with by a special procedure, a treaty body or other United Nations or similar regional complaints procedure in the field of human rights;
- The domestic remedies have not been exhausted, unless it appears that such remedies would be ineffective or unreasonably prolonged.

The National Human Rights Institutions (NHRIs), when they are established and work under the guidelines of the Principles Relating to Status of National Institutions (the Paris Principles) including in regard to quasi-judicial competence, can serve as effective means in addressing individual human rights violations.

Treaty-based Bodies

There are nine core international human rights treaties, the most recent one —on enforced disappearance—entered into force on 23 December 2010. Since the adoption of the Universal Declaration of Human Rights in 1948, all UN Member States have ratified at least one core international human rights treaty, and 80 percent have ratified four or more.

There are currently ten human rights treaty bodies, which are committees of independent experts. Nine of these treaty bodies monitor implementation of the core international human rights treaties while the tenth treaty body, the Subcommittee on Prevention of Torture, established under the Optional Protocol to the Convention against Torture, monitors places of detention in States parties to the Optional Protocol. The treaty bodies are created in accordance with the provisions of the treaty that they monitor. OHCHR supports the work of treaty bodies and assists them in harmonizing their working methods and reporting requirements through their secretariats.

UN Human Rights Committee (CCPR)

The United Nations Human Rights Committee is a United Nations body of 18 experts that meets three times a year for four-week sessions (spring session at UN headquarters in New York, summer and fall sessions at the UN Office in Geneva) to consider the five-yearly reports submitted by 162 UN member states on their compliance with the International Covenant on Civil and Political Rights, ICCPR, and to examine individual petitions concerning 112 States parties to the Optional Protocol.

The Committee is one of nine UN human rights treaty bodies, each responsible for overseeing the implementation of a particular treaty.

States that have ratified or acceded to the First Optional Protocol (currently 114 countries) have agreed to allow persons within their jurisdiction to submit complaints to the Committee requesting a determination whether provisions of the Covenant have been violated. For those countries, the Human Rights Committee functions as a mechanism for the international redress of human rights abuses, similar to the regional mechanisms afforded by the Inter-American Court of Human Rights or the European Court of Human Rights. The First Optional Protocol entered into force on 23 March 1976.

The Second Optional Protocol, in force since 11 July 1991, addresses the abolition of the death penalty and has 74 states parties.

The Human Rights Committee should not be confused with the more high-profile Commission on Human Rights, a Charter-based mechanism, or its replacement, the Human Rights Council. Whereas the Commission on Human Rights was a political forum where states debated all human rights concerns (since June 2006, replaced by the Council in that function), the Human Rights Committee is a treaty-based mechanism where a group of experts examines reports and rules on individual communications pertaining only to the International Covenant on Civil and Political Rights. It remains disputed whether the Human Rights Committee's "Views under article 5(4) of the Optional Protocol" qualify as decisions of a quasi-judicial body or simply constitute authoritative interpretations on the merits of the cases brought before them.

The members of the Human Rights Committee, who must be "of high moral character and recognized competence in the field of human rights", are elected by the member states but on an individual basis, not as representatives of their countries. They serve four-year terms, with one-half of their number elected every second year at the General Assembly.

Individual complaints (Communications) to the Committee

The United Nations Human Rights Committee has the jurisdiction to examine individual complaints (or communications) concerning the violation of rights contained within the International Covenant on Civil and Political Rights (ICCPR), by virtue of the First Optional Protocol to the Covenant. This treaty is one of five international human rights treaties that contain individual complaints procedures. In addition, there are bodies with procedures in place to consider complaints that are not within the jurisdiction of the treaty body system.

Who can bring a complaint before the Human Rights Committee

The communications procedure has been deliberately formed to be easily accessible to the general public; there is no need for legal terminology or the consultation of a lawyer to partake in the complaints process. However, consultation with a lawyer preceding the complaint is advised. The person bringing the complaint (the "author") must be someone who claims to have had his or her rights under the convention breached under Article 2 of the First Optional Protocol. If the victim is unable to issue the complaint him or herself then a representative may do so on his or her behalf provided that the third party has the written consent of the victim to represent them, or, if the victim is unable to give their own consent, the third party has provided justification for their representing the victim. Further, in accordance with Article 1 of the First Optional Protocol, the claimed violation of rights under the ICCPR must have been committed by a State party who has acceded to that Protocol or "recognised the competence of the Committee to receive such complaints".

What the complaint must include

There is no prescribed form that a complaint must conform to, however, it must be in writing (in one of the working languages of the Secretariat:

English, French, Spanish or Russian) and signed by the author or the author's representative. The complaint should contain all relevant information to the event or events that have taken place, including a chronological factual account of the events themselves, the identifying features of the victim (name, date of birth, nationality and so on), as well as the state involved, and, finally, what steps have been taken by the victim to exhaust all domestic remedies available to him or her. It is also advised that any additional documents (such as domestic court decisions and any relevant municipal laws) are provided to the Committee as part of the complaint. Finally, and perhaps most importantly, the author must establish why he or she believes that the event or events described constitute a violation of the rights granted by the ICCPR. It is important that the description of events are as detailed as possible; if necessary details are not included the author will be contacted and asked to provide them. Even though there is no prescribed form that a complaint must adhere to, examples or guidelines are provided by many NGOs and the United Nations.

The Complaints Procedure

Following the submission of a complaint the author will be advised if it has been registered and the complaint will also be sent to the State concerned for comment. Article Four of the First Optional Protocol provides that the State will have six months to submit comments on the complaint. Once the Committee has received the comments from the State these comments will be provided to the author who can then issue a response (generally within two months). Following the comments there is generally a two-stage process comprising the "Admissibility" stage and the "Merits" stage, however, due to the immense workload that the United Nations Human Rights Committee has, these two stages are usually undertaken simultaneously. The Committee assesses complaints on a closed basis in accordance with Article Five of the First Optional Protocol and for that reason only the original written complaint, the response from the State and the reply by the author will be considered. The Committee does not take any further action to verify the information that has been provided and the author or representatives of the State cannot take part via phone or video connection. If there is the potential for a substantial harm to occur that is permanent in nature, such as the execution of a death penalty or the deportation of a person who could face torture, then the author of the complaint can request that it be greeted with Urgency. Cases such as these are covered by Rule 86 of the Committee's

Rules of Procedure. Accordingly the Special Rapporteur on New Communications can issue 'interim measures' in order to prevent the harm occurring while the complaint is being considered. The Committee views any failure by the State to adhere by these interim measures a breach of their obligations under the First Optional Protocol.

Admissibility: There are a variety of criteria that the Committee can consider in order to determine whether the complaint is admissible or not. The Committee can consider one or all of these criteria, it is entirely discretionary. Some of the Factors that can determine admissibility include:

- Whether representatives have sufficient authority to be acting on behalf of a person
- Whether the author (or person being represented) is in fact a victim or sufficiently affected by an act or omission of the State. Simply complaining to the Committee as part of an attempted 'protest' against a law or policy of a State is described as an actio popularis and is not acceptable as the basis of an individual complaint to the Committee.
- Whether the complaint is within the jurisdiction of the ICCPR - there are other treaty bodies that can receive individual communications concerning other human rights treaties as well as special provisions that allow claims from outside these groups to be heard, however, no body can receive a claim that does not relate specifically to the treaty or convention that they are charged with, if this is the case, the complaint will be inadmissible ratione materiae. The right alleged to have been violated must be contained within the ICCPR in order for it to be heard. The Committee does allow for other bodies to bring complaints that the other body has received to the Committee if the ICCPR offers greater protection to that cause.
- The timing of the events - if the event or events occurred before the State concerned became a party to the First Optional Protocol then the complaint is inadmissible ratione temporis. The Committee has a list of exceptions to this general rule in regards to the ICCPR if the effects of the event continue when the State does accede to the First Optional Protocol. These include when the person is still serving a prison sentence following an unfair trial, for example.
- Whether all available domestic remedies have been exhausted. If it would be impractical or unreasonable for these to be exhausted; if, for

example, there would be too much of a delay or legal aid was not available, then the Committee can make an exception and allow the complaint to be admissible.

- Whether the complaint is an abuse of the process. If the claim is inappropriate or considered to be a waste of the Committee's time (such as frivolous claims or claims that have already been rejected by the Committee or another international mechanism) then it will be considered inadmissible.
- Finally, the complaint must not be being simultaneously considered by another international settlement mechanism. The Committee, however, qualifies this, by allowing complaints to also be submitted through the "1503" Special Procedures, or to a Special Rapporteur of the Commission on Human Rights to be considered simultaneously. They achieve these by postulating that these institutions do not constitute a separate international settlement mechanism.

Merits: When the Committee releases its view (or decision) it will outline the merits of the case or the reasons why it did or did not find that a violation had taken place. It will also include any conclusions drawn by Members whose findings differed from those of the Committee generally. This will be decided on the facts presented in the original complaint as well as taking into account the laws of the State party in conjunction with the rights contained in the ICCPR. If the State had made a reservation to the right in question when acceding to the ICCPR then generally the Committee will respect this, however, in some exceptional cases, they can come to the conclusion that the reservation itself is not acceptable.

Following a Decision

Once the Committee has issued its view, the stance that it has taken will determine what happens next. If the Committee determines that no violation of a right contained in the ICCPR has occurred then no further action will be taken. However, if the Committee decides a breach has occurred then the State must submit an 'update' to the Committee of the steps that it has taken to address the violation within three months in accordance with Article 2, paragraph 3 of the ICCPR. In Article 2, paragraph 3 the State has agreed to remedy any breaches of rights contained within the covenant. This response is also transmitted to the original author.

Notable Jurisprudence

The Committee has received thousands of complaints since its inception and due to this workload it can take a number of years before a decision is reached. During this time there have been a number of notable decisions that provide an indication of the way the Committee interprets the criteria used to determine admissibility as well as providing evidence of the practical application of the ICCPR.

Toonen v Australia: Toonen v Australia is a case decided by the Committee in 1992. The complaint in this case centred around a law in Australia that criminalised homosexual acts but had not been enforced in the country for ten years. Toonen himself had never been prosecuted under this law, however, the Committee determined that he could still be considered a victim due to the emotional anguish that the existence of such a law put him through.

Drake v New Zealand: Drake v New Zealand is a case that was decided by the Committee in 1997. Drake had been a prisoner of war in Japan during World War Two and made an individual complaint to the Committee about the actions of the New Zealand Government concerning prisoners of war following the war. One complaint was about the Treaty of San Francisco entered into between the Allies and Japan as Drake felt that his right to a remedy had been removed as a consequence of not being able to seek reparation from Japan. In addition to this, in 1988 the New Zealand Government issued reparations for those who were prisoners of war in Germany during World War Two and not those in Japan, which Drake alleged was discrimination. In both complaints the events themselves occurred before New Zealand was a party to the First Optional Protocol and so was inadmissible ratione temporis. Even if this were not the case, the claim would have been unsubstantiated as the alleged discrimination was not on any of the listed categories of discrimination of the ICCPR and therefore not within the jurisdiction of the Committee.

State reporting under the ICCPR

In common with all of the major UN human rights treaties, the ICCPR requires states that have ratified the Covenant to submit an initial report for consideration by a supervisory committee, in this case the Human Rights Committee, and thereafter to submit periodical reports at intervals of (in the case of the ICCPR) five years. The reports are expected to detail progress in implementing the treaty in domestic law and practice. The state's delegation appears before the Human Rights Committee in Geneva or New York to discuss the report, in a public process usually referred to as an 'examination' but officially termed a 'dialogue with the State Party'. At the end of a session (in which several states are considered) the committee issues 'concluding observations' on each state, using the report, the dialogue, and any other relevant information submitted by, for example, national human rights institutions or non-governmental organisations. These observations are used to commend the state for any progress in the implementation of ICCPR principles and to identify areas where improvement is expected.

The Human Rights Committee

The United Nations Human Rights Committee is the body responsible for overseeing and advising ratified states on the implementation of ICCPR treaty principles, within that state. With 160 ratified member states as of April 2012 the workload of the committee is heavy and thus the committee relies on each state at the national level to implement ICCPR principles, while acting as a periodic monitoring system. The Committee itself comprises 18 members nominated for election for their specialised knowledge in human rights and 'high moral character'.

The process of State reporting under the ICCPR

On ratifying the ICCPR, a state is then bound to report under Article 40 of the ICCPR, and has rights under Article 41 to make inter-state complaints for possible breaches of ICCPR principles. Article 40 requires that within one year an initial report is made and subsequently, periodic updates are made every four years or when specifically requested by the committee. The principal purpose of the report is to promote state compliance with the treaty principles and it should be an "honest appraisal of their conformity to the treaty obligations". Article 40(1) states that the report should set out "the measures [that the State has] adopted which give effect to the rights recognised herein and on the progress made in the enjoyment of those rights".

States are requested in the initial report to address in detail every Article in Parts I, II and III of the Covenant, particularly legal norms (the constitutional and legal framework for the implementation of Covenant rights); and explain with examples, access to remedies for any violations of Covenant rights. These reports therefore tend to be comprehensive. In periodic reports however, the Committee is concerned with the discussion of provisions identified in their concluding observations, progress on enjoyment of ICCPR rights and Articles of which there has been significant development since the last submission. The Covenant does not offer prescriptive guidelines on how to prepare a state report. The Committee instead issued general guidelines on structure in UN Doc. CCPR/C/66/GUI/Rev.2 (2001).

Procedure

Once the report has been written by the state, the procedure for consultation is as follows:

- The State party submits its report to the Human Rights Committee;
- The Human Rights Committee presents the State party with a list of issues and questions based on the concerns raised by the report (at which point there is opportunity for input from the United Nations system - NHRIs and NGO reports also called 'shadow reports');
- The State party may submit written replies to a list of issues and questions;
- The use of constructive dialogue between the Committee and the State party delegation during session (another opportunity for input from the United Nations system, NHRIs and NGOs whom may utilise);
- The Human Rights Committee issues its concluding observations on the report, inclusive of further recommendations for the State to consider in future);
- Lastly, procedures are used to follow up on implementation of the Human Rights Committees' recommendations.

Aims and objectives of the State reporting system

The aims and objectives of the state reporting system under the ICCPR were discussed in General Comment 1 of the Committee on Economic, Social and Cultural Rights (CESCR). CESCR concluded the State Reporting System was to be more than a procedural requirement, but additionally meet further aims and objectives.

"The process of reporting provides an opportunity for an individual State party to conduct a comprehensive review of the measures it has taken to bring its national law and policy into line with the provisions of the treaties to which it is a party."

NGO Reports

During the process of state reporting, NGOs may indicate their interest to the secretariat on a particular state's report and then prepare a submission to be considered alongside the state report. The input of non-governmental organisations allows for an assessment on the state of civil, social and political rights and takes into account such assessments in the view of organisation that may to be affected by ICCPR principles. The utility of NGO input has been noted by the World Conference on Human Rights in Vienna 1993 in its concluding Declaration, in the protection of human rights and in humanitarian services. NGO reports also give the public an opportunity to assist in the assessment of the government's overall adherence to the covenant or on particular matters. These reports may be assessed prior to the meeting or in some circumstances an NGO may be admitted to the meeting. Consequentially, the NGO may take a record of the meeting, facilitating dissemination of information back to the state concerned.

Nature of the State reporting process

Advantages: The process is not intended to be entirely negative, with States able to highlight in their reports progress which has been made examples of good practices. The process also allows for evaluation of internal structures of implementation and identification of further assistance the state may require. The mechanism provides an opportunity for constructive dialogue between the state and the committee rather than acting as adversarial proceedings.

Disadvantages: As a consent-based process, ensuring rights under the ICCPR internationally is fraught with difficulty. The mechanism relies on member states to implement standards by way of incorporation of ICCPR principles into municipal law or implementation through conduct. Where implementing ICCPR principles into domestic law would conflict existing policy or law, a state may ignore such a principle. New Zealand for example, has been considered slow in incorporating ICCPR principles for the reason of Parliamentary Supremacy; it may not restrict future Parliaments by strictly adopting all principles into law. A further issue is in delay between making reports and consideration by the HRC. There have been many attempts for this reason, to reform the treaty body system and make systems more effective, coherent and coordinated.

Commentators have stated that one motivation to submit these reports may be to avoid identification by other states as having failed to implement ICCPR principles, or risk the embarrassment of being blacklisted. The publication of State Reports on the internet allows for individual access to a country's progress as well as the response from the HRC. Public accessibility to reports has been further aided with a United Nations General Assembly resolution (57/300) to make available in the UN information centre of each state, copies of recent state reports, summary records and concluding observations. This stigma that may result from non-compliance does not prevent some reports being excessively late, and in some cases, erroneous. The non-invasive nature of the process means the committee is precluded from enforce recommendations made during the reporting process, therefore the power lies with the state in deciding whether the observe these observations.

Effectiveness of the State reporting system

The effectiveness of the use of state reporting has been questioned and as a result, a further mechanism for review was created in 2007; the UPR. The review was introduced to "complement" existing older mechanisms; particularly the State Reporting System. The Reports system has been regarded as weak for the fact it its success depends on the willingness of states to cooperate. Though in theory, reports should be an honest appraisal, constructive criticism of perceived failures to adhere to Covenant principles is unlikely. Further criticisms exist towards the length of the reports required as well as the onerous requirements, duplication of subject matter between various treaty reports and the lack of resources of the committee to process reports timely.

Solutions

In the reporting process, challenges typically arise in delays of reporting or consideration, non-reporting. In its 2006 Annual Report, the committee listed a number of countries overdue in reporting, for example Gambia (21 years overdue) and Equatorial Guinea (17 years overdue] and the aforementioned duplication of report requirements among treaty bodies. In his September 2002 report the former UN Secretary General Kofi Annan on 'Strengthening the United Nations; an agenda for further change' suggests one solution to the duplication issue may be to streamline reports. As "the content and timeliness of reports affects the quality of decision-making throughout the system" delays are critical and therefore, standardisation of reporting requirements will provide an efficient system and improve the state reporting process overall. A further suggestion of Annan was for "an integrated treatment of interrelated issues" through a single document to address adherence to ratified treaties.

In attempting to address issues around the state reporting process, a number of undertakings have been attempted. One such example is of the World Conference on Human Rights in its Vienna Declaration and Programme of Action, which sort to implement a system whereby Human Rights officers are assigned to states, working at the regional level, for the purpose of disseminating information, training and aiding implementation on a technical level.

Future alternatives

In response to state frustration over the workload in preparing these reports, the HRC in July 2010 proposed a new optional reporting procedure called the 'List of Issues Prior to Reporting' (LOIPR). The LOIPR system implements a new procedure whereby the committee sends the state a list of issues to address and the resulting report satisfies the requirements of Article 40 of the ICCPR. This system remains in the pilot stage until 2015 where the procedure will be reviewed "in terms of its practicality, effectiveness and capacity to improve the examination of the human rights situation in the State parties". It is intended LOIPR will allow for time to be used more efficiently and provide focus to the report. A further advantage of the procedure will be that a state will not have to submit both a periodic report and LOIPR report (though initial reports will be required). LOIPR remains an optional report and states may elect to continue with the periodic reports system or may be required by the committee to prepare a full report.

State reporting on the ICCPR in New Zealand

Since ratification of the ICCPR in December 1978, New Zealand has submitted five reports. The central criticism given by the treaty body is due to only partial incorporation of the ICCPR into domestic law with the New Zealand Bill of Rights Act 1990 (NZBORA). Some rights under the Covenant have not been recognised in the legislation, for example Article 1 'right of self determination' and Article 20 prohibition on propaganda. Further, on ratification NZ made several reservations on Articles 10 (2)(b), 10 (3), 14 (6), 20 and 22.

Committee on Economic, Social and Cultural Rights (CESCR)

The Committee on Economic, Social and Cultural Rights (CESCR) is the body of independent expertsthat monitors implementation of the International Covenant on Economic, Social and Cultural Rights by its States parties. The Committee was established under ECOSOC Resolution 1985/17 of 28 May 1985 to carry out the monitoring functions assigned to theUnited Nations Economic and Social Council (ECOSOC) in Part IV of the Covenant.

All States parties are obliged to submit regular reports to the Committee on how the rights are being implemented. States must report initially within two years of accepting the Covenant and thereafter every five years. The Committee examines each report and addresses its concerns and recommendations to the State party in the form of "concluding observations".

With regard to individual complaints, on 10 December 2008, the General Assembly unanimously adopted an Optional Protocol (GA resolution A/RES/63/117) to the International Covenant on Economic, Social and Cultural Rights which provides the Committee competence to receive and consider communications. The General Assembly took note of the adoption by the Human Rights Council by its resolution 8/2 of 18 June 2008, of the Optional Protocol . The Optional Protocol was opened for signature at a signing ceremony in 2009. In addition to the Committee on Economic, Social and Cultural rights, other committees with competence can consider individual communicationsinvolving issues related to economic, social and cultural rights in the context of its treaty.

The Committee meets in Geneva and normally holds two sessions per year, consisting of a three-week plenary and a one-week pre-sessional working group.

The Committee also publishes its interpretation of the provisions of the Covenant, known as general comments.

Committee on the Elimination of Racial Discrimination (CERD)

The International Convention on the Elimination of All Forms of Racial Discrimination (ICERD) is a United Nations convention. A second-generation human rights instrument, the Convention commits its members to the elimination of racial discrimination and the promotion of understanding among all races. Controversially, the Convention also requires its parties to outlaw hate speech and criminalize membership in racist organizations.

The Convention also includes an individual complaints mechanism, effectively making it enforceable against its parties. This has led to the development of a limited jurisprudence on the interpretation and implementation of the Convention.

The convention was adopted and opened for signature by the United Nations General Assembly on December 21, 1965, and entered into force on January 4, 1969. As of October 2011, it has 86 signatories and 175 parties.

Genesis

In December 1960, following incidents of antisemitism in several parts of the world, the United Nations General Assembly adopted a resolution condemning "all manifestations and practices of racial, religious and national hatred" as violations of the United Nations Charter and Universal Declaration of Human Rights and calling on the governments of all states to "take all necessary measures to prevent all manifestations of racial, religious and national hatred". The Economic and Social Council followed this up by drafting a resolution on "manifestations of racial prejudice and national and religious intolerance", calling on governments to educate the public against intolerance and rescind discriminatory laws. Lack of time prevented this from being considered by the General Assembly in 1961, but it was passed the next year.

During the early debate on this resolution, African nations led by the Central African Republic, Chad, Dahomey, Guinea, Côte d'Ivoire, Mali, Mauritania, and Upper Volta pushed for more concrete action on the issue, in the form of an international convention against racial discrimination. Some nations preferred a declaration rather than a binding convention, while others wanted to deal with racial and religious intolerance in a single instrument. The eventual compromise, forced by the Arab nations' reluctance to discuss antisemitism, was for two resolutions, one calling for a declaration and draft convention aimed at eliminating racial discrimination, the other doing the same for religious intolerance.

The draft Declaration on the Elimination of All Forms of Racial Discrimination was adopted by the General Assembly on November 20, 1963. The same day the General Assembly called for the Economic and Social Council and the Commission on Human Rights to make the drafting of a Convention on the subject an absolute priority. The draft was completed by mid-1964, but delays in the General Assembly meant that it could not be adopted that year. It was finally adopted on December 21, 1965.

Summary

The Convention follows the structure of the Universal Declaration of Human Rights, International Covenant on Civil and Political Rights, and International Covenant on Economic, Social and Cultural Rights, with a preamble and twenty-five articles, divided into three parts.

Part 1 (Articles 1 – 7) commits parties to the elimination of all forms of racial discrimination and to promoting understanding among all races (Article 2). Parties are obliged to not discriminate on the basis of race, not to sponsor or defend racism, and to prohibit racial discrimination within their jurisdictions. They must also review their laws and policies to ensure that they do not discriminate on the basis of race, and commit to amending or repealing those that do. Specific areas in which discrimination must be eliminated are listed in Article 5.

The Convention imposes a specific commitment on parties to eradicate racial segregation and the crime of apartheid within their jurisdictions (Article 3). Parties are also required to criminalize the incitement of racial hatred (Article 4), to ensure judicial remedies for acts of racial discrimination (Article 6), and to engage in public education to promote understanding and tolerance (Article 7).

Part 2 (Articles 8 – 16) governs reporting and monitoring of the Convention and the steps taken by the parties to implement it. It establishes the Committee on the Elimination of Racial Discrimination, and empowers it to make general recommendations to the UN General Assembly. It also establishes a dispute-resolution mechanism between parties (Articles 11 – 13), and allows parties to recognise the competence of the Committee to hear complaints from individuals about violations of the rights protected by the Convention (Article 14).

Part 3 (Articles 17 – 25) governs ratification, entry into force, and amendment of the Convention.

Core provisions

Definition of "racial discrimination"

Article 1 of the Convention defines "racial discrimination" as:

> ...any distinction, exclusion, restriction or preference based on race, colour, descent, or national or ethnic origin which has the purpose or effect of nullifying or impairing the recognition, enjoyment or exercise, on an equal

footing, of human rights and fundamental freedoms in the political, economic, social, cultural or any other field of public life.

Distinctions made on the basis of citizenship (that is, between citizens and non-citizens) are specifically excluded from the definition, as are affirmative action policies and other measures taken to redress imbalances and promote equality.

This definition does not distinguish between discrimination based on ethnicity and discrimination based on race, in part because the distinction between the ethnicity and race remains debatable among anthropologists. The inclusion of descent specifically covers discrimination on the basis of caste and other forms of inherited status.

Discrimination need not be strictly based on race or ethnicity for the Convention to apply. Rather, whether a particular action or policy discriminates is judged by its effects.

In seeking to determine whether an action has an effect contrary to the Convention, it will look to see whether that action has an unjustifiable disparate impact upon a group distinguished by race, colour, descent, or national or ethnic origin.

The question of whether an individual belongs to a particular racial group is to be decided, in the absence of justification to the contrary, by self-identification.

Prevention of discrimination

Article 2 of the Convention condemns racial discrimination and obliges parties to "undertake to pursue by all appropriate means and without delay a policy of eliminating racial discrimination in all its forms". It also obliges parties to promote understanding among all races. To achieve this, the Convention requires that signatories:

- Not practice racial discrimination in public institutions
- Not "sponsor, defend, or support" racial discrimination
- Review existing policies, and amend or revoke those that cause or perpetuate racial discrimination
- Prohibit "by all appropriate means, including legislation," racial discrimination by individuals and organisations within their jurisdictions

- Encourage groups, movements, and other means that eliminate barriers between races, and discourage racial division

Parties are obliged "when the circumstances so warrant" to use affirmative action policies for specific racial groups to guarantee "the full and equal enjoyment of human rights and fundamental freedoms". However, these measures must be finite, and "shall in no case entail as a consequence the maintenance of unequal or separate rights for different racial groups after the objectives for which they were taken have been achieved".

Article 5 expands upon on the general obligation of Article 2 and creates a specific obligation to guarantee the right of everyone to equality before the law regardless of "race, colour, or national or ethnic origin". It further lists specific rights this equality must apply to: equal treatment by courts and tribunals, security of the person and freedom from violence, the civil and political rights affirmed in the ICCPR, the economic, social and cultural rights affirmed in the ICESCR, and the right of access to any place or service used by the general public, "such as transport hotels, restaurants, cafes, theatres and parks." This list is not exhaustive, and the obligation extends to all human rights.

Article 6 obliges parties to provide "effective protection and remedies" through the courts or other institutions for any act of racial discrimination. This includes a right to a legal remedy and damages for injury suffered due to discrimination.

Condemnation of apartheid

Article 3 condemns apartheid and racial segregation and obliges parties to "prevent, prohibit and eradicate" these practices in territories under their jurisdiction. This article has since been strengthened by the recognition of apartheid as a crime against humanity in the Rome Statute of the International Criminal Court.

The Committee on the Elimination of Racial Discrimination regards this article as also entailing an obligation to eradicate the consequences of past policies of segregation, and to prevent racial segregation arising from the actions of private individuals.

Prohibition of incitement

Article 4 of the Convention condemns propaganda and organizations that attempt to justify discrimination or are based on the idea of racial supremacism. It obliges parties, "with due regard to the principles embodied in the Universal Declaration of Human Rights", to adopt "immediate and positive measures" to eradicate these forms of incitement and discrimination. Specifically, it obliges parties to criminalize hate speech, hate crimes and the financing of racist activities, and to prohibit and criminalize membership in organizations that "promote and incite" racial discrimination. A number of parties have reservations on this article, and interpret it as not permitting or requiring measures that infringe on the freedoms of speech, association or assembly.

The Committee on the Elimination of Racial Discrimination regards this article as a mandatory obligation of parties to the Convention, and has repeatedly criticized parties for failing to abide by it. It regards the obligation as consistent with the freedoms of opinion and expression affirmed in the UNDHR and ICCPR and notes that the latter specifically outlaws inciting racial discrimination, hatred and violence. It views the provisions as necessary to prevent organised racial violence and the "political exploitation of ethnic difference."

Promotion of tolerance

Article 7 obliges parties to adopt "immediate and effective measures", particularly in education, to combat racial prejudice and encourage understanding and tolerance between different racial, ethnic and national groups.

Dispute resolution mechanism

Articles 11 through 13 of the Convention establish a dispute resolution mechanism between parties. A party that believes another party is not implementing the Convention may complain to the Committee on the Elimination of Racial Discrimination. The Committee will pass on the complaint, and if it is not resolved between the two parties, may establish an ad hoc Conciliation Commission to investigate and make recommendations on the matter. This procedure has never been used. Article 22 further allows any dispute over the interpretation or application of the Convention to be referred to the International Court of Justice. This clause has been invoked only once, by Georgia against Russia.

Individual complaints mechanism

Article 14 of the Convention establishes an individual complaints mechanism similar to that of the First Optional Protocol to the International Covenant on Civil and Political Rights, Optional Protocol to the Convention on the Rights of Persons with Disabilities and Optional Protocol to the Convention on the Elimination of All Forms of Discrimination against Women. Parties may at any time recognise the competence of the Committee on the Elimination of Racial Discrimination to consider complaints from individuals or groups who claim their rights under the Convention have been violated. Such parties may establish local bodies to hear complaints before they are passed on. Complainants must have exhausted all domestic remedies, and anonymous complaints and complaints that refer to events that occurred before the country concerned joined the Optional Protocol are not permitted. The Committee can request information from and make recommendations to a party.

The individual complaints mechanism came into operation in 1982, after it had been accepted by ten states-parties. As of 2010, 58 states had recognised the competence of the Committee, and 54 cases have been dealt with by the Committee.

Reservations

A number of parties have made reservations and interpretative declarations to their application of the Convention. The Convention text forbids reservations "incompatible with the object and purpose of this Convention" or that would inhibit the operation of any body established by it. A reservation is considered incompatible or inhibitive if two-thirds of parties object to it.

Article 22

Afghanistan, Bahrain, China, Cuba, Egypt, Equatorial Guinea, India, Indonesia, Iraq, Israel, Kuwait, Lebanon, Libya, Madagascar, Morocco, Mozambique, Nepal, Saudi Arabia, Syria, Thailand, Turkey, Vietnam, and Yemen do not consider themselves bound by Article 22. Some interpret this article as allowing disputes to be referred to the International Court of Justice only with the consent of all involved parties.

Obligations beyond existing constitution

Antigua and Barbuda, the Bahamas, Barbados, Guyana, Jamaica, Nepal, Papua New Guinea, Thailand and United States interpret the Convention as not implying any obligations beyond the limits of their existing constitutions.

Hate speech

Austria, Belgium, France, Ireland, Italy, Japan, Malta, Monaco, Switzerland and Tonga all interpret Article 4 as not permitting or requiring measures that threaten the freedoms of speech, opinion, association, and assembly. Antigua and Barbuda, the Bahamas, Barbados, Fiji, Nepal, Papua New Guinea, Thailand and United Kingdom interpret the Convention as creating an obligation to enact measures against hate speech and hate crimes only when a need arises. The United States of America does not accept any obligation to enact measures under Article 4, which it views as incompatible with freedom of expression.

Immigration

Monaco and Switzerland reserve the right to apply their own legal principles on the entry of foreigners into their labour markets. The United Kingdom does not regard the Commonwealth Immigrants Act 1962 and Commonwealth Immigrants Act 1968 as constituting any form of racial discrimination.

Indigenous people

Tonga reserves the right not to apply the Convention to any restriction on the alienation of land held by indigenous Tongans. Fiji has significant reservations around Article 5, and reserves the right not to implement those provisions if they are incompatible with existing law on voting rights, the alienation of land by indigenous Fijians.

Jurisprudence

The individual complaints mechanism has led to a limited jurisprudence on the interpretation and implementation of the Convention. So far 45 complaints have been registered with the Committee; 17 of these have been deemed inadmissible, 14 have led to a finding of no violation, and in 10 cases a party has been found to have violated the Convention. Four cases are still pending.

Several cases have dealt with the treatment of Romani people in Eastern Europe. In Koptova v. Slovakia the Committee found that resolutions by several villages in Slovakia forbidding the residence of Roma were discriminatory and restricted freedom of movement and residence, and recommended the Slovak government take steps to end such practices. In L.R. v. Slovakia the Committee found that the Slovak government had failed to provide an effective remedy for discrimination suffered by Roma after the cancellation of a housing project on ethnic grounds. In Durmic v. Serbia and Montenegro the Committee found a systemic failure by the Serbian government to investigate and prosecute discrimination against Roma in access to public places.

In several cases, notably L.K. v. Netherlands and Gelle v. Denmark, the Committee has criticized parties for their failure to adequately prosecute acts of racial discrimination or incitement. In both cases, the Committee refused to accept "any claim that the enactment of law making racial discrimination a criminal act in itself represents full compliance with the obligations of States parties under the Convention". Such laws "must also be effectively implemented by the competent national tribunals and other State institutions". While the Committee accepts the discretion of prosecutors on whether or not to lay charges, this discretion "should be applied in each case of alleged racial discrimination in the light of the guarantees laid down in the Convention"

In The Jewish community of Oslo et al. v. Norway, the Committee found that the prohibition of hate speech was compatible with freedom of speech, and that the acquittal of a neo-Nazi leader by the Supreme Court of Norway on freedom of speech grounds was a violation of the Convention.

In Hagan v. Australia, the Committee ruled that, while not originally intended to demean anyone, the name of the "E. S. 'Nigger' Brown Stand" (named in honour of 1920s rugby league player Edward Stanley Brown) at a Toowoomba sports field was racially offensive and should be removed.

Impact

The impact of an international treaty can be measured in two ways: by its acceptance, and by its implementation. On the first measure, the Convention has gained near-universal acceptance by the international community, with fewer than twenty (mostly small) states yet to become parties. Most major states have also accepted the Convention's individual complaints mechanism, signaling a strong desire to be bound by the Convention's provisions.

On the second measure, the Convention has had a significant impact on national legislation, with many states adopting legislation outlawing racial discrimination by the state, in the workplace, or in the provision of services such as housing and education. Such legislation may be either civil or criminal. Examples of the former include the Race Relations Act 1971 (New Zealand), Racial Discrimination Act 1975 (Australia), Race Relations Act 1976 (UK), and Canadian Human Rights Act (Canada). Criminal provisions are used in Belgium, Denmark, France, Italy, Norway and Portugal. Despite reservations to the Convention, most western European nations have criminalized the incitement of racial hatred.

The Convention has faced persistent problems with reporting since its inception, with parties frequently failing to report fully, or even at all. As of 2008, twenty parties had failed to report for more than ten years, and thirty parties had failed to report for more than five. One party, Sierra Leone, had failed to report since 1976, while two more – Liberia and Saint Lucia had never met their reporting requirements under the Convention. The Committee has responded to this persistent failure to report by reviewing the late parties anyway – a strategy that has produced some success in gaining compliance with reporting requirements. This lack of reporting is seen by some as a significant failure of the Convention. However the reporting system has also been praised as providing "a permanent stimulus inducing individual States to enact anti-racist legislation or amend the existing one when necessary."

Committee on the Elimination of Discrimination against Women (CEDAW)

The United Nations Committee on the Elimination of Discrimination against Women (CEDAW), an expert body established in 1982, is composed of 23 experts on women's issues from around the world.

The Committee's mandate is very specific: it watches over the progress for women made in those countries that are the States parties to the 1979 Convention on the Elimination of All Forms of Discrimination against Women. A country becomes a State party by ratifying or acceding to the Convention and thereby accepting a legal obligation to counteract discrimination against women. The Committee monitors the implementation of national measures to fulfil this obligation.

At each of its sessions, the Committee reviews national reports submitted by the States parties within one year of ratification or accession, and thereafter every four years. These reports, which cover national action taken to improve the situation of women, are presented to the Committee by Government representatives. In discussions with these officials, the

CEDAW experts comment on the report and obtain additional information. This procedure of actual dialogue, developed by the Committee, has proven valuable because it allows for an exchange of views and a clearer analysis of anti-discrimination policies in the various countries.

The Committee also makes recommendations on any issue affecting women to which it believes the States parties should devote more attention. For example, at the 1989 session, the Committee discussed the high incidence of violence against women, requesting information on this problem from all countries. In 1992, the Committee adopted general recommendation 19, which requires national reports to the Committee to include statistical data on the incidence of violence against women, information on the provision of services for victims, and legislative and other measures taken to protect women against violence in their everyday lives, such as harassment at the workplace, abuse in the family and sexual violence. As of the end of 2007, the Committee has issued 25 general recommendations.

CEDAW membership

The 23 members of CEDAW, acknowledged as experts "of high moral standing and competence in the field covered by the Convention", are elected by the States parties. These elections have to meet the Convention's demands for equitable geographical distribution in membership and the requirement that CEDAW members represent "different forms of civilization as well as principal legal systems". Their terms last four years, with only half of the Committee members replaced each time elections take place. The meeting of States parties is convened every other year by the Secretary-General at UN Headquarters in New York.

Past and present members of the Committee

As of the end of 2007, a total of 110 experts have served as members of the Committee since 1982.

Past and present members of the Committee

The officers of the Committee consist of a Chairperson, three Vice-Chairpersons and a Rapporteur. While the length of the terms of office is laid down in the Convention, the rules of procedure add that the officers shall be eligible for re-election "provided that the principle of rotation is upheld".

The rules of procedure identify the general powers of the Chairperson. Under the rules, the Chairperson guides the proceedings of the Committee, including the direction of the discussion and decision-making process. Procedurally, the Chairperson works closely with the UN Secretariat in the preparation of the session, in ensuring the timely conduct of business, including the preparation of documents, the presence of States parties for the consideration of reports, and the general provision of backup to the Committee.

The Chairperson has been increasingly called upon to represent the Committee at various international activities and events, including international conferences and other intergovernmental meetings of the United Nations. The Chairperson participates on behalf of the Committee in the annual meeting of the persons chairing UN human rights treaty bodies, which makes recommendations to the General Assembly.

As of the thirty-ninth session of the Committee (2007), eleven experts had served as its Chairperson.

Committee against Torture (CAT)

The Committee Against Torture (CAT) is the body of 10 independent experts that monitors implementation of the Convention against Torture and Other Cruel, Inhuman or Degrading Treatment or Punishment by its State parties.

All States parties are obliged to submit regular reports to the Committee on how the rights are being implemented. States must report initially one year after acceding to the Convention and then every four years. The Committee examines each report and addresses its concerns and recommendations to the State party in the form of "concluding observations".

In addition to the reporting procedure, the Convention establishes three other mechanisms through which the Committee performs its monitoring functions: the Committee may also, under certain circumstances, considerindividual complaints or communications from individuals claiming that their rights under the Convention have been violated, undertake inquiries, and consider inter-state complaints.

The Optional Protocol to the Convention, which entered into force in June 2006, creates the Subcommittee on Prevention of Torture (SPT). The SPT has a mandate to visit places where persons are deprived of their liberty in the States parties. Under the Optional Protocol, States parties shall establish a independent national preventive mechanisms for the prevention of torture at the domestic level which has also a mandate to inspect places of detention.

The CAT meets in Geneva and normally holds twosessions per year consisting of a four week session in April/May and another four week session in November.

The Committee also publishes its interpretation of the content of the provisions of the Convention, known asgeneral comments on thematic issues

Subcommittee on Prevention of Torture (SPT)

The mandate of the United Nations Subcommittee onPrevention of Torture and Other Cruel, Inhuman or Degrading Treatment or Punishment (SPT) is twofold: to visit all places of detention in States Parties and to provide assistance and advice to both States Parties and National Preventive Mechanisms.

Independent Experts

The SPT is composed of 10 independent and impartial experts serving in their individual capacity from different backgrounds and from various countries, which have ratified or acceded to the OPCAT. After the fiftieth ratification of or accession, the number of the members of the SPT has increased to twenty-five.

SPT membership is multidisciplinary, including lawyers, doctors and inspection experts, among others. Members are elected by States Parties for a four-year term; the term of half the members elected at the first election will expire at the end of two years. They are eligible for re-election once if re-nominated.

Visits

The SPT visits police stations, prisons (military and civilian), detention centres (e.g. pre-trial detention centres, immigration detention centres, juvenile justice establishments, etc.), mental health and social care institutions and any other places where people are or may be deprived of their liberty. It recommends action to be taken to improve the treatment of detainees, including conditions of detention.

The visits are conducted by at least two members of the SPT. These members may be accompanied, if needed, by experts of demonstrated professional experience and knowledge in the field. These experts are selected from a roster of experts prepared on the basis of proposals made by States Parties, the Office of the United Nations High Commissioner for Human Rights and the United Nations Centre for International Crime Prevention. In preparing the roster, the States Parties concerned may propose no more than five national experts.

Access

Under the OPCAT, the SPT has unrestricted access to all places of detention, their installations and facilities and to all relevant information relating to the treatment and conditions of detention of persons deprived of their liberty. The SPT must also be granted access to have private interviews with the persons deprived of their liberty, without witnesses, and to any other person who in the SPT's view may supply relevant information.

The States Parties undertake to ensure that there are no sanctions or reprisals for providing information to SPT members.

Assistance and Advice

According to the OPCAT, the SPT's mandate includes advising and assisting States in the establishment of the NPMs. These national mechanisms have the mandate to examine regularly the treatment of persons deprived of their liberty and make recommendations to the States' authorities in order to improve the conditions of detention. In the framework of the close cooperation between the SPT and the States Parties, the SPT will make itself available for ongoing dialogue concerning the NPMs. Advising States in the development of effective national mechanisms is a key element in the work of the SPT and will form an important part of each visit.

The SPT advises States Parties about reinforcing the powers, independence and capacity of NPMs. The SPT also provides NPMs with advice on and assistance in reinforcing their independence and capacities and strengthening safeguards against ill-treatment of persons deprived of their liberty. The SPT works in close collaboration with the NPMs, in order to ensure ongoing monitoring of all places of detention.

The OPCAT requires that the composition of the NPMs be established in accordance with a process providing all necessary guarantees of the independence of the NPMs, including the pluralist representation of civil society.

Principles

The SPT is guided by core principles: confidentiality, impartiality, non-selectivity, universality and objectivity. The OPCAT is based on co-operation between the SPT and the States Parties. During its visits, the SPT's members meet with State officials, NPMs, representatives of national human rights institutions, non-governmental organizations, as well as with any other person who can provide information relevant to the mandate.

The SPT communicates its recommendations and observations confidentially to the State, and if necessary, to the national preventive mechanisms. The SPT will publish the report, together with comments from the State Party, whenever requested to do so by the State Party.

However, if the State Party makes part of the report public, the SPT may publish all or part of the report. Moreover, if a country refuses to co-operate or fails to take steps to improve the situation in light of the SPT's recommendations, the SPT may request the Committee against Torture to make a public statement or to publish the SPT report.

The SPT presents a public annual report on its activities to the Committee against Torture.

Committee on the Rights of the Child (CRC)

The Committee on the Rights of the Child (CRC) is the body of independent experts that monitors implementation of theConvention on the Rights of the Child by its State parties. It also monitors implementation of two optional protocols to the Convention, on involvement of children in armed conflictand on sale of children, child prostitution and child pornography. On 19 December 2011, the UN General Assembly approved a third optional protocol on a Communications Procedure, which will allow individual children to submit complaints regarding specific violations of their rights under the Convention and its first two optional protocols. The Protocol opens for signature in 2012 and will enter into force upon ratification by 10 UN Member States.

All States parties are obliged to submit regular reports to the Committee on how the rights are being implemented. States must report initially two years after acceding to the Convention and then every five years. The Committee examines each report and addresses its concerns and recommendations to the State party in the form of "concluding observations".

The Committee reviews additional reports which must be submitted by States who have acceded to the two Optional Protocols to the Convention.

The Committee will soon be able to consider individual complaints by children. In the meantime, violations of child rights may be raised before other committees with competence to consider individual complaints.

The Committee meets in Geneva and normally holds threesessions per year consisting of a three-week plenary and a one-week pre-sessional working group. In 2010, the Committee considered reports in two parallel chambers of 9 members each, "as an exceptional and temporary measure", in order to clear the backlog of reports.

The Committee also publishes its interpretation of the content of human rights provisions, known as general comments on thematic issues and organizes days of general discussion.

Committee on Migrant Workers (CMW)

The Committee on the Protection of the Rights of All Migrant Workers and Members of their Families (CMW) is the body of independent experts that monitors implementation of the International Convention on the Protection of the Rights of All Migrant Workers and Members of Their Families by its State parties. It held its first session in March 2004.

All States parties are obliged to submit regular reports to the Committee on how the rights are being implemented. States must report initially one year after acceding to the Convention and then every five years. The Committee will examine each report and address its concerns and recommendations to the State party in the form of "concluding observations".

The Committee will also, under certain circumstances, be able to consider individual complaints or communications from individuals claiming that their rights under the Convention have been violated once 10 States parties have accepted this procedure in accordance with article 77 of the Convention. At the moment, two States have accepted this procedure.

The Committee meets in Geneva and normally holds two sessions per year.

The Committee also organizes days of general discussion and can publish statements on themes related to its work and interpretations of the content of the provisions in the Convention (general comments).

Committee on the Rights of Persons with Disabilities (CRPD)

The Committee on the Rights of Persons with Disabilities is one of the human rights bodies in the Office of the High Commissioner for Human Rights of the United Nations. It is tasked with monitoring the implementation of the Convention on the Rights of Persons with Disabilities. It initially consisted of 12 independent human rights experts, with half elected for two-year terms and half elected for four years. Thereafter, members will be elected for four-year terms, with half the members elected every two years. As the Convention has achieved 80 ratifications, the committee was expanded to 18 members.

All states parties are required to submit regular reports to the Committee outlining the legislative, judicial, policy and other measures they have taken to implement the rights affirmed in the Convention. The first report is due within two years of ratifying the Convention; thereafter reports are due every four years. The Committee will examine each report and address its concerns and recommendations to the state party in the form of "concluding observations".

The initial membership of the Committee was elected by secret ballot at the first conference of states' parties to the Convention on 3 November 2008 in New York. The first chair, elected at the first session in February 2009, was Mohammed Al-Tarawneh[citation needed], who was succeeded with effect from February 2010 by Ron McCallum.

Committee on Enforced Disappearances (CED)

The Committee on Enforced Disappearances (CED) is the body of independent experts which monitors implementation of the Convention by the States Parties.

All States parties are obliged to submit regular reports to the Committee on how the rights are being implemented.

States must report initially within two years of accepting the Convention. The Committee examines each report and shall make such suggestions and general recommendations on the report as it may consider appropriate and shall forward these to the State Party concerned.

In accordance with article 31, a State Party may at the time of ratification of this Convention or at any time afterwards declare that it recognizes the competence of the Committee to receive and consider communications from or on behalf of individuals subject to its jurisdiction claiming to be victims of a violation by this State Party of provisions of this Convention.

The Committee shall meet in Geneva and normally hold two sessions per year.

References

Ball, Olivia; Gready, Paul (2006). *The no-nonsense guide to human rights*. Oxford: New Internationalist.

Beitz, Charles R. (2009). *The idea of human rights*. Oxford: Oxford University Press.

Donnelly, Jack (2003). *Universal human rights in theory and practice* (2nd ed.). Ithaca: Cornell University Press.

Freeman, Michael (2002). *Human rights : an interdisciplinary approach*. Cambridge: Polity Press.

Moyn, Samuel (2010). *The last utopia: human rights in history*. Cambridge, Mass.: Belknap Press of Harvard University Press.

4

United Nations System for Human Rights Protection

Under the mandate of the UN charter, the and the multilateral UN human rights treaties, the United Nations (UN) as an intergovernmental body seeks to apply international jurisdiction for universal human-rights legislation· Within the UN machinery, human-rights issues are primarily the concern of the United Nations Security Council and the United Nations Human Rights Council, and there are numerous committees within the UN with responsibilities for safeguarding different human-rights treaties. The most senior body of the UN in the sphere of human rights is the Office of the High Commissioner for Human Rights. The United Nations has an international mandate to: achieve international co-operation in solving international problems of an economic, social, cultural, or humanitarian character, and in promoting and encouraging respect for human rights and for fundamental freedoms for all without distinction as to race, gender, language, or religion.

There are 193 member states, including every internationally recognized sovereign state in the world but Vatican City. From its offices around the world, the UN and its specialized agencies decide on substantive and administrative issues in regular meetings held throughout the year. The organization has six principal organs: the General Assembly (the main deliberative assembly); the Security Council (for deciding certain resolutions for peace and security); the Economic and Social Council (for assisting in promoting international economic and social cooperation and development); the Secretariat (for providing studies, information, and facilities needed by the UN); the International Court of Justice (the primary judicial organ); and the United Nations Trusteeship Council (which is currently inactive). Other prominent UN System agencies include the World Health Organization (WHO), the World Food Programme (WFP) and United Nations Children's Fund (UNICEF). The UN's most prominent position is Secretary-General which has been held by Ban Ki-moon of South Korea since 2007.

The United Nations Headquarters resides in international territory in New York City, with further main offices at Geneva, Nairobi, and Vienna. The organization is financed from assessed and voluntary contributions from its member states, and has six official languages: Arabic, Chinese, English, French, Russian, and Spanish.

History of UN

The League of Nations failed to prevent World War II (1939–1945). Because of the widespread recognition that humankind could not afford a third world war, the United Nations was established to replace the flawed League of Nations in 1945 in order to maintain international peace and promote cooperation in solving international economic, social and humanitarian problems. The earliest concrete plan for a new world organization was begun under the aegis of the U.S. State Department in 1939. Franklin D. Roosevelt first coined the term 'United Nations' as a term to describe the Allied countries. The term was first officially used on 1 January 1942, when 26 governments signed the Atlantic Charter, pledging to continue the war effort. On 25 April 1945, the UN Conference on International Organization began in San Francisco, attended by 50 governments and a number of non-governmental organizations involved in drafting the United Nations Charter. The UN officially came into existence on 24 October 1945 upon ratification of the Charter by the five then-permanent members of the Security Council—France, the Republic of China, the Soviet Union, the United Kingdom and the United States—and by a majority of the other 46 signatories. The first meetings of the General Assembly, with 51 nations represented, and the Security Council, took place in Methodist Central Hall Westminster in London in January 1946.

The organization was based at the Sperry Gyroscope Corporation's facility in Lake Success, New York, from 1946–1952, before moving to the United Nations Headquarters building in Manhattan upon its completion.

Since its creation, there has been controversy and criticism of the United Nations. In the United States, an early opponent of the UN was the John Birch Society, which began a "get US out of the UN" campaign in 1959, charging that the UN's aim was to establish a "One World Government." After the Second World War, the French Committee of National Liberation was late to be recognized by the US as the government of France, and so the country was initially excluded from the conferences that aimed at creating the new organization. Charles de Gaulle criticized the UN, famously calling it a machin ("contraption"), and was not convinced that a global security alliance would help maintain world peace, preferring direct defence treaties between countries.

Legal Basis of Establishment

Shortly after its establishment the UN sought recognition as an international legal person due to the case of Reparations for Injuries Suffered in the Service of the United Nations with the advisory opinion delivered by the International Court of Justice (ICJ). The question arose whether the United Nations, as an organisation, had "the capacity to bring an international claim against a government regarding injuries that the organisation alleged had been caused by that state."

The Court stated: the Organization was intended to exercise and enjoy, and is in fact exercising and enjoying functions and rights, which can only be explained on the basis of the possession of a large measure of international personality and the capacity to operate upon an international plane ... Accordingly, the Court has come to the conclusion that the Organization is an international person. That is not the same thing as saying that it is a State, which it certainly is not, or that its legal personality and rights and duties are the same as those of a State ... What it does mean is that it is a subject of international law and capable of possessing international rights and duties, and that it has capacity to maintain its rights by bringing international claims.

Organization

The United Nations' system is based on five principal organs (formerly six – the Trusteeship Council suspended operations in 1994, upon the independence of Palau, the last remaining UN trustee territory); the General Assembly, the Security Council, the Economic and Social Council (ECOSOC), the Secretariat, and the International Court of Justice.

Four of the five principal organs are located at the main United Nations Headquarters located on international territory in New York City. The International Court of Justice is located in The Hague, while other major agencies are based in the UN offices at Geneva, Vienna, and Nairobi. Other UN institutions are located throughout the world.

The six official languages of the United Nations, used in intergovernmental meetings and documents, are Arabic, Chinese, English, French, Russian, and Spanish. The Secretariat uses two working languages, English and French. Four of the official languages are the national languages of the permanent members of the Security Council (the United Kingdom and the United States share English as a de facto official language); Spanish and Arabic are the languages of the two largest blocs of official languages outside of the permanent members (Spanish being official in 20 countries, Arabic in 26). Five of the official languages were chosen when the UN was founded; Arabic was added later in 1973. The United Nations Editorial Manual states that the standard for English language documents is British usage and Oxford spelling, the Chinese writing standard is Simplified Chinese. This replaced Traditional Chinese in 1971 when the UN representation of China was changed from the Republic of China to the People's Republic of China.

General Assembly

The General Assembly is the main deliberative assembly of the United Nations. Composed of all United Nations member states, the assembly meets in regular yearly sessions under a president elected from among the member states. Over a two-week period at the start of each session, all members have the opportunity to address the assembly. Traditionally, the Secretary-General makes the first statement, followed by the president of the assembly. The first session was convened on 10 January 1946 in the Methodist Central Hall Westminster in London and included representatives of 51 nations.

When the General Assembly votes on important questions, a two-thirds majority of those present and voting is required. Examples of important questions include: recommendations on peace and security; election of members to organs; admission, suspension, and expulsion of members; and, budgetary matters. All other questions are decided by majority vote. Each member country has one vote. Apart from approval of budgetary matters, resolutions are not binding on the members. The Assembly may make recommendations on any matters within the scope of the UN, except matters of peace and security that are under Security Council consideration.

Conceivably, the one state, one vote power structure could enable states comprising just eight percent of the world population to pass a resolution by a two-thirds vote. However, as no more than recommendations, it is difficult to imagine a situation in which a recommendation by member states constituting just eight percent of the world's population, would be adhered to by the remaining ninety-two percent of the population, should they object. Likewise, countries representing a 3.4% of the world population could form a majority on any of the questions that are decided by majority vote.

Security Council

The Security Council is charged with maintaining peace and security among countries. While other organs of the United Nations can only make 'recommendations' to member governments, the Security Council has the power to make binding decisions that member governments have agreed to carry out, under the terms of Charter Article 25. The decisions of the Council are known as United Nations Security Council resolutions.

The Security Council is made up of 15 member states, consisting of 5 permanent members–China, France, Russia, the United Kingdom and the United States–and 10 non-permanent members, currently Azerbaijan, India, South Africa, Colombia, Morocco, Togo, Germany, Pakistan, Guatemala, and Portugal. The five permanent members hold veto power over substantive but not procedural resolutions allowing a permanent member to block adoption but not to block the debate of a resolution unacceptable to it. The ten temporary seats are held for two-year terms with member states voted in by the General Assembly on a regional basis. The presidency of the Security Council is rotated alphabetically each month.

Secretariat

The United Nations Secretariat is headed by the Secretary-General, assisted by a staff of international civil servants worldwide. It provides studies, information, and facilities needed by United Nations bodies for their meetings. It also carries out tasks as directed by the UN Security Council, the UN General Assembly, the UN Economic and Social Council, and other UN bodies. The United Nations Charter provides that the staff be chosen by application of the "highest standards of efficiency, competence, and integrity," with due regard for the importance of recruiting on a wide geographical basis.

The Charter provides that the staff shall not seek or receive instructions from any authority other than the UN. Each UN member country is enjoined to respect the international character of the Secretariat and not seek to influence its staff. The Secretary-General alone is responsible for staff selection.

The Secretary-General's duties include helping resolve international disputes, administering peacekeeping operations, organizing international conferences, gathering information on the implementation of Security Council decisions, and consulting with member governments regarding various initiatives. Key Secretariat offices in this area include the Office of the Coordinator of Humanitarian Affairs and the Department of Peacekeeping Operations. The Secretary-General may bring to the attention of the Security Council any matter that, in his or her opinion, may threaten international peace and security.

Secretary-General

The Secretariat is headed by the Secretary-General, who acts as the de facto spokesperson and leader of the UN. The current Secretary-General is Ban Ki-moon, who took over from Kofi Annan in 2007 and has been elected for a second term to conclude at the end of 2016.

Envisioned by Franklin D. Roosevelt as a "world moderator", the position is defined in the UN Charter as the organization's "chief administrative officer", but the Charter also states that the Secretary-General can bring to the Security Council's attention "any matter which in his opinion may threaten the maintenance of international peace and security", giving the position greater scope for action on the world stage. The position has evolved into a dual role of an administrator of the UN organization, and a diplomat and mediator addressing disputes between member states and finding consensus to global issues.

The Secretary-General is appointed by the General Assembly, after being recommended by the Security Council, where the permanent members have veto power. The General Assembly can theoretically override the Security Council's recommendation if a majority vote is not achieved, although this has not happened so far. There are no specific criteria for the post, but over the years, it has become accepted that the post shall be held for one or two terms of five years, that the post shall be appointed on the basis of geographical rotation, and that the Secretary-General shall not originate from one of the five permanent Security Council member states.

International Court of Justice

The International Court of Justice (ICJ), located in The Hague, Netherlands, is the primary judicial organ of the United Nations. Established in 1945 by the United Nations Charter, the Court began work in 1946 as the successor to the Permanent Court of International Justice. The Statute of the International Court of Justice, similar to that of its predecessor, is the main constitutional document constituting and regulating the Court.

It is based in the Peace Palace in The Hague, Netherlands, sharing the building with the Hague Academy of International Law, a private centre for the study of international law. Several of the Court's current judges are either alumni or former faculty members of the Academy. Its purpose is to adjudicate disputes among states. The court has heard cases related to war crimes, illegal state interference and ethnic cleansing, among others, and continues to hear cases.

International Criminal Court

The International Criminal Court (ICC), it came into being on 1 July 2002 with the entering into force of the Rome Statute of the International Criminal Court which was adopted on 17 July 1998. It is the first permanent international court charged with trying those who commit the most serious crimes under international law, including war crimes, genocide, crimes against humanity and the crime of aggression (although it cannot exercise jurisdiction over this crime prior to 2017). The ICC is functionally independent of the UN in terms of personnel and financing, but some meetings of the ICC governing body, the Assembly of the States Parties to the Rome Statute, are held at the United Nations. There is a "relationship agreement" between the ICC and the UN that governs how the two institutions regard each other legally.

Economic and Social Council

The Economic and Social Council (ECOSOC) assists the General Assembly in promoting international economic and social cooperation and development. ECOSOC has 54 members, all of which are elected by the General Assembly for a three-year term. The president is elected for a one-year term and chosen amongst the small or middle powers represented on ECOSOC. ECOSOC meets once a year in July for a four-week session. Since 1998, it has held another meeting each April with finance ministers heading key committees of the World Bank and the International Monetary Fund (IMF). Viewed separate from the specialized bodies it coordinates, ECOSOC's functions include information gathering, advising member nations, and making recommendations. In addition, ECOSOC is well-positioned to provide policy coherence and coordinate the overlapping functions of the UN's subsidiary bodies and it is in these roles that it is most active.

Permanent Forum on Indigenous Issues

The United Nations Permanent Forum on Indigenous Issues (UNPFII or PFII) is the UN's central coordinating body for matters relating to the concerns and rights of the world's indigenous peoples. The forum, which evolved from the United Nations Working Group on Indigenous Populations, is an advisory body within the framework of the United Nations System that reports to the UN's Economic and Social Council (ECOSOC); however, it performs an advisory function in relation to other branches of the United Nations system. It also works with other U.N. bodies as they address indigenous rights through Conventions such as the International Labour Organization's Convention No.169 and the Convention on Biological Diversity (Article 8j).

The Forum's mandate is to:

- Provide expert advice and recommendations to the Economic and Social Council and to the various programmes, funds and agencies of the United Nations System through the Council;
- Raise awareness and promote the integration and coordination of activities related to indigenous issues within the UN system;
- Prepare and disseminate information on these issues.

Since the passage of the Declaration on the Rights of Indigenous Peoples in 2007, much of the work of UNPFII has surrounded the compliance of U.N. member states to the standards of that declaration. However, it performs many other international functions as well.

Specialized institutions

Many UN organizations and agencies exist to work on particular issues. Some of the most well-known agencies are the International Atomic Energy Agency, the Food and Agriculture Organization, UNESCO (United Nations Educational, Scientific and Cultural Organization), the World Bank and the World Health Organization.

It is through these agencies that the UN performs most of its humanitarian work. Examples include mass vaccination programmes (through the WHO), the avoidance of famine and malnutrition (through the work of the WFP) and the protection of vulnerable and displaced people (for example, by the UNHCR).

The United Nations Charter stipulates that each primary organ of the UN can establish various specialized agencies to fulfil its duties.

Membership

With the addition of South Sudan on 14 July 2011, there are currently 193 United Nations member states, including all fully recognized independent states apart from Vatican City (the Holy See, which holds sovereignty over the state of Vatican City, is a permanent observer, for details see Holy See and the United Nations).

The United Nations Charter outlines the rules for membership:

- Membership in the United Nations is open to all other peace-loving states that accept the obligations contained in the present Charter and, in the judgment of the Organization, are able and willing to carry out these obligations.
- The admission of any such state to membership in the United Nations will be effected by a decision of the General Assembly upon the recommendation of the Security Council.

Group of 77

The Group of 77 at the UN is a loose coalition of developing nations, designed to promote its members' collective economic interests and create an enhanced joint negotiating capacity in the United Nations. There were 77 founding members of the organization, but the organization has since expanded to 130 member countries. The group was founded on 15 June 1964 by the "Joint Declaration of the Seventy-Seven Countries" issued at the

United Nations Conference on Trade and Development (UNCTAD). The first major meeting was in Algiers in 1967, where the Charter of Algiers was adopted and the basis for permanent institutional structures was begun.

Objectives of UN

Peacekeeping and Security

The UN, after approval by the Security Council, sends peacekeepers to regions where armed conflict has recently ceased or paused to enforce the terms of peace agreements and to discourage combatants from resuming hostilities. Since the UN does not maintain its own military, peacekeeping forces are voluntarily provided by member states of the UN. The forces, also called the "Blue Helmets", who enforce UN accords, are awarded United Nations Medals, which are considered international decorations instead of military decorations. The peacekeeping force as a whole received the Nobel Peace Prize in 1988.

The founders of the UN had envisaged that the organization would act to prevent conflicts between nations and make future wars impossible, however the outbreak of the Cold War made peacekeeping agreements extremely difficult because of the division of the world into hostile camps. Following the end of the Cold War, there were renewed calls for the UN to become the agency for achieving world peace, as several dozen ongoing conflicts continue to rage around the globe.

A 2005 RAND Corp study found the UN to be successful in two out of three peacekeeping efforts. It compared UN nation-building efforts to those of the United States, and found that seven out of eight UN cases are at peace, as compared with four out of eight US cases at peace. Also in 2005, the Human Security Report documented a decline in the number of wars, genocides and human rights abuses since the end of the Cold War, and presented evidence, albeit circumstantial, that international activism—mostly spearheaded by the UN—has been the main cause of the decline in armed conflict since the end of the Cold War. Situations where the UN has not only acted to keep the peace but also occasionally intervened include the Korean War (1950–1953), and the authorization of intervention in Iraq after the Persian Gulf War in 1990.

The UN has also drawn criticism for perceived failures. In many cases, member states have shown reluctance to achieve or enforce Security Council resolutions, an issue that stems from the UN's intergovernmental nature—seen by some as simply an association of 193 member states who must reach consensus, not an independent organization. Disagreements in the Security Council about military action and intervention are seen as having failed to prevent the 1971 Bangladesh atrocities, the 1994 Rwandan Genocide, failed to provide humanitarian aid and intervene in the Second Congo War, failed to intervene in the 1995 Srebrenica massacre and protect a refugee haven by authorizing peacekeepers to use force, failure to deliver food to starving people in Somalia, failure to implement provisions of Security Council resolutions related to the Israeli-Palestinian conflict, and continuing failure to prevent genocide or provide assistance in Darfur. UN peacekeepers have also been accused of child rape, sexual abuse or soliciting prostitutes during various peacekeeping missions, starting in 2003, in the Congo, Haiti, Liberia, Sudan and what is now South Sudan, Burundi and Côte d'Ivoire. In 2004, former Israeli ambassador to the UN Dore Gold criticized what it called the organization's moral relativism in the face of (and occasional support of) genocide and terrorism that occurred between the moral clarity of its founding period and the present day. Gold specifically mentions Yasser Arafat's 1988 invitation to address the General Assembly as a low point in the UN's history.

In addition to peacekeeping, the UN is also active in encouraging disarmament. Regulation of armaments was included in the writing of the United Nations Charter in 1945 and was envisioned as a way of limiting the use of human and economic resources for the creation of them. However, the advent of nuclear weapons came only weeks after the signing of the charter and immediately halted concepts of arms limitation and disarmament, resulting in the first resolution of the first ever General Assembly meeting calling for specific proposals for "the elimination from national armaments of atomic weapons and of all other major weapons adaptable to mass destruction". The principal forums for disarmament issues are the General Assembly First Committee, the UN Disarmament Commission, and the Conference on Disarmament, and considerations have been made of the merits of a ban on testing nuclear weapons, outer space arms control, the banning of chemical weapons and land mines, nuclear and conventional disarmament, nuclear-weapon-free zones, the reduction of military budgets, and measures to strengthen international security.

The UN is one of the official supporters of the World Security Forum, a major international conference on the effects of global catastrophes and disasters, which took place in the United Arab Emirates in October 2008.

Human Rights and Humanitarian Assistance

The pursuit of human rights was a central reason for creating the UN. World War II atrocities and genocide led to a ready consensus that the new organization must work to prevent any similar tragedies in the future. An early objective was creating a legal framework for considering and acting on complaints about human rights violations. The UN Charter obliges all member nations to promote "universal respect for, and observance of, human rights" and to take "joint and separate action" to that end. The Universal Declaration of Human Rights, though not legally binding, was adopted by the General Assembly in 1948 as a common standard of achievement for all. The Assembly regularly takes up human rights issues.

The UN and its agencies are central in upholding and implementing the principles enshrined in the Universal Declaration of Human Rights. A case in point is support by the UN for countries in transition to democracy. Technical assistance in providing free and fair elections, improving judicial structures, drafting constitutions, training human rights officials, and transforming armed movements into political parties have contributed significantly to democratization worldwide. The UN has helped run elections in countries with little or no democratic history, including recently in Afghanistan and East Timor. The UN is also a forum to support the right of women to participate fully in the political, economic, and social life of their countries. The UN contributes to raising consciousness of the concept of human rights through its covenants and its attention to specific abuses through its General Assembly, Security Council resolutions, or International Court of Justice rulings.

The purpose of the United Nations Human Rights Council, established in 2006, is to address human rights violations. The Council is the successor to the United Nations Commission on Human Rights, which was often criticized for the high-profile positions it gave to member states that did not guarantee the human rights of their own citizens. The council has 47 members distributed by region, which each serve three-year terms, and may not serve three consecutive terms. A candidate to the body must be approved by a majority of the General Assembly. In addition, the council has strict rules for membership, including a universal human rights review. While some members with questionable human rights records have been elected, it is fewer than before with the increased focus on each member state's human rights record.

The rights of some 370 million indigenous peoples around the world are also a focus for the UN, with a Declaration on the Rights of Indigenous Peoples being approved by the General Assembly in 2007. The declaration outlines the individual and collective rights to culture, language, education, identity, employment and health, thereby addressing post-colonial issues that had confronted indigenous peoples for centuries. The declaration aims to maintain, strengthen and encourage the growth of indigenous institutions, cultures and traditions. It also prohibits discrimination against indigenous peoples and promotes their active participation in matters that concern their past, present and future. The United Nations Permanent Forum on Indigenous Issues is the UN's central coordinating body for matters relating to the concerns and rights of the world's indigenous peoples. The forum is an advisory body within the framework of the United Nations System that reports to the UN's Economic and Social Council.

In conjunction with other organizations such as the Red Cross, the UN provides food, drinking water, shelter and other humanitarian services to populaces suffering from famine, displaced by war, or afflicted by other disasters. Major humanitarian branches of the UN are the World Food Programme (which helps feed more than 100 million people a year in 80 countries), the office of the High Commissioner for Refugees with projects in over 116 countries, as well as peacekeeping projects in over 24 countries.

In 2011, the United Nations passed its first resolution recognizing LGBT rights, and followed up with a report documenting violations of the rights of LGBT people, including hate crime, criminalization of homosexuality, and discrimination. In July 2012, the South African and Brazilian ambassadors demanded further discussion on discrimination against LGBT people. The joint statement said that sexual orientation and gender identiy is a human rights issue. This was rejected by a group lead by the Organisation of Islamic Cooperation.

Social and Economic Development

The UN is involved in supporting development, e.g. by the formulation of the Millennium Development Goals. The UN Development Programme

(UNDP) is the largest multilateral source of grant technical assistance in the world. Organizations like the World Health Organization (WHO), UNAIDS, and The Global Fund to Fight AIDS, Tuberculosis and Malaria are leading institutions in the battle against diseases around the world, especially in poor countries. The UN Population Fund is a major provider of reproductive services. 32 UN agencies performing tasks on development are coordinating their efforts through the United Nations Development Group or UNDG.

The UN also promotes human development through some related agencies, particularly the UNDP. The World Bank Group and International Monetary Fund (IMF), for example, are independent, specialized agencies and observers within the UN framework, according to a 1947 agreement. They were initially formed as separate from the UN through the Bretton Woods Agreement in 1944.

The UNDP annually publishes the Human Development Index (HDI), a comparative measure ranking countries by poverty, literacy, education, life expectancy, and other factors.

The Millennium Development Goals (declared in the United Nations Millennium Declaration, signed in September 2000) are eight goals that all of the then 192 United Nations member states have agreed to try to achieve by the year 2015.

Mandates

From time to time, the different bodies of the United Nations pass resolutions that contain operating paragraphs that begin with the words "requests", "calls upon", or "encourages", which the Secretary-General interprets as a mandate to set up a temporary organization or do something. These mandates can be as little as researching and publishing a written report, or mounting a full-scale peacekeeping operation.

Although the specialized institutions, such as the WHO, were originally set up by this means, they are not the same as mandates because they are permanent organizations that exist independently of the UN with their own membership structure. One could say that original mandate was simply to cover the process of setting up the institution, and has therefore long expired. Most mandates expire after a limited period and require renewal from the body, which set them up.

One of the outcomes of the 2005 World Summit was a mandate (labelled id 17171) for the Secretary-General to "review all mandates older than five years originating from resolutions of the General Assembly and other organs". To facilitate this review and to finally bring coherence to the organization, the Secretariat has produced an on-line registry of mandates to draw together the reports relating to each one and create an overall picture.

Greening the Blue

On 5 June 2007, World Environment Day, Secretary-General Ban Ki-moon made public his ambition to make the United Nations more efficient in its operations: "I would like to see our renovated Headquarters complex eventually become a globally acclaimed model of efficient use of energy and resources. Beyond New York, the initiative should include the other United Nations headquarters and offices around the globe." The UN's progress towards achieving this goal is communicated through the initiative Greening the Blue.

Others

Over the lifetime of the UN, over 80 colonies have attained independence. The General Assembly adopted the Declaration on the Granting of Independence to Colonial Countries and Peoples in 1960 with no votes against but abstentions from all major colonial powers. Through the UN Committee on Decolonization, created in 1962, the UN has focused considerable attention on decolonization. It has also supported the new states that have arisen as a result of self-determination initiatives. The committee has overseen the decolonization of every country larger than 20,000 km^2 and removed them from the United Nations list of Non-Self-Governing Territories, besides Western Sahara, a country larger than the UK only relinquished by Spain in 1975.

The UN declares and coordinates international observances, periods of time to observe some issue of international interest or concern. Using the symbolism of the UN, a specially designed logo for the year, and the infrastructure of the United Nations System, various days and years have become catalysts to advancing key issues of concern on a global scale. For example, World Tuberculosis Day, Earth Day and International Year of Deserts and Desertification.

FUNDING

The UN is financed from assessed and voluntary contributions from member states. The General Assembly approves the regular budget and determines the assessment for each member. This is broadly based on the relative capacity of each country to pay, as measured by their gross national income (GNI), with adjustments for external debt and low per capita income.

The Assembly has established the principle that the UN should not be overly dependent on any one member to finance its operations. Thus, there is a 'ceiling' rate, setting the maximum amount any member is assessed for the regular budget. In December 2000, the Assembly revised the scale of assessments to reflect current global circumstances. As part of that revision, the regular budget ceiling was reduced from 25% to 22%. For the least developed countries (LDCs), a ceiling rate of 0.01% is applied. In addition to the ceiling rates, the minimum amount assessed to any member nation (or 'floor' rate) is set at 0.001% of the UN budget. Refer to the table for major contributors.

A large share of UN expenditures addresses the core UN mission of peace and security. The peacekeeping budget for the 2005–2006 fiscal year was approximately US$5 billion, •2.5 billion (compared to approximately US$1.5 billion, •995 million for the UN core budget over the same period), with some 70,000 troops deployed in 17 missions around the world. UN peace operations are funded by assessments, using a formula derived from the regular funding scale, but including a weighted surcharge for the five permanent Security Council members, who must approve all peacekeeping operations. This surcharge serves to offset discounted peacekeeping assessment rates for less developed countries. As of 1 January 2011, the top 10 providers of assessed financial contributions to United Nations peacekeeping operations were: the United States, Japan, the United Kingdom, Germany, France, Italy, China, Canada, Spain and the Republic of Korea.

Special UN programmes not included in the regular budget (such as UNICEF, the WFP and UNDP) are financed by voluntary contributions from other member governments. Most of this is financial contributions, but some is in the form of agricultural commodities donated for afflicted populations. Since their funding is voluntary, many of these agencies suffer severe shortages during economic recessions. In July 2009, the World Food

Programme reported that it has been forced to cut services because of insufficient funding. It has received barely a quarter of the total it needed for the 09/10 financial year.

The UN and its agencies are immune to the laws of the countries where they operate, safeguarding UN's impartiality with regard to the host and member countries.

Despite their independence in matters of human resources policy, the UN and its agencies voluntarily apply the laws of member states regarding same-sex marriages, allowing decisions about the status of employees in a same-sex partnership to be based on nationality. The UN and its agencies recognize same-sex marriages only if the employees are citizens of countries that recognize the marriage. This practice is not specific to the recognition of same-sex marriage but reflects a common practice of the UN for a number of human resources matters. It has to be noted though that some agencies provide limited benefits to domestic partners of their staff and that some agencies do not recognise same-sex marriage or domestic partnership of their staff.

The Charter of the United Nations

The Charter of the United Nations is the foundational treaty of the international organization called the United Nations. It was signed at the San Francisco War Memorial and Performing Arts Center in San Francisco, United States, on 26 June 1945, by 50 of the 51 original member countries (Poland, the other original member, which was not represented at the conference, signed it two months later). It entered into force on 24 October 1945, after being ratified by the five permanent members of the Security Council—the Republic of China (later replaced by the People's Republic of China), France, the Union of Soviet Socialist Republics (later replaced by the Russian Federation), the United Kingdom, and the United States—and a majority of the other signatories. Today, 193 countries are the members of the United Nations.

As a charter, it is a constituent treaty, and all members are bound by its articles. Furthermore, the Charter states that obligations to the United Nations prevail over all other treaty obligations Most countries in the world have now ratified the Charter. One notable exception is the Vatican City State, which has chosen to remain a permanent observer state and therefore is not a full signatory to the Charter.

Introductory Note

The Charter of the United Nations was signed on 26 June 1945, in San Francisco, at the conclusion of the United Nations Conference on International Organization, and came into force on 24 October 1945. The Statute of the International Court of Justice is an integral part of the Charter.

Amendments to Articles 23, 27 and 61 of the Charter were adopted by the General Assembly on 17 December 1963 and came into force on 31 August 1965. A further amendment to Article 61 was adopted by the General Assembly on 20 December 1971, and came into force on 24 September 1973. An amendment to Article 109, adopted by the General Assembly on 20 December 1965, came into force on 12 June 1968.

The amendment to Article 23 enlarges the membership of the Security Council from eleven to fifteen. The amended Article 27 provides that decisions of the Security Council on procedural matters shall be made by an affirmative vote of nine members (formerly seven) and on all other matters by an affirmative vote of nine members (formerly seven), including the concurring votes of the five permanent members of the Security Council.

The amendment to Article 61, which entered into force on 31 August 1965, enlarged the membership of the Economic and Social Council from eighteen to twenty-seven. The subsequent amendment to that Article, which entered into force on 24 September 1973, further increased the membership of the Council from twenty-seven to fifty-four.

The amendment to Article 109, which relates to the first paragraph of that Article, provides that a General Conference of Member States for the purpose of reviewing the Charter may be held at a date and place to be fixed by a two-thirds vote of the members of the General Assembly and by a vote of any nine members (formerly seven) of the Security Council. Paragraph 3 of Article 109, which deals with the consideration of a possible review conference during the tenth regular session of the General Assembly, has been retained in its original form in its reference to a "vote, of any seven members of the Security Council", the paragraph having been acted upon in 1955 by the General Assembly, at its tenth regular session, and by the Security Council.

Preamble

We the peoples of the united nations determined

- to save succeeding generations from the scourge of war, which twice in our lifetime has brought untold sorrow to mankind, and
- to reaffirm faith in fundamental human rights, in the dignity and worth of the human person, in the equal rights of men and women and of nations large and small, and
- to establish conditions under which justice and respect for the obligations arising from treaties and other sources of international law can be maintained, and
- to promote social progress and better standards of life in larger freedom,

And for these ends

- to practice tolerance and live together in peace with one another as good neighbours, and
- to unite our strength to maintain international peace and security, and
- to ensure, by the acceptance of principles and the institution of methods, that armed force shall not be used, save in the common interest, and
- to employ international machinery for the promotion of the economic and social advancement of all peoples,

Have resolved to combine our efforts to accomplish these aims

Accordingly, our respective Governments, through representatives assembled in the city of San Francisco, who have exhibited their full powers found to be in good and due form, have agreed to the present Charter of the United Nations and do hereby establish an international organization to be known as the United Nations.

Chapter I: Purposes And Principles

Article 1

The Purposes of the United Nations are:

1. To maintain international peace and security, and to that end: to take effective collective measures for the prevention and removal of threats to the peace, and for the suppression of acts of aggression or other breaches of the peace, and to bring about by peaceful means, and in conformity with the principles of justice and international law, adjustment or settlement of international disputes or situations which might lead to a breach of the peace;

2. To develop friendly relations among nations based on respect for the principle of equal rights and self-determination of peoples, and to take other appropriate measures to strengthen universal peace;
3. To achieve international co-operation in solving international problems of an economic, social, cultural, or humanitarian character, and in promoting and encouraging respect for human rights and for fundamental freedoms for all without distinction as to race, sex, language, or religion; and
4. To be a centre for harmonizing the actions of nations in the attainment of these common ends.

Article 2

The Organization and its Members, in pursuit of the Purposes stated in Article 1, shall act in accordance with the following Principles.

1. The Organization is based on the principle of the sovereign equality of all its Members.
2. All Members, in order to ensure to all of them the rights and benefits resulting from membership, shall fulfill in good faith the obligations assumed by them in accordance with the present Charter.
3. All Members shall settle their international disputes by peaceful means in such a manner that international peace and security, and justice, are not endangered.
4. All Members shall refrain in their international relations from the threat or use of force against the territorial integrity or political independence of any state, or in any other manner inconsistent with the Purposes of the United Nations.
5. All Members shall give the United Nations every assistance in any action it takes in accordance with the present Charter, and shall refrain from giving assistance to any state against which the United Nations is taking preventive or enforcement action.
6. The Organization shall ensure that states which are not Members of the United Nations act in accordance with these Principles so far as may be necessary for the maintenance of international peace and security.
7. Nothing contained in the present Charter shall authorize the United Nations to intervene in matters which are essentially within the

domestic jurisdiction of any state or shall require the Members to submit such matters to settlement under the present Charter; but this principle shall not prejudice the application of enforcement measures under Chapter Vll.

Chapter II: Membership

Article 3

The original Members of the United Nations shall be the states which, having participated in the United Nations Conference on International Organization at San Francisco, or having previously signed the Declaration by United Nations of 1 January 1942, sign the present Charter and ratify it in accordance with Article 110.

Article 4

1. Membership in the United Nations is open to all other peace-loving states which accept the obligations contained in the present Charter and, in the judgment of the Organization, are able and willing to carry out these obligations.
2. The admission of any such state to membership in the United Nations will be effected by a decision of the General Assembly upon the recommendation of the Security Council.

Article 5

A Member of the United Nations against which preventive or enforcement action has been taken by the Security Council may be suspended from the exercise of the rights and privileges of membership by the General Assembly upon the recommendation of the Security Council. The exercise of these rights and privileges may be restored by the Security Council.

Article 6

A Member of the United Nations which has persistently violated the Principles contained in the present Charter may be expelled from the Organization by the General Assembly upon the recommendation of the Security Council.

Chapter III: Organs

Article 7

1. There are established as principal organs of the United Nations: a General Assembly, a Security Council, an Economic and Social

Council, a Trusteeship Council, an International Court of Justice and a Secretariat.

2. Such subsidiary organs as may be found necessary may be established in accordance with the present Charter.

Article 8

The United Nations shall place no restrictions on the eligibility of men and women to participate in any capacity and under conditions of equality in its principal and subsidiary organs.

Chapter IV: The General Assembly

Composition

Article 9

1. The General Assembly shall consist of all the Members of the United Nations.
2. Each Member shall have not more than five representatives in the General Assembly.

Functions and powers

Article 10

The General Assembly may discuss any questions or any matters within the scope of the present Charter or relating to the powers and functions of any organs provided for in the present Charter, and, except as provided in Article 12, may make recommendations to the Members of the United Nations or to the Security Council or to both on any such questions or matters.

Article 11

1. The General Assembly may consider the general principles of co-operation in the maintenance of international peace and security, including the principles governing disarmament and the regulation of armaments, and may make recommendations with regard to such principles to the Members or to the Security Council or to both.
2. The General Assembly may discuss any questions relating to the maintenance of international peace and security brought before it by any Member of the United Nations, or by the Security Council, or by a state which is not a Member of the United Nations in accordance

with Article 35, paragraph 2, and, except as provided in Article 12, may make recommendations with regard to any such questions to the state or states concerned or to the Security Council or to both. Any such question on which action is necessary shall be referred to the Security Council by the General Assembly either before or after discussion.

3. The General Assembly may call the attention of the Security Council to situations which are likely to endanger international peace and security.
4. The powers of the General Assembly set forth in this Article shall not limit the general scope of Article 10.

Article 12

1. While the Security Council is exercising in respect of any dispute or situation the functions assigned to it in the present Charter, the General Assembly shall not make any recommendation with regard to that dispute or situation unless the Security Council so requests.
2. The Secretary-General, with the consent of the Security Council, shall notify the General Assembly at each session of any matters relative to the maintenance of international peace and security which are being dealt with by the Security Council and shall similarly notify the General Assembly, or the Members of the United Nations if the General Assembly is not in session, immediately the Security Council ceases to deal with such matters.

Article 13

1. The General Assembly shall initiate studies and make recommendations for the purpose of: a. promoting international co-operation in the political field and encouraging the progressive development of international law and its codification; b. promoting international co-operation in the economic, social, cultural, educational, and health fields, and assisting in the realization of human rights and fundamental freedoms for all without distinction as to race, sex, language, or religion.
2. The further responsibilities, functions and powers of the General Assembly with respect to matters mentioned in paragraph 1 (b) above are set forth in Chapters IX and X.

Article 14

Subject to the provisions of Article 12, the General Assembly may recommend measures for the peaceful adjustment of any situation, regardless of origin, which it deems likely to impair the general welfare or friendly relations among nations, including situations resulting from a violation of the provisions of the present Charter setting forth the Purposes and Principles of the United Nations.

Article 15

1. The General Assembly shall receive and consider annual and special reports from the Security Council; these reports shall include an account of the measures that the Security Council has decided upon or taken to maintain international peace and security.
2. The General Assembly shall receive and consider reports from the other organs of the United Nations.

Article 16

The General Assembly shall perform such functions with respect to the international trusteeship system as are assigned to it under Chapters XII and XIII, including the approval of the trusteeship agreements for areas not designated as strategic.

Article 17

1. The General Assembly shall consider and approve the budget of the Organization.
2. The expenses of the Organization shall be borne by the Members as apportioned by the General Assembly.
3. The General Assembly shall consider and approve any financial and budgetary arrangements with specialized agencies referred to in Article 57 and shall examine the administrative budgets of such specialized agencies with a view to making recommendations to the agencies concerned.

VOTING

Article 18

1. Each member of the General Assembly shall have one vote.

2. Decisions of the General Assembly on important questions shall be made by a two-thirds majority of the members present and voting. These questions shall include: recommendations with respect to the maintenance of international peace and security, the election of the non-permanent members of the Security Council, the election of the members of the Economic and Social Council, the election of members of the Trusteeship Council in accordance with paragraph 1 (c) of Article 86, the admission of new Members to the United Nations, the suspension of the rights and privileges of membership, the expulsion of Members, questions relating to the operation of the trusteeship system, and budgetary questions.
3. Decisions on other questions, including the determination of additional categories of questions to be decided by a two-thirds majority, shall be made by a majority of the members present and voting.

Article 19

A Member of the United Nations which is in arrears in the payment of its financial contributions to the Organization shall have no vote in the General Assembly if the amount of its arrears equals or exceeds the amount of the contributions due from it for the preceding two full years. The General Assembly may, nevertheless, permit such a Member to vote if it is satisfied that the failure to pay is due to conditions beyond the control of the Member.

Procedure

Article 20

The General Assembly shall meet in regular annual sessions and in such special sessions as occasion may require. Special sessions shall be convoked by the Secretary-General at the request of the Security Council or of a majority of the Members of the United Nations.

Article 21

The General Assembly shall adopt its own rules of procedure. It shall elect its President for each session.

Article 22

The General Assembly may establish such subsidiary organs as it deems necessary for the performance of its functions.

Chapter V: The Security Council

Composition

Article 23

1. The Security Council shall consist of fifteen Members of the United Nations. The Republic of China, France, the Union of Soviet Socialist Republics, the United Kingdom of Great Britain and Northern Ireland, and the United States of America shall be permanent members of the Security Council. The General Assembly shall elect ten other Members of the United Nations to be non-permanent members of the Security Council, due regard being specially paid, in the first instance to the contribution of Members of the United Nations to the maintenance of international peace and security and to the other purposes of the Organization, and also to equitable geographical distribution.
2. The non-permanent members of the Security Council shall be elected for a term of two years. In the first election of the non-permanent members after the increase of the membership of the Security Council from eleven to fifteen, two of the four additional members shall be chosen for a term of one year. A retiring member shall not be eligible for immediate re-election.
3. Each member of the Security Council shall have one representative.

Functions and powers

Article 24

1. In order to ensure prompt and effective action by the United Nations, its Members confer on the Security Council primary responsibility for the maintenance of international peace and security, and agree that in carrying out its duties under this responsibility the Security Council acts on their behalf.
2. In discharging these duties the Security Council shall act in accordance with the Purposes and Principles of the United Nations. The specific powers granted to the Security Council for the discharge of these duties are laid down in Chapters VI, VII, VIII, and XII.
3. The Security Council shall submit annual and, when necessary, special reports to the General Assembly for its consideration.

Article 25

The Members of the United Nations agree to accept and carry out the decisions of the Security Council in accordance with the present Charter.

Article 26

In order to promote the establishment and maintenance of international peace and security with the least diversion for armaments of the world's human and economic resources, the Security Council shall be responsible for formulating, with the assistance of the Military Staff Committee referred to in Article 47, plans to be submitted to the Members of the United Nations for the establishment of a system for the regulation of armaments.

VOTING

Article 27

1. Each member of the Security Council shall have one vote.
2. Decisions of the Security Council on procedural matters shall be made by an affirmative vote of nine members.
3. Decisions of the Security Council on all other matters shall be made by an affirmative vote of nine members including the concurring votes of the permanent members; provided that, in decisions under Chapter VI, and under paragraph 3 of Article 52, a party to a dispute shall abstain from voting.

PROCEDURE

Article 28

1. The Security Council shall be so organized as to be able to function continuously. Each member of the Security Council shall for this purpose be represented at all times at the seat of the Organization.
2. The Security Council shall hold periodic meetings at which each of its members may, if it so desires, be represented by a member of the government or by some other specially designated representative.
3. The Security Council may hold meetings at such places other than the seat of the Organization as in its judgment will best facilitate its work.

Article 29

The Security Council may establish such subsidiary organs as it deems necessary for the performance of its functions.

Article 30

The Security Council shall adopt its own rules of procedure, including the method of selecting its President.

Article 31

Any Member of the United Nations which is not a member of the Security Council may participate, without vote, in the discussion of any question brought before the Security Council whenever the latter considers that the interests of that Member are specially affected.

Article 32

Any Member of the United Nations which is not a member of the Security Council or any state which is not a Member of the United Nations, if it is a party to a dispute under consideration by the Security Council, shall be invited to participate, without vote, in the discussion relating to the dispute. The Security Council shall lay down such conditions as it deems just for the participation of a state which is not a Member of the United Nations.

Chapter VI: Pacific Settlement of Disputes

Article 33

1. The parties to any dispute, the continuance of which is likely to endanger the maintenance of international peace and security, shall, first of all, seek a solution by negotiation, enquiry, mediation, conciliation, arbitration, judicial settlement, resort to regional agencies or arrangements, or other peaceful means of their own choice.
2. The Security Council shall, when it deems necessary, call upon the parties to settle their dispute by such means.

Article 34

The Security Council may investigate any dispute, or any situation which might lead to international friction or give rise to a dispute, in order to determine whether the continuance of the dispute or situation is likely to endanger the maintenance of international peace and security.

Article 35

1. Any Member of the United Nations may bring any dispute, or any situation of the nature referred to in Article 34, to the attention of the Security Council or of the General Assembly.
2. A state which is not a Member of the United Nations may bring to the attention of the Security Council or of the General Assembly any dispute to which it is a party if it accepts in advance, for the purposes

of the dispute, the obligations of pacific settlement provided in the present Charter.

3. The proceedings of the General Assembly in respect of matters brought to its attention under this Article will be subject to the provisions of Articles 11 and 12.

Article 36

1. The Security Council may, at any stage of a dispute of the nature referred to in Article 33 or of a situation of like nature, recommend appropriate procedures or methods of adjustment.
2. The Security Council should take into consideration any procedures for the settlement of the dispute which have already been adopted by the parties.
3. In making recommendations under this Article the Security Council should also take into consideration that legal disputes should as a general rule be referred by the parties to the International Court of Justice in accordance with the provisions of the Statute of the Court.

Article 37

1. Should the parties to a dispute of the nature referred to in Article 33 fail to settle it by the means indicated in that Article, they shall refer it to the Security Council.
2. If the Security Council deems that the continuance of the dispute is in fact likely to endanger the maintenance of international peace and security, it shall decide whether to take action under Article 36 or to recommend such terms of settlement as it may consider appropriate.

Article 38

Without prejudice to the provisions of Articles 33 to 37, the Security Council may, if all the parties to any dispute so request, make recommendations to the parties with a view to a pacific settlement of the dispute.

Chapter VII: Action With Respect to Threats to the Peace, Breaches of the Peace, and Acts of Aggression

Article 39

The Security Council shall determine the existence of any threat to the peace, breach of the peace, or act of aggression and shall make recommendations, or decide what measures shall be taken in accordance with Articles 41 and 42, to maintain or restore international peace and security.

Article 40

In order to prevent an aggravation of the situation, the Security Council may, before making the recommendations or deciding upon the measures provided for in Article 39, call upon the parties concerned to comply with such provisional measures as it deems necessary or desirable. Such provisional measures shall be without prejudice to the rights, claims, or position of the parties concerned. The Security Council shall duly take account of failure to comply with such provisional measures.

Article 41

The Security Council may decide what measures not involving the use of armed force are to be employed to give effect to its decisions, and it may call upon the Members of the United Nations to apply such measures. These may include complete or partial interruption of economic relations and of rail, sea, air, postal, telegraphic, radio, and other means of communication, and the severance of diplomatic relations.

Article 42

Should the Security Council consider that measures provided for in Article 41 would be inadequate or have proved to be inadequate, it may take such action by air, sea, or land forces as may be necessary to maintain or restore international peace and security. Such action may include demonstrations, blockade, and other operations by air, sea, or land forces of Members of the United Nations.

Article 43

1. All Members of the United Nations, in order to contribute to the maintenance of international peace and security, undertake to make available to the Security Council, on its call and in accordance with a special agreement or agreements, armed forces, assistance, and facilities, including rights of passage, necessary for the purpose of maintaining international peace and security.
2. Such agreement or agreements shall govern the numbers and types of forces, their degree of readiness and general location, and the nature of the facilities and assistance to be provided.

3. The agreement or agreements shall be negotiated as soon as possible on the initiative of the Security Council. They shall be concluded between the Security Council and Members or between the Security Council and groups of Members and shall be subject to ratification by the signatory states in accordance with their respective constitutional processes.

Article 44

When the Security Council has decided to use force it shall, before calling upon a Member not represented on it to provide armed forces in fulfilment of the obligations assumed under Article 43, invite that Member, if the Member so desires, to participate in the decisions of the Security Council concerning the employment of contingents of that Member's armed forces.

Article 45

In order to enable the United Nations to take urgent military measures, Members shall hold immediately available national air-force contingents for combined international enforcement action. The strength and degree of readiness of these contingents and plans for their combined action shall be determined within the limits laid down in the special agreement or agreements referred to in Article 43, by the Security Council with the assistance of the Military Staff Committee.

Article 46

Plans for the application of armed force shall be made by the Security Council with the assistance of the Military Staff Committee.

Article 47

1. There shall be established a Military Staff Committee to advise and assist the Security Council on all questions relating to the Security Council's military requirements for the maintenance of international peace and security, the employment and command of forces placed at its disposal, the regulation of armaments, and possible disarmament.
2. The Military Staff Committee shall consist of the Chiefs of Staff of the permanent members of the Security Council or their representatives. Any Member of the United Nations not permanently represented on the Committee shall be invited by the Committee to be associated with it when the efficient discharge of the Committee's responsibilities requires the participation of that Member in its work.

3. The Military Staff Committee shall be responsible under the Security Council for the strategic direction of any armed forces placed at the disposal of the Security Council. Questions relating to the command of such forces shall be worked out subsequently.
4. The Military Staff Committee, with the authorization of the Security Council and after consultation with appropriate regional agencies, may establish regional sub-committees.

Article 48

1. The action required to carry out the decisions of the Security Council for the maintenance of international peace and security shall be taken by all the Members of the United Nations or by some of them, as the Security Council may determine.
2. Such decisions shall be carried out by the Members of the United Nations directly and through their action in the appropriate international agencies of which they are members.

Article 49

The Members of the United Nations shall join in affording mutual assistance in carrying out the measures decided upon by the Security Council.

Article 50

If preventive or enforcement measures against any state are taken by the Security Council, any other state, whether a Member of the United Nations or not, which finds itself confronted with special economic problems arising from the carrying out of those measures shall have the right to consult the Security Council with regard to a solution of those problems.

Article 51

Nothing in the present Charter shall impair the inherent right of individual or collective self-defence if an armed attack occurs against a Member of the United Nations, until the Security Council has taken measures necessary to maintain international peace and security. Measures taken by Members in the exercise of this right of self-defence shall be immediately reported to the Security Council and shall not in any way affect the authority and responsibility of the Security Council under the present Charter to take at any time such action as it deems necessary in order to maintain or restore international peace and security.

Chapter VIII: Regional Arrangements

Article 52

1. Nothing in the present Charter precludes the existence of regional arrangements or agencies for dealing with such matters relating to the maintenance of international peace and security as are appropriate for regional action provided that such arrangements or agencies and their activities are consistent with the Purposes and Principles of the United Nations.
2. The Members of the United Nations entering into such arrangements or constituting such agencies shall make every effort to achieve pacific settlement of local disputes through such regional arrangements or by such regional agencies before referring them to the Security Council.
3. The Security Council shall encourage the development of pacific settlement of local disputes through such regional arrangements or by such regional agencies either on the initiative of the states concerned or by reference from the Security Council.
4. This Article in no way impairs the application of Articles 34 and 35.

Article 53

1. The Security Council shall, where appropriate, utilize such regional arrangements or agencies for enforcement action under its authority. But no enforcement action shall be taken under regional arrangements or by regional agencies without the authorization of the Security Council, with the exception of measures against any enemy state, as defined in paragraph 2 of this Article, provided for pursuant to Article 107 or in regional arrangements directed against renewal of aggressive policy on the part of any such state, until such time as the Organization may, on request of the Governments concerned, be charged with the responsibility for preventing further aggression by such a state.
2. The term enemy state as used in paragraph 1 of this Article applies to any state which during the Second World War has been an enemy of any signatory of the present Charter.

Article 54

The Security Council shall at all times be kept fully informed of activities undertaken or in contemplation under regional arrangements or by regional agencies for the maintenance of international peace and security.

Chapter Ix: International Economic And Social Co-Operation

Article 55

With a view to the creation of conditions of stability and well-being which are necessary for peaceful and friendly relations among nations based on respect for the principle of equal rights and self-determination of peoples, the United Nations shall promote:

a. higher standards of living, full employment, and conditions of economic and social progress and development;

b. solutions of international economic, social, health, and related problems; and international cultural and educational cooperation; and

c. universal respect for, and observance of, human rights and fundamental freedoms for all without distinction as to race, sex, language, or religion.

Article 56

All Members pledge themselves to take joint and separate action in co-operation with the Organization for the achievement of the purposes set forth in Article 55.

Article 57

1. The various specialized agencies, established by intergovernmental agreement and having wide international responsibilities, as defined in their basic instruments, in economic, social, cultural, educational, health, and related fields, shall be brought into relationship with the United Nations in accordance with the provisions of Article 63.
2. Such agencies thus brought into relationship with the United Nations are hereinafter referred to as specialized agencies.

Article 58

The Organization shall make recommendations for the co-ordination of the policies and activities of the specialized agencies.

Article 59

The Organization shall, where appropriate, initiate negotiations among the states concerned for the creation of any new specialized agencies required for the accomplishment of the purposes set forth in Article 55.

Article 60

Responsibility for the discharge of the functions of the Organization set forth in this Chapter shall be vested in the General Assembly and, under the authority of the General Assembly, in the Economic and Social Council, which shall have for this purpose the powers set forth in Chapter X.

Chapter X: The Economic And Social Council

Composition

Article 61

1. The Economic and Social Council shall consist of fifty-four Members of the United Nations elected by the General Assembly.
2. Subject to the provisions of paragraph 3, eighteen members of the Economic and Social Council shall be elected each year for a term of three years. A retiring member shall be eligible for immediate re-election.
3. At the first election after the increase in the membership of the Economic and Social Council from twenty-seven to fifty-four members, in addition to the members elected in place of the nine members whose term of office expires at the end of that year, twenty-seven additional members shall be elected. Of these twenty-seven additional members, the term of office of nine members so elected shall expire at the end of one year, and of nine other members at the end of two years, in accordance with arrangements made by the General Assembly.
4. Each member of the Economic and Social Council shall have one representative.

Functions and powers

Article 62

1. The Economic and Social Council may make or initiate studies and reports with respect to international economic, social, cultural, educational, health, and related matters and may make recommendations with respect to any such matters to the General Assembly to the Members of the United Nations, and to the specialized agencies concerned.

2. It may make recommendations for the purpose of promoting respect for, and observance of, human rights and fundamental freedoms for all.
3. It may prepare draft conventions for submission to the General Assembly, with respect to matters falling within its competence.
4. It may call, in accordance with the rules prescribed by the United Nations, international conferences on matters falling within its competence.

Article 63

1. The Economic and Social Council may enter into agreements with any of the agencies referred to in Article 57, defining the terms on which the agency concerned shall be brought into relationship with the United Nations. Such agreements shall be subject to approval by the General Assembly.
2. It may co-ordinate the activities of the specialized agencies through consultation with and recommendations to such agencies and through recommendations to the General Assembly and to the Members of the United Nations.

Article 64

1. The Economic and Social Council may take appropriate steps to obtain regular reports from the specialized agencies. It may make arrangements with the Members of the United Nations and with the specialized agencies to obtain reports on the steps taken to give effect to its own recommendations and to recommendations on matters falling within its competence made by the General Assembly.
2. It may communicate its observations on these reports to the General Assembly.

Article 65

The Economic and Social Council may furnish information to the Security Council and shall assist the Security Council upon its request.

Article 66

1. The Economic and Social Council shall perform such functions as fall within its competence in connection with the carrying out of the recommendations of the General Assembly.

2. It may, with the approval of the General Assembly, perform services at the request of Members of the United Nations and at the request of specialized agencies.

3. It shall perform such other functions as are specified elsewhere in the present Charter or as may be assigned to it by the General Assembly.

VOTING

Article 67

1. Each member of the Economic and Social Council shall have one vote.

2. Decisions of the Economic and Social Council shall be made by a majority of the members present and voting.

PROCEDURE

Article 68

The Economic and Social Council shall set up commissions in economic and social fields and for the promotion of human rights, and such other commissions as may be required for the performance of its functions.

Article 69

The Economic and Social Council shall invite any Member of the United Nations to participate, without vote, in its deliberations on any matter of particular concern to that Member.

Article 70

The Economic and Social Council may make arrangements for representatives of the specialized agencies to participate, without vote, in its deliberations and in those of the commissions established by it, and for its representatives to participate in the deliberations of the specialized agencies.

Article 71

The Economic and Social Council may make suitable arrangements for consultation with non-governmental organizations which are concerned with matters within its competence. Such arrangements may be made with international organizations and, where appropriate, with national organizations after consultation with the Member of the United Nations concerned.

Article 72

1. The Economic and Social Council shall adopt its own rules of procedure, including the method of selecting its President.
2. The Economic and Social Council shall meet as required in accordance with its rules, which shall include provision for the convening of meetings on the request of a majority of its members.

Chapter XI: Declaration Regarding Non-Self-Governing Territories

Article 73

Members of the United Nations which have or assume responsibilities for the administration of territories whose peoples have not yet attained a full measure of self-government recognize the principle that the interests of the inhabitants of these territories are paramount, and accept as a sacred trust the obligation to promote to the utmost, within the system of international peace and security established by the present Charter, the well-being of the inhabitants of these territories, and, to this end:

a. to ensure, with due respect for the culture of the peoples concerned, their political, economic, social, and educational advancement, their just treatment, and their protection against abuses;
b. to develop self-government, to take due account of the political aspirations of the peoples, and to assist them in the progressive development of their free political institutions, according to the particular circumstances of each territory and its peoples and their varying stages of advancement;
c. to further international peace and security;
d. to promote constructive measures of development, to encourage research, and to co-operate with one another and, when and where appropriate, with specialized international bodies with a view to the practical achievement of the social, economic, and scientific purposes set forth in this Article; and
e. to transmit regularly to the Secretary-General for information purposes, subject to such limitation as security and constitutional considerations may require, statistical and other information of a technical nature relating to economic, social, and educational conditions in the territories for which they are respectively responsible other than those territories to which Chapters XII and XIII apply.

Article 74

Members of the United Nations also agree that their policy in respect of the territories to which this Chapter applies, no less than in respect of their metropolitan areas, must be based on the general principle of good-neighbourliness, due account being taken of the interests and well-being of the rest of the world, in social, economic, and commercial matters.

Chapter XII: International Trusteeship System

Article 75

The United Nations shall establish under its authority an international trusteeship system for the administration and supervision of such territories as may be placed thereunder by subsequent individual agreements. These territories are hereinafter referred to as trust territories.

Article 76

The basic objectives of the trusteeship system, in accordance with the Purposes of the United Nations laid down in Article 1 of the present Charter, shall be:

a. to further international peace and security;

b. to promote the political, economic, social, and educational advancement of the inhabitants of the trust territories, and their progressive development towards self-government or independence as may be appropriate to the particular circumstances of each territory and its peoples and the freely expressed wishes of the peoples concerned, and as may be provided by the terms of each trusteeship agreement;

c. to encourage respect for human rights and for fundamental freedoms for all without distinction as to race, sex, language, or religion, and to encourage recognition of the interdependence of the peoples of the world; and

d. to ensure equal treatment in social, economic, and commercial matters for all Members of the United Nations and their nationals, and also equal treatment for the latter in the administration of justice, without prejudice to the attainment of the foregoing objectives and subject to the provisions of Article 80.

Article 77

1. The trusteeship system shall apply to such territories in the following

categories as may be placed thereunder by means of trusteeship agreements:

2. a. territories now held under mandate;
3. b. territories which may be detached from enemy states as a result of the Second World War; and
4. c. territories voluntarily placed under the system by states responsible for their administration.
5. It will be a matter for subsequent agreement as to which territories in the foregoing categories will be brought under the trusteeship system and upon what terms.

Article 78

The trusteeship system shall not apply to territories which have become Members of the United Nations, relationship among which shall be based on respect for the principle of sovereign equality.

Article 79

The terms of trusteeship for each territory to be placed under the trusteeship system, including any alteration or amendment, shall be agreed upon by the states directly concerned, including the mandatory power in the case of territories held under mandate by a Member of the United Nations, and shall be approved as provided for in Articles 83 and 85.

Article 80

1. Except as may be agreed upon in individual trusteeship agreements, made under Articles 77, 79, and 81, placing each territory under the trusteeship system, and until such agreements have been concluded, nothing in this Chapter shall be construed in or of itself to alter in any manner the rights whatsoever of any states or any peoples or the terms of existing international instruments to which Members of the United Nations may respectively be parties.
2. Paragraph 1 of this Article shall not be interpreted as giving grounds for delay or postponement of the negotiation and conclusion of agreements for placing mandated and other territories under the trusteeship system as provided for in Article 77.

Article 81

The trusteeship agreement shall in each case include the terms under which the trust territory will be administered and designate the authority which will exercise the administration of the trust territory. Such authority, hereinafter called the administering authority, may be one or more states or the Organization itself.

Article 82

There may be designated, in any trusteeship agreement, a strategic area or areas which may include part or all of the trust territory to which the agreement applies, without prejudice to any special agreement or agreements made under Article 43.

Article 83

1. All functions of the United Nations relating to strategic areas, including the approval of the terms of the trusteeship agreements and of their alteration or amendment shall be exercised by the Security Council.
2. The basic objectives set forth in Article 76 shall be applicable to the people of each strategic area.
3. The Security Council shall, subject to the provisions of the trusteeship agreements and without prejudice to security considerations, avail itself of the assistance of the Trusteeship Council to perform those functions of the United Nations under the trusteeship system relating to political, economic, social, and educational matters in the strategic areas.

Article 84

It shall be the duty of the administering authority to ensure that the trust territory shall play its part in the maintenance of international peace and security. To this end the administering authority may make use of volunteer forces, facilities, and assistance from the trust territory in carrying out the obligations towards the Security Council undertaken in this regard by the administering authority, as well as for local defence and the maintenance of law and order within the trust territory.

Article 85

1. The functions of the United Nations with regard to trusteeship agreements for all areas not designated as strategic, including the approval of the terms of the trusteeship agreements and of their alteration or amendment, shall be exercised by the General Assembly.

2. The Trusteeship Council, operating under the authority of the General Assembly shall assist the General Assembly in carrying out these functions.

Chapter Xiii: The Trusteeship Council

Composition

Article 86

1. The Trusteeship Council shall consist of the following Members of the United Nations:
2. a. those Members administering trust territories;
3. b. such of those Members mentioned by name in Article 23 as are not administering trust territories; and
4. c. as many other Members elected for three-year terms by the General Assembly as may be necessary to ensure that the total number of members of the Trusteeship Council is equally divided between those Members of the United Nations which administer trust territories and those which do not.
5. Each member of the Trusteeship Council shall designate one specially qualified person to represent it therein.

Functions And Powers

Article 87

The General Assembly and, under its authority, the Trusteeship Council, in carrying out their functions, may:

a. consider reports submitted by the administering authority;
b. accept petitions and examine them in consultation with the administering authority;
c. provide for periodic visits to the respective trust territories at times agreed upon with the administering authority; and
d. take these and other actions in conformity with the terms of the trusteeship agreements.

Article 88

The Trusteeship Council shall formulate a questionnaire on the political, economic, social, and educational advancement of the inhabitants of each trust territory, and the administering authority for each trust territory within the competence of the General Assembly shall make an annual report to the General Assembly upon the basis of such questionnaire.

Voting

Article 89

1. Each member of the Trusteeship Council shall have one vote.
2. Decisions of the Trusteeship Council shall be made by a majority of the members present and voting.

Procedure

Article 90

1. The Trusteeship Council shall adopt its own rules of procedure, including the method of selecting its President.
2. The Trusteeship Council shall meet as required in accordance with its rules, which shall include provision for the convening of meetings on the request of a majority of its members.

Article 91

The Trusteeship Council shall, when appropriate, avail itself of the assistance of the Economic and Social Council and of the specialized agencies in regard to matters with which they are respectively concerned.

Chapter XIV: The International Court Of Justice

Article 92

The International Court of Justice shall be the principal judicial organ of the United Nations. It shall function in accordance with the annexed Statute, which is based upon the Statute of the Permanent Court of International Justice and forms an integral part of the present Charter.

Article 93

1. All Members of the United Nations are *ipso facto* parties to the Statute of the International Court of Justice.
2. A state which is not a Member of the United Nations may become a party to the Statute of the International Court of Justice on conditions to be determined in each case by the General Assembly upon the recommendation of the Security Council.

Article 94

1. Each Member of the United Nations undertakes to comply with the decision of the International Court of Justice in any case to which it is a party.
2. If any party to a case fails to perform the obligations incumbent upon it under a judgment rendered by the Court, the other party may have recourse to the Security Council, which may, if it deems necessary, make recommendations or decide upon measures to be taken to give effect to the judgment.

Article 95

Nothing in the present Charter shall prevent Members of the United Nations from entrusting the solution of their differences to other tribunals by virtue of agreements already in existence or which may be concluded in the future.

Article 96

a. The General Assembly or the Security Council may request the International Court of Justice to give an advisory opinion on any legal question.
b. Other organs of the United Nations and specialized agencies, which may at any time be so authorized by the General Assembly, may also request advisory opinions of the Court on legal questions arising within the scope of their activities.

Chapter XV: The Secretariat

Article 97

The Secretariat shall comprise a Secretary-General and such staff as the Organization may require. The Secretary-General shall be appointed by the General Assembly upon the recommendation of the Security Council. He shall be the chief administrative officer of the Organization.

Article 98

The Secretary-General shall act in that capacity in all meetings of the General Assembly, of the Security Council, of the Economic and Social Council, and of the Trusteeship Council, and shall perform such other functions as are entrusted to him by these organs. The Secretary-General shall make an annual report to the General Assembly on the work of the Organization.

Article 99

The Secretary-General may bring to the attention of the Security Council any matter which in his opinion may threaten the maintenance of international peace and security.

Article 100

1. In the performance of their duties the Secretary-General and the staff shall not seek or receive instructions from any government or from any other authority external to the Organization. They shall refrain from any action which might reflect on their position as international officials responsible only to the Organization.
2. Each Member of the United Nations undertakes to respect the exclusively international character of the responsibilities of the Secretary-General and the staff and not to seek to influence them in the discharge of their responsibilities.

Article 101

1. The staff shall be appointed by the Secretary-General under regulations established by the General Assembly.
2. Appropriate staffs shall be permanently assigned to the Economic and Social Council, the Trusteeship Council, and, as required, to other organs of the United Nations. These staffs shall form a part of the Secretariat.
3. The paramount consideration in the employment of the staff and in the determination of the conditions of service shall be the necessity of securing the highest standards of efficiency, competence, and integrity. Due regard shall be paid to the importance of recruiting the staff on as wide a geographical basis as possible.

Chapter XVI: Miscellaneous Provisions

Article 102

1. Every treaty and every international agreement entered into by any Member of the United Nations after the present Charter comes into force shall as soon as possible be registered with the Secretariat and published by it.
2. No party to any such treaty or international agreement which has not been registered in accordance with the provisions of paragraph 1 of this Article may invoke that treaty or agreement before any organ of the United Nations.

Article 103

In the event of a conflict between the obligations of the Members of the United Nations under the present Charter and their obligations under any other international agreement, their obligations under the present Charter shall prevail.

Article 104

The Organization shall enjoy in the territory of each of its Members such legal capacity as may be necessary for the exercise of its functions and the fulfilment of its purposes.

Article 105

1. The Organization shall enjoy in the territory of each of its Members such privileges and immunities as are necessary for the fulfilment of its purposes.
2. Representatives of the Members of the United Nations and officials of the Organization shall similarly enjoy such privileges and immunities as are necessary for the independent exercise of their functions in connexion with the Organization.
3. The General Assembly may make recommendations with a view to determining the details of the application of paragraphs 1 and 2 of this Article or may propose conventions to the Members of the United Nations for this purpose.

Chapter XVII: Transitional Security Arrangements

Article 106

Pending the coming into force of such special agreements referred to in Article 43 as in the opinion of the Security Council enable it to begin the exercise of its responsibilities under Article 42, the parties to the Four-Nation Declaration, signed at Moscow, 30 October 1943, and France, shall, in accordance with the provisions of paragraph 5 of that Declaration, consult with one another and as occasion requires with other Members of the United Nations with a view to such joint action on behalf of the Organization as may be necessary for the purpose of maintaining international peace and security.

Article 107

Nothing in the present Charter shall invalidate or preclude action, in relation to any state which during the Second World War has been an enemy of any signatory to the present Charter, taken or authorized as a result of that war by the Governments having responsibility for such action.

Chapter XVIII: Amendments

Article 108

Amendments to the present Charter shall come into force for all Members of the United Nations when they have been adopted by a vote of two thirds of the members of the General Assembly and ratified in accordance with their respective constitutional processes by two thirds of the Members of the United Nations, including all the permanent members of the Security Council.

Article 109

1. A General Conference of the Members of the United Nations for the purpose of reviewing the present Charter may be held at a date and place to be fixed by a two-thirds vote of the members of the General Assembly and by a vote of any nine members of the Security Council. Each Member of the United Nations shall have one vote in the conference.
2. Any alteration of the present Charter recommended by a two-thirds vote of the conference shall take effect when ratified in accordance with their respective constitutional processes by two thirds of the Members of the United Nations including all the permanent members of the Security Council.
3. If such a conference has not been held before the tenth annual session of the General Assembly following the coming into force of the present Charter, the proposal to call such a conference shall be placed on the agenda of that session of the General Assembly, and the conference shall be held if so decided by a majority vote of the members of the General Assembly and by a vote of any seven members of the Security Council.

Chapter XIX: Ratification and Signature

Article 110

1. The present Charter shall be ratified by the signatory states in accordance with their respective constitutional processes.

2. The ratifications shall be deposited with the Government of the United States of America, which shall notify all the signatory states of each deposit as well as the Secretary-General of the Organization when he has been appointed.
3. The present Charter shall come into force upon the deposit of ratifications by the Republic of China, France, the Union of Soviet Socialist Republics, the United Kingdom of Great Britain and Northern Ireland, and the United States of America, and by a majority of the other signatory states. A protocol of the ratifications deposited shall thereupon be drawn up by the Government of the United States of America which shall communicate copies thereof to all the signatory states.
4. The states signatory to the present Charter which ratify it after it has come into force will become original Members of the United Nations on the date of the deposit of their respective ratifications.

Article 111

The present Charter, of which the Chinese, French, Russian, English, and Spanish texts are equally authentic, shall remain deposited in the archives of the Government of the United States of America. Duly certified copies thereof shall be transmitted by that Government to the Governments of the other signatory states.

IN FAITH WHEREOF the representatives of the Governments of the United Nations have signed the present Charter. DONE at the city of San Francisco the twenty-sixth day of June, one thousand nine hundred and forty-five.

References

Robertson, Arthur Henry; Merrills, John Graham (1996). *Human Rights in the World: An Introduction to the Study of the International Protection of Human Rights*. Manchester University Press.

Gerald M. Steinberg, Anne Herzberg and Jordan Berman (2012). *Best Practices for Human Rights and Humanitarian NGO Fact-Finding*. Martinus Nijhoff Publisher.

Steiner, J. & Alston, Philip. (1996). *International Human Rights in Context: Law, Politics, Morals.* Oxford: Clarendon Press.

Shute, Stephen & Hurley, Susan (eds.). (1993). *On Human Rights: The Oxford Amnesty Lectures.* New York: BasicBooks.

5

International Court of Justice

The International Court of Justice (French: Cour internationale de Justice; commonly referred to as the World Court or ICJ) is the primary judicial organ of the United Nations. It is based in the Peace Palace in The Hague, the Netherlands. Its main functions are to settle legal disputes submitted to it by states and to provide advisory opinions on legal questions submitted to it by duly authorised international organs, agencies, and the UN General Assembly.

Activities

Established in 1945 by the UN Charter, the Court began work in 1946 as the successor to the Permanent Court of International Justice. The Statute of the International Court of Justice, similar to that of its predecessor, is the main constitutional document constituting and regulating the Court.

The Court's workload covers a wide range of judicial activity. To date, the ICJ has dealt with relatively few cases. However, since the 1980s there has been a clear increase in willingness to use the Court, especially among developing countries. After the court ruled that the U.S.'s covert war against Nicaragua was in violation of international law (Nicaragua v. United States), the United States withdrew from compulsory jurisdiction in 1986. The United States accepts the court's jurisdiction only on a case-by-case basis. Chapter XIV of the United Nations Charter authorizes the UN Security Council to enforce World Court rulings. However, such enforcement is subject to the veto power of the five permanent members of the Council.

Composition

The ICJ is composed of fifteen judges elected to nine year terms by the UN General Assembly and the UN Security Council from a list of persons nominated by the national groups in the Permanent Court of Arbitration. The election process is set out in Articles 4–19 of the ICJ statute. Elections are staggered with five judges elected every three years, in order to ensure continuity within the court.

Should a judge die in office, the practice has generally been to elect a judge of the same nationality to complete the term. No two may be nationals of the same country. According to Article 9, the membership of the Court is supposed to represent the "main forms of civilization and of the principal legal systems of the world". Essentially, this has meant common law, civil law and socialist law (now post-communist law). Since its creation, four of the five permanent members of the Security Council (France, Russia, the United Kingdom, and the United States) have always had a judge on the Court. The exception was China (the Republic of China until 1971, the People's Republic of China from 1971 onwards), which did not have a judge on the Court from 1967–1985, because it did not put forward a candidate. The rule on a geopolitical composition of the bench exists despite the fact that there is no provision for it in the Statute of the ICJ.

Article 6 of the Statute provides that all judges should be "elected regardless of their nationality among persons of high moral character", who are either qualified for the highest judicial office in their home states or known as lawyers with sufficient competence in international law. Judicial independence is dealt with specifically in Articles 16–18. Judges of the ICJ are not able to hold any other post, nor act as counsel. In practice the Members of the Court have their own interpretation of these rules. This allows them to be involved in outside arbitration and hold professional posts as long as there is no conflict of interest. A judge can be dismissed only by a unanimous vote of other members of the Court. Despite these provisions, the independence of ICJ judges has been questioned. For example, during the Nicaragua Case, the USA issued a communiqué suggesting that it could not present sensitive material to the Court because of the presence of judges from Eastern bloc states.

Judges may deliver joint judgments or give their own separate opinions. Decisions and Advisory Opinions are by majority and, in the event of an equal division, the President's vote becomes decisive. Judges may also deliver separate dissenting opinions.

Ad hoc Judges

Article 31 of the statute sets out a procedure whereby ad hoc judges sit on contentious cases before the Court. This system allows any party to a contentious case to nominate a judge of their choosing. It is possible that as many as seventeen judges may sit on one case.

This system may seem strange when compared with domestic court processes, but its purpose is to encourage states to submit cases to the Court. For example, if a state knows it will have a judicial officer who can participate in deliberation and offer other judges local knowledge and an understanding of the state's perspective, that state may be more willing to submit to the Court's jurisdiction. Although this system does not sit well with the judicial nature of the body, it is usually of little practical consequence. Ad hoc judges usually (but not always) vote in favor of the state that appointed them and thus cancel each other out.

Chambers

Generally, the Court sits as full bench, but in the last fifteen years it has on occasion sat as a chamber. Articles 26–29 of the statute allow the Court to form smaller chambers, usually 3 or 5 judges, to hear cases. Two types of chambers are contemplated by Article 26: firstly, chambers for special categories of cases, and second, the formation of ad hoc chambers to hear particular disputes. In 1993 a special chamber was established, under Article 26(1) of the ICJ statute, to deal specifically with environmental matters (although this chamber has never been used).

Ad hoc chambers are more frequently convened. For example, chambers were used to hear the Gulf of Maine Case (Canada/USA). In that case, the parties made clear they would withdraw the case unless the Court appointed judges to the chamber who were acceptable to the parties. Judgments of chambers may have less authority than full Court judgments, or may diminish the proper interpretation of universal international law informed by a variety of cultural and legal perspectives. On the other hand, the use of chambers might encourage greater recourse to the Court and thus enhance international dispute resolution.

Jurisdiction

The International Court of Justice has jurisdiction in two types of cases: contentious issues between states in which the court produces binding rulings between states that agree, or have previously agreed, to submit to the ruling of the court; and advisory opinions, which provide reasoned, but non-binding, rulings on properly submitted questions of international law, usually at the request of the United Nations General Assembly. Advisory opinions do not have to concern particular controversies between states, though they often do.

Contentious Issues

The key principle is that the Court only has jurisdiction on the basis of consent. The court has no true compulsory jurisdiction. Jurisdiction is often a key question for the Court, because it is challenged by the respondent. At the Preliminary Objections phase, a respondent may challenge (i) jurisdiction and/or (ii) admissibility of the case. Article 36 outlines four bases on which the Court's jurisdiction may be founded.

Only states may be parties in contentious cases before the ICJ. Individuals, corporations, parts of a federal state, NGOs, UN organs and self-determination groups are excluded from direct participation in cases, although the Court may receive information from public international organisations. This does not preclude non-state interests from being the subject of proceedings if one state brings the case against another. For example, a state may, in case of "diplomatic protection", bring a case on behalf of one of its nationals or corporations.

Special Agreement

First, 36(1) provides that parties may refer cases to the Court (jurisdiction founded on "special agreement" or "compromis"). This method is based on explicit consent and is, perhaps, the most effective basis for the Court's jurisdiction. It is effective because the parties concerned have a desire for the Court to resolve the dispute, and are thus more likely to comply with the Court's judgment. Parties will usually define the nature of the dispute between them and the legal questions on which they wish the Court to rule.

Compromissory Clause

Second, 36(1) also gives the Court jurisdiction over "matters specifically provided for ... in treaties and conventions in force". Most modern treaties will contain a compromissory clause, providing for dispute resolution by the ICJ. For instance, Article 32(2) of the United Nations Convention Against Illicit Traffic in Narcotic Drugs and Psychotropic Substances provides for mediation and other dispute-resolution options, but also states that "[a]ny such dispute which cannot be settled ... shall be referred, at the request of any one of the States Parties to the dispute, to the International Court of Justice for decision".

Cases founded on compromissory clauses have not been as effective as cases founded on special agreement, since a state may have no interest in having the matter examined by the Court and may refuse to comply with a judgment. Since the 1970s the use of such compromissory clauses has declined. Many modern treaties set out their own dispute-resolution regime, often based on forms of arbitration.

In 1987, upon the initiative of Mikhail Gorbachev, all of the permanent members of the Security Council began negotiations for expanding the compulsory jurisdiction of the ICJ. The content of these negotiations is to date unknown, and no agreements were reached.

Optional Clause Declarations

Thirdly, Article 36(2) allows states to make declarations accepting the Court's jurisdiction as compulsory ("optional clause declarations"). Not all countries accept the compulsory jurisdiction of the International Court of Justice, ICJ. For example, Australia accepts compulsory ICJ jurisdiction "with reservations" whereas Brazil has not accepted compulsory ICJ jurisdiction.

Succession from PCIJ

Finally, 36(5) provides for jurisdiction on the basis of declarations made under the Permanent Court of International Justice's statute. Article 37 of the ICJ's statute similarly transfers jurisdiction under any compromissory clause in a treaty that gave jurisdiction to the PCIJ.

Advisory Opinion

An advisory opinion is a function of the court open only to specified United Nations bodies and agencies. On receiving a request, the Court decides which States and organizations might provide useful information and gives them an opportunity to present written or oral statements. The Court's advisory procedure is otherwise modelled on that for contentious proceedings, and the sources of applicable law are the same.

In principle the Court's advisory opinions are consultative in character and as such do not generally result in judgments that aim to resolve specific controversies. Certain instruments or regulations can, however, provide in advance that the advisory opinion shall be specifically binding on particular agencies or states.

The advisory opinions of the court are influential and widely respected interpretations of the law, but they are not authoritative, and they are inherently non-binding under the Statute of the Court. Examples of advisory opinions can be found in the section advisory opinions in the List of International Court of Justice cases article.

The ICJ and the Security Council

The relationship between the ICJ and the Security Council, and the separation of their powers, was considered by the Court in 1992, in the Pan Am case. The Court had to consider an application from Libya for the order of provisional measures to protect its rights, which, it alleged, were being infringed by the threat of economic sanctions by the UK and USA.

The problem was that these sanctions had been authorised by the Security Council, which resulted with a potential conflict between the Chapter VII functions of the Security Council and the judicial function of the Court. The Court decided, by eleven votes to five, that it could not order the requested provisional measures because the rights claimed by Libya, even if legitimate under the Montreal Convention, could no longer be upheld since the action was justified by the Security Council.

In accordance with Article 103 of the UN Charter, obligations under the Charter took precedence over other treaty obligations.

There was a marked reluctance on the part of a majority of the Court to become involved in a dispute in such a way as to bring it potentially into conflict with the Council. The Court stated in the Nicaragua case (Jurisdiction) that there is no necessary inconsistency between action by the Security Council and adjudication by the ICJ. However, where there is room for conflict, the balance appears to be in favour of the Security Council.

Should either party fail "to perform the obligations incumbent upon it under a judgment rendered by the Court", the Security Council may be called upon to "make recommendations or decide upon measures" if the security council deems such actions necessary. In practice, the Court's powers have been limited by the unwillingness of the losing party to abide by the Court's ruling, and by the Security Council's unwillingness to enforce consequences. However, in theory, "so far as the parties to the case are concerned, a judgment of the Court is binding, final and without appeal," and "by signing the Charter, a State Member of the United Nations undertakes to comply with any decision of the International Court of Justice in a case to which it is a party".

For example, in Nicaragua v. United States the United States of America had previously accepted the Court's compulsory jurisdiction upon its creation in 1946 but withdrew its acceptance following the Court's judgment in 1984 that called on the United States to "cease and to refrain" from the "unlawful use of force" against the government of Nicaragua. In a split decision, the majority of the Court ruled the United States was "in breach of its obligation under customary international law not to use force against another state" and ordered the US pay reparations, although it never did.

Examples of cases include:

- A complaint by the United States in 1980 that Iran was detaining American diplomats in Tehran in violation of international law.
- A dispute between Tunisia and Libya over the delimitation of the continental shelf between them.
- A dispute over the course of the maritime boundary dividing the U.S. and Canada in the Gulf of Maine area.
- A complaint by the Federal Republic of Yugoslavia against the member states of the North Atlantic Treaty Organisation regarding their actions in the Kosovo War. This was denied on 15 December 2004 due to lack of jurisdiction, because the FRY was not a party to the ICJ statute at the time it made the application.

The last example can be used as evidence of the Court's failure to take on politically controversial cases; as the Court has no means to enforce its rulings, its survival is dependent on its political legitimacy. That would be endangered if it constantly came with rulings which states have no interest of taking into consideration. This is one of the Court's major shortcomings: its rulings must be considered in a political context.

Sources of International Law

Sources of international law are the materials and processes out of which the rules and principles regulating the international community are developed. They have been influenced by a range of political and legal theories. During the 19th century, it was recognised by legal positivists that a sovereign could limit its authority to act by consenting to an agreement according to the principle pacta sunt servanda. This consensual view of international law was reflected in the 1920 Statute of the Permanent Court of International Justice, and preserved in Article 38(1) of the 1946 Statute of the International Court of Justice.

Article 38(1) is generally recognised as a definitive statement of the sources of international law. It requires the Court to apply, among other things, (a) international conventions "expressly recognized by the contesting states", and (b) "international custom, as evidence of a general practice accepted as law". To avoid the possibility of non liquet, sub-paragraph (c) added the requirement that the general principles applied by the Court were those that had been "the general principles of the law recognized by civilized nations". As it is states that by consent determine the content of international law, sub-paragraph (d) acknowledges that the Court is entitled to refer to "judicial decisions" and the most highly qualified juristic writings "as subsidiary means for the determination of rules of law".

On the question of preference between sources of international law, rules established by treaty will take preference if such an instrument exists. It is also argued however that international treaties and international custom are sources of international law of equal validity; this is that new custom may supersede older treaties and new treaties may override older custom. Certainly, judicial decisions and juristic writings are regarded as auxiliary sources of international law, whereas it is unclear whether the general principles of law recognized by 'civilized nations' should be recognized as a principal or auxiliary source of international law.

It may be argued that the practice of international organizations, most notably that of the United Nations, as it appears in the resolutions of the Security Council and the General Assembly, are an additional source of international law, even though it is not mentioned as such in Article 38(1) of the 1946 Statute of the International Court of Justice. Article 38(1) is closely based on the corresponding provision of the 1920 Statute of the Permanent Court of International Justice, thus predating the role that international organizations have come to play in the international plane. That is, the provision of Article 38(1) may be regarded as dated, and this can most vividly be seen in the mention made to 'civilized nations', a mentioning that appears all the more quaint after the decolonization process that took place in the early 1960s and the participation of nearly all nations of the world in the United Nations.

It is also possible, though less common, for a treaty to be modified by practices arising between the parties to that treaty. The other situation in which a rule would take precedence over a treaty provision would be where the rule has the special status of being part of the jus cogens.

International Custom

Article 38.1(b) of the ICJ Statute refers to "international custom" as a source of international law, specifically emphasizing the two requirements of state practice plus acceptance of the practice as obligatory or opinio juris sive necessitatis (usually abbreviated as opinio juris).

Derived from the consistent practice of (originally) Western states accompanied by opinio juris (the conviction of States that the consistent practice is required by a legal obligation), customary international law is differentiated from acts of comity by the presence of opinio juris (although in some instances, acts of comity have developed into customary international law, i.e. diplomatic immunity). Treaties have gradually displaced much customary international law. This development is similar to the replacement of customary or common law by codified law in municipal legal settings, but customary international law continues to play a significant role in international law.

State Practice

When examining state practice to determine relevant rules of international law, it is necessary to take into account every activity of the organs and officials of states that relate to that purpose. There has been continuing debate over where a distinction should be drawn as to the weight that should be attributed to what states do, rather than what they say represents the law. In its most extreme form, this would involve rejecting what states say as practice and relegating it to the status of evidence of opinio juris. A more moderate version would evaluate what a state says by reference to the occasion on which the statement was made. It is only relatively powerful countries with extensive international contacts and interests that have regular opportunities of contributing by deed to the practice of international law. The principal means of contribution to state practice for the majority of states will be at meetings of international organisations, particularly the UN General Assembly, by voting and otherwise expressing their view on matters under consideration. Moreover, there are circumstances in which what states say may be the only evidence of their view as to what conduct is required in a particular situation.

The notion of practice establishing a customary rule implies that the practice is followed regularly, or that such state practice must be "common, consistent and concordant". Given the size of the international community, the practice does not have to encompass all states or be completely uniform. There has to be a sufficient degree of participation, especially on the part of states whose interests are likely be most affected, and an absence of substantial dissent. There have been a number of occasions on which the ICJ has rejected claims that a customary rule existed because of a lack of consistency in the practice brought to its attention.

Within the context of a specific dispute, however, it is not necessary to establish the generality of practice. A rule may apply if a state has accepted the rule as applicable to it individually, or because the two states belong to a group of states between which the rule applies.

A dissenting state is entitled to deny the opposability of a rule in question if it can demonstrate its persistent objection to that rule, either as a member of a regional group or by virtue of its membership of the international community. It is not easy for a single state to maintain its dissent. Also, rules of the jus cogens have a universal character and apply to all states, irrespective of their wishes.

Demand for rules that are responsive to increasingly rapid changes has led to the suggestion that there can be, in appropriate circumstances, such a concept as "instant custom". Even within traditional doctrine, the ICJ has recognised that passage of a short period of time is not necessarily a bar to the formation of a new rule. Because of this, the question is sometimes raised as to whether the word "custom" is suitable to a process that could occur with great rapidity.

Opinio Juris

A wealth of state practice does not usually carry with it a presumption that opinio juris exists. "Not only must the acts concerned amount to a settled practice, but they must also be such, or be carried out in such a way, as to be evidence of a belief that this practice is rendered obligatory by the existence of a rule of law requiring it."

In cases where practice (of which evidence is given) comprises abstentions from acting, consistency of conduct might not establish the existence of a rule of customary international law. The fact that no nuclear weapons have been used since 1945, for example, does not render their use illegal on the basis of a customary obligation because the necessary opinio juris was lacking.

Although the ICJ has frequently referred to opinio juris as being an equal footing with state practice, the role of the psychological element in the creation of customary law is uncertain.

Jus cogens

A peremptory norm or jus cogens (Latin for "compelling law" or "strong law") is a principle of international law considered so fundamental that it overrides all other sources of international law, including even the Charter of the United Nations. The principle of jus cogens is enshrined in Article 53 of the Vienna Convention on the Law of Treaties:

For the purposes of the present Convention, a peremptory norm of general international law is a norm accepted and recognised by the international community of States as a whole as a norm from which no derogation is permitted and which can be modified only by a subsequent norm of general international law having the same character.

Rules of jus cogens generally require or forbid the state to do particular acts or respect certain rights. However, some define criminal offences which the state must enforce against individuals. Generally included on lists of such norms are prohibitions of such crimes and internationally wrongful acts as waging aggressive war, war crimes, crimes against humanity, piracy, genocide, apartheid, slavery and torture.

The evidence supporting the emergence of a rule of jus cogens will be essentially similar to that required to establish the creation of a new rule of customary international law. Indeed, jus cogens could be thought of as a special principle of custom with a superadded opinio juris. The European Court of Human Rights has stressed the international public policy aspect of the jus cogens.

Treaties as Law

Treaties can play the role of contracts between two or more parties, such as an extradition treaty or a defence pact. Treaties can also be legislation to regulate a particular aspect of international relations, or form the constitutions of international organisations. Whether or not all treaties can be regarded as sources of law, they are sources of obligation for the parties to them. Article 38(1)(a), which uses the term "international conventions", concentrates upon treaties as a source of contractual obligation but also acknowledges the possibility of a state expressly accepting the obligations of a treaty to which it is not formally a party.

For a treaty-based rule to be a source of law, rather than simply a source of obligation, it must either be capable of affecting non-parties or have consequences for parties more extensive than those specifically imposed by the treaty itself.

Treaties as Custom

Some treaties are the result of codifying existing customary law, such as laws governing the global commons, and jus ad bellum. While the purpose is to establish a code of general application, its effectiveness depends upon the number of states that ratify or accede to the particular convention. Relatively few such instruments have a sufficient number of parties to be regarded as international law in their own right. The most obvious examples are the 1949 Geneva Conventions for the Protection of War Victims.

Most multi-lateral treaties fall short of achieving such a near universal degree of formal acceptance, and are dependent upon their provisions being regarded as representing customary international law and, by this indirect route, as binding upon non-parties. This outcome is possible in a number of ways:

- When the treaty rule reproduces an existing rule of customary law, the rule will be clarified in terms of the treaty provision. A notable example is the Vienna Convention on the Law of Treaties 1969, which was considered by the ICJ to be law even before it had been brought into force.

- When a customary rule is in the process of development, its incorporation in a multilateral treaty may have the effect of consolidating or crystallising the law in the form of that rule. It is not always easy to identify when this occurs. Where the practice is less developed, the treaty provision may not be enough to crystallise the rule as part of customary international law.

Even if the rule is new, the drafting of the treaty provision may be the impetus for its adoption in the practice of states, and it is the subsequent acceptance of the rule by states that renders it effective as part of customary law. If a broad definition is adopted of state practice, the making of a treaty would fall within the definition. Alternatively, it is possible to regard the treaty as the final act of state practice required to establish the rule in question, or as the necessary articulation of the rule to give it the opinio juris of customary international law.

Convention-based "instant custom" has been identified by the ICJ on several occasions as representing customary law without explanation of whether the provision in question was supported by state practice. This has happened with respect to a number of provisions of the Vienna Convention on the Law of Treaties 1969. If "instant custom" is valid as law, it could deny to third parties the normal consequences of non-accession to the treaty.

General Principles of Law

The scope of general principles of law, to which Article 38(1) of the Statute of the ICJ refers, is unclear and controversial but may include such legal principles that are common to a large number of systems of municipal law. Given the limits of treaties or custom as sources of international law, Article 38(1) may be looked upon as a directive to the Court to fill any gap in the law and prevent a non liquet by reference to the general principles.

In earlier stages of the development of international law, rules were frequently drawn from municipal law. In the 19th century, legal positivists rejected the idea that international law could come from any source that did not involve state will or consent, but were prepared to allow for the application of general principles of law, provided that they had in some way been accepted by states as part of the legal order. Thus Article 38(1)(c), for example, speaks of general principles "recognised" by states. An area that demonstrates the adoption of municipal approaches is the law applied to the relationship between international officials and their employing organisations, although today the principles are regarded as established international law.

The significance of general principles has undoubtedly been lessened by the increased intensity of treaty and institutional relations between states. Nevertheless, the concepts of estoppel and equity have been employed in the adjudication of international disputes. For example, a state that has, by its conduct, encouraged another state to believe in the existence of a certain legal or factual situation, and to rely upon that belief, may be estopped from asserting a contrary situation in its dealings. The principle of good faith was said by the ICJ to be "[o]ne of the basic principles governing the creation and performance of legal obligations". Similarly, there have been frequent references to equity. It is generally agreed that equity cannot be employed to subvert legal rules (that is, operate contra legem). This "equity as law" perception is reinforced by references to equitable principles in the text of the United Nations Convention on the Law of the Sea 1982, though this may be little more than an admission as to the existence, and legitimation, of the discretion of the adjudicator.

However, the principles of estoppel and equity in the international context do not retain all the connotations they do under common law. The reference to the principles as "general" signify that, if rules were to be adapted from municipal law, they should be at a sufficient level of generality to encompass similar rules existing in many municipal systems. Principles of municipal law should be regarded as sources of inspiration rather than as sources of rules of direct application.

Judicial Decisions and Juristic Writings

According to Article 38(1)(d) of its Statute, the ICJ is also to apply "judicial decisions and the teachings of the most highly qualified publicists of the various nations, as subsidiary means for the determination of rules of law". It is difficult to tell what influence these materials have on the development of the law. Pleadings in cases before the ICJ are often replete with references to case law and to legal literature.

Judicial decisions

The decisions of international and municipal courts and the publications of academics can be referred to, not as a source of law as such, but as a means of recognizing the law established in other sources. In practice the

International Court of Justice does not refer to domestic decisions although it does invoke its previous case-law.

There is no rule of stare decisis in international law. The decision of the Court has no binding force except between the parties and in respect of that particular case. Nevertheless, often the Court would refer to its past decisions and advisory opinions to support its explanation of a present case.

Often the International Court of Justice will consider General Assembly resolutions as indicative of customary international law.

Juristic writings

Article 38(1)(d) of the International Court of Justice Statute states that the 'teachings of the most highly qualified publicists of the various nations' are also among the 'subsidiary means for the determination of the rules of law'. The scholarly works of prominent jurists are not sources of international law but are essential in developing the rules that are sourced in treaties, custom and the general principles of law. This is accepted practice in the interpretation of international law and was utilised by the United States Supreme Court in The Paquete Habana case (175 US (1900) 677 at 700-1).

PROCEDURE

The ICJ is vested with the power to make its own rules. Court procedure is set out in Rules of Court of the International Court of Justice 1978 (as amended on 29 September 2005).

Cases before the ICJ will follow a standard pattern. The case is lodged by the applicant who files a written memorial setting out the basis of the Court's jurisdiction and the merits of its claim. The respondent may accept the Court's jurisdiction and file its own memorial on the merits of the case.

Preliminary Objections

A respondent who does not wish to submit to the jurisdiction of the Court may raise Preliminary Objections. Any such objections must be ruled upon before the Court can address the merits of the applicant's claim. Often a separate public hearing is held on the Preliminary Objections and the Court will render a judgment. Respondents normally file Preliminary Objections to the jurisdiction of the Court and/or the admissibility of the case. Inadmissibility refers to a range of arguments about factors the Court should take into account in deciding jurisdiction; for example, that the issue is not justiciable or that it is not a "legal dispute".

In addition, objections may be made because all necessary parties are not before the Court. If the case necessarily requires the Court to rule on the rights and obligations of a state that has not consented to the Court's jurisdiction, the Court will not proceed to issue a judgment on the merits. If the Court decides it has jurisdiction and the case is admissible, the respondent will then be required to file a Memorial addressing the merits of the applicant's claim. Once all written arguments are filed, the Court will hold a public hearing on the merits.

Once a case has been filed, any party (but usually the Applicant) may seek an order from the Court to protect the status quo pending the hearing of the case. Such orders are known as Provisional (or Interim) Measures and are analogous to interlocutory injunctions in United States law. Article 41 of the statute allows the Court to make such orders. The Court must be satisfied to have prima facie jurisdiction to hear the merits of the case before granting provisional measures.

Applications to Intervene

In cases where a third state's interests are affected, that state may be permitted to intervene in the case, and participate as a full party. Under Article 62, a state "with an interest of a legal nature" may apply; however, it is within the Court's discretion whether or not to allow the intervention. Intervention applications are rare — the first successful application occurred in 1991.

Judgment and Remedies

Once deliberation has taken place, the Court will issue a majority opinion. Individual judges may issue separate opinions (if they agree with the outcome reached in the judgment of the court but differ in their reasoning) or dissenting opinions (if they disagree with the majority). No appeal is possible, though any party may ask for the court to clarify if there is a dispute as to the meaning or scope of the court's judgment.

References

Rosenne S., (2003)."Rosenne's the world court: what it is and how it works *6th ed* (Leiden: Martinus Nijhoff.

Van Der Wolf W. & De Ruiter D., (2011). "The International Court of Justice: Facts and Documents About the History and Work of the Court". *International Courts Association.*

6

The International Criminal Court

The International Criminal Court (commonly referred to as the ICC or ICCt) is a permanent tribunal to prosecute individuals for genocide, crimes against humanity, war crimes, and the crime of aggression (although it cannot, until at least 2017, exercise jurisdiction over the crime of aggression).

It came into being on 1 July 2002—the date its founding treaty, the Rome Statute of the International Criminal Court, came into force—and it can prosecute only crimes committed on or after that date. The Court's official seat is in The Hague, Netherlands, but its proceedings may take place anywhere.

As of July 2012, 121 states are states parties to the Statute of the Court, including all of South America, nearly all of Europe and roughly half the countries in Africa. A further 32 countries, including Russia, have signed but not ratified the Rome Statute; one of them, Ivory Coast, has accepted the Court's jurisdiction. The law of treaties obliges these states to refrain from "acts which would defeat the object and purpose" of the treaty until they declare they do not intend to become a party to the treaty. Three of these states—Israel, Sudan and the United States—have informed the UN Secretary General that they no longer intend to become states parties and, as such, have no legal obligations arising from their former representatives' signature of the Statute. 41 United Nations member states have neither signed nor ratified or acceded to the Rome Statute; some of them, including China and India, are critical of the Court. The Palestinian National Authority, which neither is nor represents a United Nations member state, has formally accepted the jurisdiction of the Court. On 3 April 2012, the ICC Prosecutor declared himself unable to determine that Palestine is a "state" for the purposes of the Rome Statute.

In June 2010, two amendments to the Rome Statute of the International Criminal Court were adopted by the Review Conference in Kampala, Uganda. The first amendment criminalizes the use of certain kinds of weapons in non-international conflicts whose use was already forbidden in international conflicts. It is in force in one state party (San Marino); it will enter into force for its second ratifying state, Liechtenstein, on 8 May 2013, its third ratifying state, Samoa, on 25 September 2013, and its fourth ratifying state, Trinidad and Tobago, on 13 November 2013. The second amendment specifies the crime of aggression. It is in force in no state party but will enter into force for its first ratifying state, Liechtenstein, on 8 May 2013, its second ratifying state, Samoa, on 25 September 2013, and its third ratifying state, Trinidad and Tobago, on 13 November 2013. However, the Court will only have jurisdiction over the crime of aggression after it enters into force for 30 states parties and after the Assembly of States Parties has voted in favour of allowing the Court to have jurisdiction after 1 January 2017.

The Court can generally exercise jurisdiction only in three cases, viz. if the accused is a national of a state party, if the alleged crime took place on the territory of a state party or if a situation is referred to the Court by the United Nations Security Council. It is designed to complement existing national judicial systems: it can exercise its jurisdiction only when national courts are unwilling or unable to investigate or prosecute such crimes. Primary responsibility to investigate and punish crimes is therefore left to individual states.

To date, the Court has opened investigations into seven situations in Africa: the Democratic Republic of the Congo; Uganda; the Central African Republic; Darfur, Sudan; the Republic of Kenya; the Libyan Arab Jamahiriya and the Republic of Côte d'Ivoire. Of these seven, three were referred to the Court by the concerned states parties themselves (Uganda, Democratic Republic of the Congo and the Central African Republic), two were referred by the United Nations Security Council (Darfur and Libya) and two were begun proprio motu by the Prosecutor (Kenya and Côte d'Ivoire). Additionally, the government of Mali has referred the situation in the country to the Prosecutor. As Mali is a state party to the Rome Statute, the Prosecutor can now directly open a formal investigation once she has concluded the preliminary examination.

It has publicly indicted 30 people, proceedings against 24 of whom are ongoing. The ICC has issued arrest warrants for 21 individuals and summonses to nine others. Five individuals are in custody; one of them has been found guilty and sentenced (with an appeal lodged) while four of them are being tried. Ten individuals remain at large as fugitives (although one is reported to have died). Additionally, three individuals have been arrested by national authorities, but have not yet been transferred to the Court. Proceedings against six individuals have finished following the death of two and the dismissal of charges against the other four.

As of November 2012, the Court's first trial, the Lubanga trial in the situation of the DR Congo, is in the appeals phase after the accused was found guilty and sentenced to 14 years in prison and a reparations regime was established. The Katanga-Chui trial regarding the DR Congo was concluded in May 2012; the judgment with regard to Mr Ngudjolo Chui is to be delivered on 18 December 2012. The Bemba trial regarding the Central African Republic is ongoing with the defence presenting its evidence. A fourth trial chamber, for the Banda-Jerbo trial in the situation of Darfur, Sudan, has been established. There are a fifth and a sixth trial both scheduled to begin in April 2013 in the Kenya situation, namely the Ruto-Sang and the Muthaura-Kenyatta trials for which a single Trial Chamber is responsible. The confirmation of charges hearing dates in the Gbagbo case in the Côte d'Ivoire situation will be announced shortly.

History of ICC

The establishment of an international tribunal to judge political leaders accused of war crimes was first made during the Paris Peace Conference in 1919 by the Commission of Responsibilities. The issue was addressed again at a conference held in Geneva under the auspices of the League of Nations on 1–16 November 1937, which resulted in the conclusion of the first convention stipulating the establishment of a permanent international court to try acts of international terrorism. The convention was signed by 13 governments, but was never ratified, and the convention never entered into effect.

The United Nations stated that the General Assembly first recognised the need for a permanent international court to deal with atrocities of the kind committed during World War II in 1948, following the Nuremberg and Tokyo Tribunals. At the request of the General Assembly, the International Law Commission drafted two statutes by the early 1950s but these were shelved as the Cold War made the establishment of an international criminal court politically unrealistic.

Benjamin B. Ferencz, an investigator of Nazi war crimes after World War II and the Chief Prosecutor for the United States Army at the Einsatzgruppen Trial, one of the twelve military trials held by the U.S. authorities at Nuremberg, later became a vocal advocate of the establishment of an international rule of law and of an International Criminal Court. In his first book published in 1975, entitled Defining International Aggression - The Search for World Peace, he argued for the establishment of such an international court.

The idea was revived in 1989 when A. N. R. Robinson, then Prime Minister of Trinidad and Tobago, proposed the creation of a permanent international court to deal with the illegal drug trade. While work began on a draft statute, the international community established ad hoc tribunals to try war crimes in the former Yugoslavia and Rwanda, established in 1994, further highlighting the need for a permanent international criminal court.

In June 1989, motivated in part by an effort to combat drug trafficking, Trinidad and Tobago resurrected a pre-existing proposal for the establishment of an ICC and the UN GA asked that the ILC resume its work on drafting a statute.In June 1989, motivated in part by an effort to combat drug trafficking, Trinidad and Tobago resurrected a pre-existing proposal for the establishment of an ICC and the UN GA asked that the ILC resume its work on drafting a statute. The conflicts in Bosnia-Herzegovina and Croatia as well as in Rwanda in the early 1990s and the mass commission of crimes against humanity, war crimes, and genocide led the UN Security Council to establish two separate temporary ad hoc tribunals to hold individuals accountable for these atrocities, further highlighting the need for a permanent international criminal court.

In 1994, the ILC presented its final draft statute for an ICC to the UN GA and recommended that a conference of plenipotentiaries be convened to negotiate a treaty and enact the Statute. To consider major substantive issues in the draft statute, the General Assembly established the Ad Hoc Committee on the Establishment of an International Criminal Court, which met twice in 1995.

After considering the Committee's report, the UN GA created the Preparatory Committee on the Establishment of the ICC to prepare a consolidated draft text. From 1996 to 1998, six sessions of the UN Preparatory Committee were held at the United Nations headquarters in New York, in which NGOs provided input into the discussions and attended meetings under the umbrella of the NGO Coalition for an ICC (CICC). In January 1998, the Bureau and coordinators of the Preparatory Committee convened for an Inter-Sessional meeting in Zutphen, the Netherlands to technically consolidate and restructure the draft articles into a draft.

Following years of negotiations, the General Assembly convened a conference in Rome in June 1998, with the aim of finalizing a treaty. On 17 July 1998, the Rome Statute of the International Criminal Court was adopted by a vote of 120 to 7, with 21 countries abstaining. The seven countries that voted against the treaty were China, Iraq, Israel, Libya, Qatar, United States, and Yemen.

The Rome Statute became a binding treaty on 11 April 2002, when the number of countries that had ratified it reached sixty. The Statute legally came into force on 1 July 2002, and the ICC can only prosecute crimes committed after that date. The first bench of 18 judges was elected by an Assembly of States Parties in February 2003. They were sworn in at the inaugural session of the Court on 11 March 2003. The Court issued its first arrest warrants on 8 July 2005, and the first pre-trial hearings were held in 2006.

During a Review Conference of the International Criminal Court Statute in Kampala, Uganda, two amendments to the Rome Statute of the International Criminal Court were adopted on 10 and 11 June 2010. The second amendment concerns the definition of the crime of aggression.

State Parties

As of July 2012, 121 states are states parties to the Statute of the Court, including all of South America, nearly all of Europe and roughly half the countries in Africa. A further 32 countries, including Russia, have signed but not ratified the Rome Statute; one of them, Ivory Coast, has accepted the Court's jurisdiction. The law of treaties obliges these states to refrain from "acts which would defeat the object and purpose" of the treaty until they declare they do not intend to become a party to the treaty. Three of these states—Israel, Sudan and the United States—have informed the UN

Secretary General that they no longer intend to become states parties and, as such, have no legal obligations arising from their former representatives' signature of the Statute. 41 United Nations member states have neither signed nor ratified or acceded to the Rome Statute; some of them, including China and India, are critical of the Court. The Palestinian National Authority, which neither is nor represents a United Nations member state, has formally accepted the jurisdiction of the Court. On 3 April 2012, the ICC Prosecutor declared himself unable to determine that Palestine is a "state" for the purposes of the Rome Statute.

In January 2009, the Office of the Prosecutor of the International Criminal Court received an official communication from the Minister of Justice of the Palestinian Authority (PA), Ali Kashan, which expressed the PA's readiness to recognize the jurisdiction of the ICC over "the territory of Palestine." The PA's declaration purported to invoke Article 12 (3) of the Rome Statute, which specifically enables "a state which is not a party to this Statute" to request that the ICC exercise its jurisdiction on an ad hoc basis with respect to an alleged crime on that state's territory or involving its nationals.

In April 2012, the ICC rejected the request. "International arenas are routinely hijacked for political purposes, but today's decision was markedly different," said Anne Herzberg, legal adviser for NGO Monitor. According to the Jerusalem Post, "had the ICC accepted the PA's recognition of its jurisdiction, it would have also tacitly accepted its statehood."

Jurisdiction

Article 5 of the Rome Statute grants the Court jurisdiction over four groups of crimes, which it refers to as the "most serious crimes of concern to the international community as a whole": the crime of genocide, crimes against humanity, war crimes, and the crime of aggression. The Statute defines each of these crimes except for aggression. The crime of genocide is unique because the crime must be committed with 'intent to destroy'. Crimes against humanity are specifically listed prohibited acts when committed as part of a widespread or systematic attack directed against any civilian population. The Statute provides that the Court will not exercise its jurisdiction over the crime of aggression until such time as the states parties agree on a definition of the crime and set out the conditions under which it may be prosecuted.

In June 2010, the ICC's first review conference in Kampala, Uganda adopted amendments defining "crimes of aggression" and expanding the ICC's jurisdiction over them. The ICC will not be allowed to prosecute for this crime until at least 2017. Furthermore, it expanded the term of war crimes for the use of certain weapons in an armed conflict not of an international character.

Many states wanted to add terrorism and drug trafficking to the list of crimes covered by the Rome Statute; however, the states were unable to agree on a definition for terrorism and it was decided not to include drug trafficking as this might overwhelm the Court's limited resources. India lobbied to have the use of nuclear weapons and other weapons of mass destruction included as war crimes but this move was also defeated. India has expressed concern that "the Statute of the ICC lays down, by clear implication, that the use of weapons of mass destruction is not a war crime. This is an extraordinary message to send to the international community."

Some commentators have argued that the Rome Statute defines crimes too broadly or too vaguely. For example, China has argued that the definition of 'war crimes' goes beyond that accepted under customary international law.

Territorial Jurisdiction

During the negotiations that led to the Rome Statute, a large number of states argued that the Court should be allowed to exercise universal jurisdiction. However, this proposal was defeated due in large part to opposition from the United States. A compromise was reached, allowing the Court to exercise jurisdiction only under the following limited circumstances:

- where the person accused of committing a crime is a national of a state party (or where the person's state has accepted the jurisdiction of the Court);
- where the alleged crime was committed on the territory of a state party (or where the state on whose territory the crime was committed has accepted the jurisdiction of the Court); or
- where a situation is referred to the Court by the UN Security Council.

Temporal Jurisdiction

The Court's jurisdiction does not apply retroactively: it can only prosecute crimes committed on or after 1 July 2002 (the date on which the Rome Statute entered into force). Where a state becomes party to the Rome Statute after that date, the Court can exercise jurisdiction automatically with respect to crimes committed after the Statute enters into force for that state.

Complementarity

The ICC is intended as a court of last resort, investigating and prosecuting only where national courts have failed. Article 17 of the Statute provides that a case is inadmissible if:

"(a) The case is being investigated or prosecuted by a State which has jurisdiction over it, unless the State is unwilling or unable genuinely to carry out the investigation or prosecution;

(b) The case has been investigated by a State which has jurisdiction over it and the State has decided not to prosecute the person concerned, unless the decision resulted from the unwillingness or inability of the State genuinely to prosecute;

(c) The person concerned has already been tried for conduct which is the subject of the complaint, and a trial by the Court is not permitted under article 20, paragraph 3;

(d) The case is not of sufficient gravity to justify further action by the Court."

Article 20, paragraph 3, specifies that, if a person has already been tried by another court, the ICC cannot try them again for the same conduct unless the proceedings in the other court:

"(a) Were for the purpose of shielding the person concerned from criminal responsibility for crimes within the jurisdiction of the Court; or (b) Otherwise were not conducted independently or impartially in accordance with the norms of due process recognized by international law and were conducted in a manner which, in the circumstances, was inconsistent with an intent to bring the person concerned to justice."

Structure of ICC

The ICC is governed by an Assembly of States Parties. The Court consists of four main organs: the Presidency, the Judicial Divisions, the Office of the Prosecutor, and the Registry.

Assembly of States Parties

The Court's management oversight and legislative body, the Assembly of States Parties, consists of one representative from each state party. Each state party has one vote and "every effort" has to be made to reach decisions by consensus. If consensus cannot be reached, decisions are made by vote. The Assembly is presided over by a president and two vice-presidents, who are elected by the members to three-year terms.

The Assembly meets in full session once a year in New York or The Hague, and may also hold special sessions where circumstances require. Sessions are open to observer states and non-governmental organizations.

The Assembly elects the judges and prosecutors, decides the Court's budget, adopts important texts (such as the Rules of Procedure and Evidence), and provides management oversight to the other organs of the Court. Article 46 of the Rome Statute allows the Assembly to remove from office a judge or prosecutor who "is found to have committed serious misconduct or a serious breach of his or her duties" or "is unable to exercise the functions required by this Statute".

The states parties cannot interfere with the judicial functions of the Court. Disputes concerning individual cases are settled by the Judicial Divisions.

Presidency

The Presidency is responsible for the proper administration of the Court (apart from the Office of the Prosecutor). It comprises the President and the First and Second Vice-Presidents—three judges of the Court who are elected to the Presidency by their fellow judges for a maximum of two three-year terms. The current President is Sang-Hyun Song, who was elected on 11 March 2009.

Judicial Divisions

The Judicial Divisions consist of the 18 judges of the Court, organized into three chambers—the Pre-Trial Chamber, Trial Chamber and Appeals Chamber—which carry out the judicial functions of the Court. Judges are elected to the Court by the Assembly of States Parties. They serve nine-year terms and are not generally eligible for re-election. All judges must be nationals of states parties to the Rome Statute, and no two judges may be nationals of the same state. They must be "persons of high moral character, impartiality and integrity who possess the qualifications required in their respective States for appointment to the highest judicial offices".

The Prosecutor or any person being investigated or prosecuted may request the disqualification of a judge from "any case in which his or her impartiality might reasonably be doubted on any ground". Any request for the disqualification of a judge from a particular case is decided by an absolute majority of the other judges. A judge may be removed from office if he or she "is found to have committed serious misconduct or a serious breach of his or her duties" or is unable to exercise his or her functions. The removal of a judge requires both a two-thirds majority of the other judges and a two-thirds majority of the states parties.

Office of the Prosecutor

The Office of the Prosecutor is responsible for conducting investigations and prosecutions. It is headed by the Chief Prosecutor, who is assisted by one or more Deputy Prosecutors. The Rome Statute provides that the Office of the Prosecutor shall act independently; as such, no member of the Office may seek or act on instructions from any external source, such as states, international organisations, non-governmental organisations or individuals.

The Prosecutor may open an investigation under three circumstances:

- when a situation is referred to him or her by a state party;
- when a situation is referred to him or her by the United Nations Security Council, acting to address a threat to international peace and security; or
- when the Pre-Trial Chamber authorises him or her to open an investigation on the basis of information received from other sources, such as individuals or non-governmental organisations.

Any person being investigated or prosecuted may request the disqualification of a prosecutor from any case "in which their impartiality might reasonably be doubted on any ground". Requests for the disqualification of prosecutors are decided by the Appeals Chamber. A prosecutor may be removed from office by an absolute majority of the states parties if he or she "is found to have committed serious misconduct or a serious breach of his or her duties" or is unable to exercise his or her functions. However, critics of the Court argue that there are "insufficient checks and balances on the authority of the ICC prosecutor and judges" and "insufficient protection against politicized prosecutions or other abuses". Henry Kissinger says the checks and balances are so weak that the prosecutor "has virtually unlimited discretion in practice".

As of 16 June 2012, the Prosecutor has been Fatou Bensouda of Gambia who had been elected as the new Prosecutor on 12 December 2011. She has been elected for nine years. Her predecessor, Luis Moreno Ocampo of Argentina, had been in office from 2003 to 2012.

Registry

The Registry is responsible for the non-judicial aspects of the administration and servicing of the Court. This includes, among other things, "the administration of legal aid matters, court management, victims and witnesses matters, defence counsel, detention unit, and the traditional services provided by administrations in international organisations, such as finance, translation, building management, procurement and personnel". The Registry is headed by the Registrar, who is elected by the judges to a five-year term. The current Registrar is Silvana Arbia, who was elected on 28 February 2008.

Headquarters, Offices and Detention Unit

The official seat of the Court is in The Hague, Netherlands, but its proceedings may take place anywhere.

The Court is currently housed in interim premises on the eastern edge of The Hague. It intends to construct the ICC Permanent Premises in the Alexanderkazerne, to the north of The Hague. The land and financing for the new construction have been provided by the Netherlands, and architects schmidt hammer lassen have been retained to design the project.

The ICC also maintains a liaison office in New York and field offices in places where it conducts its activities. As of 18 October 2007, the Court had field offices in Kampala, Kinshasa, Bunia, Abéché and Bangui.

The ICC's detention centre comprises twelve cells on the premises of the Scheveningen branch of the Haaglanden Penal Institution, The Hague. Suspects held by the International Criminal Tribunal for the former Yugoslavia are held in the same prison and share some facilities, like the fitness room, but have no contact with suspects held by the ICC. The detention unit is close to the ICC's future headquarters in the Alexanderkazerne.

As of July 2012, the detention centre houses one person convicted by the court, Thomas Lubanga, and four suspects: Germain Katanga, Mathieu Ngudjolo Chui, Jean-Pierre Bemba and Laurent Gbagbo. Additionally, former Liberian President Charles Taylor is held there. Taylor was tried under the mandate and auspices of the Special Court for Sierra Leone, but his trial was held at the ICC's facilities in The Hague because of political and security concerns about holding the trial in Freetown. On 26 April 2012, Taylor was convicted on eleven charges.

The ICC does not have its own witness protection program, but rather must rely on national programs to keep witnesses safe.

Procedures

Trial

Trials are conducted under a hybrid common law and civil law judicial system, but it has been argued the procedural orientation and character of the court is still evolving. A majority of the 3 judges present, as triers of fact, may reach a decision, which must include a full and reasoned statement. Trials are supposed to be public, but proceedings are often closed, and such exceptions to a public trial have not been enumerated in detail. In camera proceedings are allowed for protection of witnesses or defendants as well as for confidential or sensitive evidence. Hearsay and other indirect evidence is not generally prohibited, but it has been argued the court is guided by hearsay exceptions which are prominent in common law systems. There is no subpoena or other means to compel witnesses to come before the court, although the court has some power to compel testimony of those who are, such as fines.

Rights of the Accused

The Rome Statute provides that all persons are presumed innocent until proven guilty beyond reasonable doubt, and establishes certain rights of the accused and persons during investigations. These include the right to be fully informed of the charges against him or her; the right to have a lawyer appointed, free of charge; the right to a speedy trial; and the right to examine the witnesses against him or her.

Some argue that the protections offered by the ICC are insufficient. According to the Heritage Foundation "Americans who appear before the court would be denied such basic constitutional rights as trial by a jury of one's peers, protection from double jeopardy, and the right to confront one's accusers." However, the Human Rights Watch argues that the ICC standards are sufficient, saying, "the ICC has one of the most extensive lists of due process guarantees ever written", including "presumption of innocence; right to counsel; right to present evidence and to confront witnesses; right to remain silent; right to be present at trial; right to have charges proved beyond a reasonable doubt; and protection against double jeopardy".

According to David Scheffer, who led the US delegation to the Rome Conference and who voted against adoption of the treaty, "when we were negotiating the Rome treaty, we always kept very close tabs on, 'Does this meet U.S. constitutional tests, the formation of this court and the due process rights that are accorded defendants?' And we were very confident at the end of Rome that those due process rights, in fact, are protected, and that this treaty does meet a constitutional test."

To ensure "equality of arms" between defence and prosecution teams, the ICC has established an independent Office of Public Counsel for the Defence (OPCD) to provide logistical support, advice and information to defendants and their counsel. The OPCD also helps to safeguard the rights of the accused during the initial stages of an investigation. However, Thomas Lubanga's defence team say they were given a smaller budget than the Prosecutor and that evidence and witness statements were slow to arrive.

The trial court procedures are similar to the US Guantanamo military commissions.

Victim Participation and Reparations

One of the great innovations of the Statute of the International Criminal Court and its Rules of Procedure and Evidence is the series of rights granted to victims. For the first time in the history of international criminal justice, victims have the possibility under the Statute to present their views and observations before the Court.

Participation before the Court may occur at various stages of proceedings and may take different forms, although it will be up to the judges to give directions as to the timing and manner of participation.

Participation in the Court's proceedings will in most cases take place through a legal representative and will be conducted "in a manner which is not prejudicial or inconsistent with the rights of the accused and a fair and impartial trial".

The victim-based provisions within the Rome Statute provide victims with the opportunity to have their voices heard and to obtain, where appropriate, some form of reparation for their suffering. It is this balance between retributive and restorative justice that will enable the ICC, not only to bring criminals to justice but also to help the victims themselves obtain justice.

Article 43(6) establishes a Victims and Witnesses Unit to provide "protective measures and security arrangements, counseling and other appropriate assistance for witnesses, victims who appear before the Court, and others who are at risk on account of testimony given by such witnesses." Article 68 sets out procedures for the "Protection of the victims and witnesses and their participation in the proceedings." The Court has also established an Office of Public Counsel for Victims, to provide support and assistance to victims and their legal representatives. Article 79 of the Rome Statute establishes a Trust Fund to make financial reparations to victims and their families.

Participation of Victims in Proceedings

The Rome Statute contains provisions which enable victims to participate in all stages of the proceedings before the Court.

Hence victims may file submissions before the Pre-Trial Chamber when the Prosecutor requests its authorisation to investigate. They may also file submissions on all matters relating to the competence of the Court or the admissibility of cases.

More generally, victims are entitled to file submissions before the Court chambers at the pre-trial stage, during the proceedings or at the appeal stage.

The rules of procedure and evidence stipulate the time for victim participation in proceedings before the Court. They must send a written application to the Court Registrar and more precisely to the Victims' Participation and Reparation Section, which must submit the application to the competent Chamber which decides on the arrangements for the victims' participation in the proceedings. The Chamber may reject the application if it considers that the person is not a victim. Individuals who wish to make applications to participate in proceedings before the Court must therefore provide evidence proving they are victims of crimes which come under the competence of the Court in the proceedings commenced before it. The Section prepared standard forms and a booklet to make it easier for victims to file their petition to participate in the proceedings.

It should be stipulated that a petition may be made by a person acting with the consent of the victim, or in their name when the victim is a child or if any disability makes this necessary.

Victims are free to choose their legal representative who must be equally as qualified as the counsel for the defence (this may be a lawyer or person with experience as a judge or prosecutor) and be fluent in one of the Court's two working languages (English or French).

To ensure efficient proceedings, particularly in cases with many victims, the competent Chamber may ask victims to choose a shared legal representative. If the victims are unable to appoint one, the Chamber may ask the Registrar to appoint one or more shared legal representatives. The Victims' Participation and Reparation Section is responsible for assisting victims with the organisation of their legal representation before the Court. When a victim or a group of victims does not have the means to pay for a shared legal representative appointed by the Court, they may request financial aid from the Court to pay counsel. Counsel may participate in the proceedings before the Court by filing submissions and attending the hearings.

The Registry, and within it the Victims' Participation and Reparation Section, has many obligations with regard to notification of the proceedings to the victims to keep them fully informed of progress. Thus, it is stipulated that the Section must notify victims, who have communicated with the Court in a given case or situation, of any decisions by the Prosecutor not to open an investigation or not to commence a prosecution, so that these victims can file submissions before the Pre-Trial Chamber responsible for checking the decisions taken by the Prosecutor under the conditions laid down in the Statute. The same notification is required before the confirmation hearing in the Pre-Trial Chamber to allow the victims to file all the submissions they require. All decisions taken by the Court are then notified to the victims who participated in the proceedings or to their counsel. The Victims' Participation and Reparation Section has wide discretion to use all possible means to give adequate publicity to the proceedings before the Court (local media, requests for co-operation sent to Governments, aid requested from NGOs or other means).

Reparation for Victims

For the first time in the history of humanity, an international court has the power to order an individual to pay reparation to another individual; it is also the first time that an international criminal court has had such power.

Pursuant to article 75, the Court may lay down the principles for reparation for victims, which may include restitution, indemnification and rehabilitation. On this point, the Rome Statute of the International Criminal Court has benefited from all the work carried out with regard to victims, in particular within the United Nations.

The Court must also enter an order against a convicted person stating the appropriate reparation for the victims or their beneficiaries. This reparation may also take the form of restitution, indemnification or rehabilitation. The Court may order this reparation to be paid through the Trust Fund for Victims, which was set up by the Assembly of States Parties in September 2002.

To be able to apply for reparation, victims have to file a written application with the Registry, which must contain the evidence laid down in Rule 94 of the Rules of Procedure and Evidence. The Victims' Participation and Reparation Section prepared standard forms to make this easier for victims. They may also apply for protective measures for the purposes of confiscating property from the persons prosecuted.

The Victims' Participation and Reparation Section is responsible for giving all appropriate publicity to these reparation proceedings to enable victims to make their applications. These proceedings take place after the person prosecuted has been declared guilty of the alleged facts.

The Court has the option of granting individual or collective reparation, concerning a whole group of victims or a community, or both. If the Court decides to order collective reparation, it may order that reparation to be made through the Victims' Fund and the reparation may then also be paid to an inter-governmental, international or national organisation.

Co-operation by States Not Party to Rome Statute

One of the principles of international law is that a treaty does not create either obligations or rights for third states (pacta tertiis nec nocent nec prosunt) without their consent, and this is also enshrined in the 1969 Vienna Convention on the Law of Treaties. The co-operation of the non-party states with the ICC is envisioned by the Rome Statute of the International Criminal Court to be of voluntary nature. However, even states that have not acceded to the Rome Statute might still be subjects to an obligation to co-operate with ICC in certain cases. When a case is referred to the ICC by the UN Security Council all UN member states are obliged to co-operate, since its decisions are binding for all of them. Also, there is an obligation to respect and ensure respect for international humanitarian law, which stems from the Geneva Conventions and Additional Protocol I, which reflects the absolute nature of IHL. Although the wording of the Conventions might not be precise as to what steps have to be taken, it has been argued that it at least requires non-party states to make an effort not to block actions of ICC in response to serious violations of those Conventions. In relation to co-operation in investigation and evidence gathering, it is implied from the Rome Statute that the consent of a non-party state is a prerequisite for ICC Prosecutor to conduct an investigation within its territory, and it seems that it is even more necessary for him to observe any reasonable conditions raised by that state, since such restrictions exist for states party to the Statute. Taking into account the experience of the ICTY (which worked with the principle of the primacy, instead of complementarity) in relation to co-operation, some scholars have expressed their pessimism as to the possibility of ICC to obtain co-operation of non-party states.

As for the actions that ICC can take towards non-party states that do not co-operate, the Rome Statute stipulates that the Court may inform the Assembly of States Parties or Security Council, when the matter was referred by it, when non-party state refuses to co-operate after it has entered into an ad hoc arrangement or an agreement with the Court.

Amnesties and National Reconciliation Processes

It is unclear to what extent the ICC is compatible with reconciliation processes that grant amnesty to human rights abusers as part of agreements to end conflict. Article 16 of the Rome Statute allows the Security Council to prevent the Court from investigating or prosecuting a case, and Article 53 allows the Prosecutor the discretion not to initiate an investigation if he or she believes that "an investigation would not serve the interests of justice". Former ICC President Philippe Kirsch has said that "some limited amnesties may be compatible" with a country's obligations genuinely to investigate or prosecute under the Statute.

It is sometimes argued that amnesties are necessary to allow the peaceful transfer of power from abusive regimes. By denying states the right to offer amnesty to human rights abusers, the International Criminal Court may make it more difficult to negotiate an end to conflict and a transition to democracy. For example, the outstanding arrest warrants for four leaders of the Lord's Resistance Army are regarded by some as an obstacle to ending the insurgency in Uganda. Czech politician Marek Benda argues that "the ICC as a deterrent will in our view only mean the worst dictators will try to retain power at all costs". However, the United Nations and the International Committee of the Red Cross maintain that granting amnesty to those accused of war crimes and other serious crimes is a violation of international law.

Relationships with Other Agencies

United Nations

Unlike the International Court of Justice, the ICC is legally independent from the United Nations. However, the Rome Statute grants certain powers to the United Nations Security Council. Because the ICC cannot look into anything that happened before its establishment in 2002, it cannot be said that the ICC is functionally independent from the UN. Article 13 allows the Security Council to refer to the Court situations that would not otherwise fall under the Court's jurisdiction (as it did in relation to the situations in Darfur and Libya, which the Court could not otherwise have prosecuted as neither Sudan nor Libya are state parties). Article 16 allows the Security Council to require the Court to defer from investigating a case for a period of 12 months. Such a deferral may be renewed indefinitely by the Security Council. This sort of an arrangement gives the ICC some of the advantages inhering in the organs of the United Nations such as using the enforcement powers of the Security Council but it also creates a risk of being tainted with the political controversies of the Security Council.

The Court cooperates with the UN in many different areas, including the exchange of information and logistical support. The Court reports to the UN each year on its activities, and some meetings of the Assembly of States Parties are held at UN facilities. The relationship between the Court and the UN is governed by a "Relationship Agreement between the International Criminal Court and the United Nations".

Nongovernmental Organizations

During the 1970s and 1980s, international human rights and humanitarian Nongovernmental Organizations (or NGOs) began to proliferate at exponential rates. Concurrently, the quest to find a way to punish international crimes shifted from being the exclusive responsibility of legal experts to being shared with international human rights activism.

NGOs helped birth the ICC through advocacy and championing for the prosecution of perpetrators of crimes against humanity. NGOs closely monitor the organization's declarations and actions, ensuring that the work that is being executed on behalf of the ICC is fulfilling its objectives and responsibilities to civil society. According to Benjamin Schiff, "From the Statute Conference onward, the relationship between the ICC and the NGOs has probably been closer, more consistent, and more vital to the Court than have analogous relations between NGOs and any other international organization."

There are a number of NGOs working on a variety of issues related to the ICC. The NGO Coalition for the International Criminal Court has served as a sort of umbrella for NGOs to coordinate with each other on similar objectives related to the ICC. The CICC has 2,500 member organizations in 150 different countries.

The original steering committee included representatives from the World Federalist Movement, the International Commission of Jurists, Amnesty International, the Lawyers Committee for Human Rights, Human Rights Watch, Parliamentarians for Global Action, and No Peace Without Justice. Today, many of the NGOs with which the ICC cooperates are members of the CICC. These organizations come from a range of backgrounds, spanning from major international NGOs such as Human Rights Watch and Amnesty International, to smaller, more local organizations focused on peace and justice missions. Many work closely with states, such as the International Criminal Law Network, founded and predominantly funded by The Hague municipality and the Dutch Ministries of Defense and Foreign Affairs. The CICC also claims organizations that are themselves federations, such as the International Federation of Human Rights Leagues (FIDH).

CICC members ascribe to three principles that permit them to work under the umbrella of the CICC, so long as their objectives match them:

- Promoting worldwide ratification and implementation of the Rome Statute of the ICC
- Maintaining the integrity of the Rome Statute of the ICC, and
- Ensuring the ICC will be as fair, effective and independent as possible

The NGOs that work under the CICC do not normally pursue agendas exclusive to the work of the Court, rather they may work for broader causes, such as general human rights issues, victims' rights, gender rights, rule of law, conflict mediation, and peace. The CICC coordinates their efforts to improve the efficiency of NGOs' contributions to the Court and to pool their influence on major common issues. From the ICC side, it has been useful to have the CICC channel NGO contacts with the Court so that its officials do not have to interact individually with thousands of separate organizations.

NGOs have been crucial to the evolution of the ICC, as they assisted in the creation of the normative climate that urged states to seriously consider the Court's formation. Their legal experts helped shape the Statute, while their lobbying efforts built support for it. They advocate Statute ratification globally and work at expert and political levels within member states for passage of necessary domestic legislation. NGOs are greatly represented at meetings for the Assembly of States Parties and they use the ASP meetings to press for decisions promoting their priorities. Many of these NGOs have reasonable access to important officials at the ICC because of their involvement during the Statute process. They are engaged in monitoring, commenting upon, and assisting in the ICC's activities.

The ICC many time depends on NGOs to interact with local populations. The Registry Public Information Office personnel and Victims Participation and Reparations Section officials hold seminars for local leaders, professionals and the media to spread the word about the Court. These are the kinds of events that are often hosted or organized by local NGOs. Because there can be challenges with determining which of these NGOs are legitimate, CICC regional representatives often have the ability to help screen and identify trustworthy organizations.

However, NGOs are also "sources of criticism, exhortation and pressure upon" the ICC. The ICC heavily depends on NGOs for its operations. Although NGOs and states cannot directly impact the judicial nucleus of the organization, they can impart information on crimes, can help locate victims and witnesses, and can promote and organize victim participation.

NGOs outwardly comment on the Court's operations, "push for expansion of its activities especially in the new justice areas of outreach in conflict areas, in victims' participation and reparations, an in upholding due-process standards and defense 'equality of arms' and so implicitly set an agenda for the future evolution of the ICC." The relatively uninterrupted progression of NGO involvement with the ICC may mean that NGOs have become repositories of more institutional historical knowledge about the ICC than have national representatives to it and have greater expertise than some of the organization's employees themselves. While NGOs look to mold the ICC to satisfy the interests and priorities that they have worked for since the early 1990s, they unavoidably press against the limits imposed upon the ICC by the states that are members of the organization. NGOs can pursue their own mandates, irrespective of whether they are compatible with those of other NGOs, while the ICC must respond to the complexities of its own mandate as well as those of the states and NGOs.

Another issue has been that NGOs possess “”exaggerated senses of their ownership over the organization and, having been vital to and successful in promoting the Court, were not managing to redefine their roles to permit the Court its necessary independence." Additionally, because there does exist such a gap between the large human rights organizations and the smaller peace-oriented organizations, it is difficult for ICC officials to manage and gratify all of their NGOs. "ICC officials recognize that the NGOs pursue their own agendas, and that they will seek to pressure the ICC in the direction of their own priorities rather than necessarily understanding or being fully sympathetic to the myriad constraints and pressures under which the Court operates." Both the ICC and the NGO community avoid criticizing each other publicly or vehemently, although NGOs have released advisory and cautionary messages regarding the ICC. They avoid taking stances that could potentially give the Court's adversaries, particularly the US, more motive to berate the organization.

Finance

The ICC is financed by contributions from the states parties. The amount payable by each state party is determined using the same method as the United Nations: each state's contribution is based on the country's capacity to pay, which reflects factors such as a national income and population. The maximum amount a single country can pay in any year is limited to 22% of the Court's budget; Japan paid this amount in 2008. The Court spent •80.5 million in 2007, and the Assembly of States Parties has approved a budget of •90,382,100 for 2008 and •101,229,900 for 2009. As of September 2008, the ICC's staff consisted of 571 persons from 83 states.

Investigations of ICC

So far, the International Criminal Court has opened investigations into seven situations in Africa: the Democratic Republic of the Congo; Uganda; the Central African Republic; Darfur, Sudan; the Republic of Kenya; the Libyan Arab Jamahiriya and the Republic of Côte d'Ivoire. Of these seven, three were referred to the Court by the concerned states parties themselves (Uganda, Democratic Republic of the Congo and the Central African Republic), two were referred by the United Nations Security Council (Darfur and Libya) and two were begun proprio motu by the Prosecutor (Kenya and Côte d'Ivoire). Additionally, the government of Mali has referred the situation in the country to the Prosecutor. As Mali is a state party to the Rome Statute, the Prosecutor can now directly open a formal investigation once she has concluded the preliminary examination.

The Court publicly indicted 30 people, proceedings against 24 of whom are ongoing. The ICC has issued arrest warrants for 21 individuals and summonses to nine others. Five individuals are in custody; one of them has been found guilty and sentenced (with an appeal lodged) while four of them are being tried. Ten individuals remain at large as fugitives (although one is reported to have died). Additionally, three individuals have been arrested by national authorities, but have not yet been transferred to the Court. Proceedings against six individuals have finished following the death of two and the dismissal of charges against the other four.

As of end September 2010, the Office of the Prosecutor had received 8,874 communications about alleged crimes. After initial review, 4,002 of these communications were dismissed as "manifestly outside the jurisdiction of the Court".

How an Investigation is Opened

The Prosecutor may open an investigation under three circumstances:

- when a situation is referred to him by a state party;
- when a situation is referred to him by the United Nations Security Council, acting to address a threat to international peace and security;

or

- when the Pre-Trial Chamber authorises him to open an investigation on the basis of information received from other sources, such as individuals or non-governmental organisations.

Of the seven situations the Prosecutor has investigated to date, three were referred by states parties, two were referred by the Security Council, and in two the Pre-Trial Chamber authorised him to open an investigation based on information received from other sources.

Active Investigations

Uganda

In December 2003, the government of Uganda, a state party, referred to the Prosecutor the situation concerning the Lord's Resistance Army in Northern Uganda. The Prosecutor decided to open an investigation into this matter on 29 July 2004, and on 5 July the situation was assigned to Pre-Trial Chamber II.

On 8 July 2005, the Court issued its first public arrest warrants for five senior leaders of the LRA alleging:

Leader Joseph Kony committed the crimes against humanity of murder, enslavement, sexual enslavement, rape and serious bodily injury and the war crimes of murder, cruel treatment of civilians, attacking civilians, pillage, inducing rape and enlisting child soldiers

Kony's deputy, Vincent Otti, committed the crimes against humanity of murder, sexual enslavement and serious bodily injury and the war crimes of inducing rape, attacking civilians, enlisting child soldiers, cruel treatment of civilians, pillage and murder

Army Commander of the LRA, Okot Odiambo committed the crime against humanity of enslavement and war crimes of attacking civilians, pillage and enlisting child soldiers; Odiambo reportedly led an attack on Barlonyo refugee camp (Aromo sub-county, Erute north constituency,Lira District) in February 2004 when more than 300 people were massacred.

LRA commander Raska Lukwiya committed the crime against humanity of enslavement and the war crimes of cruel treatment of civilians, attacking civilians and pillage

LRA commander Dominic Ongwen committed the crimes against humanity of murder, enslavement and serious bodily injury and the war crimes of murder, cruel treatment of civilians, attacking civilians and pillage

None of the indictees have yet been arrested but Lukwiya was killed in fighting on 12 August 2006, and Otti is said to have been killed in 2007, apparently by Kony. The other three suspects are believed to be either in Southern Sudan or the northwestern Ituri Province of the Democratic Republic of the Congo.

The government of Uganda is currently in peace talks with the LRA. The LRA's leaders have repeatedly demanded immunity from ICC prosecution in return for an end to the insurgency. The government of Uganda says it is considering establishing a national tribunal that meets international standards, thereby allowing the ICC warrants to be set aside.

Democratic Republic of the Congo

In March 2004, the government of the Democratic Republic of the Congo, a state party, referred to the Prosecutor "the situation of crimes within the jurisdiction of the Court allegedly committed anywhere in the territory of the DRC since the entry into force of the Rome Statute, on 1 July 2002." On 23 June, the Prosecutor decided to open an investigation into the matter and on 4 July the case was allocated to Pre-Trial Chamber I. In February 2008, at the time of the arrest of the third suspect, the Prosecutor announced that this arrest had closed the ICC investigations in Ituri.

Thomas Lubanga

On 17 March 2006, Thomas Lubanga, former leader of the Union of Congolese Patriots militia in Ituri, became the first person to be arrested under a warrant issued by the court; he will be the first suspect to face trial at the ICC. A sealed (secret) warrant had been issued for his arrest on 10 February 2006 for the war crime of using child soldiers. He was flown to the court the same day in a French military aircraft. The prosecutor has stated that his trial will only be on the allegation of using child soldiers, and other allegations will be followed up in a subsequent prosecution.

Originally, Lubanga's trial was due to begin on 23 June 2008, but it was halted on 13 June when the Court ruled that the Prosecutor's refusal to disclose potentially exculpatory material had breached Lubanga's right to a fair trial. The Prosecutor had obtained the evidence from the United Nations and other sources on condition of confidentiality, but judges ruled that the Prosecutor had incorrectly applied the relevant provision of the Rome Statute and, as a consequence, "the trial process has been ruptured to such a degree that it is now impossible to piece together the constituent elements of a fair trial". The Court lifted this suspension on 18 November 2008; Lubanga's trial began on 26 January 2009.

On 14 March 2012, the Court, by unanimous verdict of the Trial Chamber, found Lubanga guilty as a co-perpetrator in the use of child soldiers.

Germain Katanga and Mathieu Ngudjolo Chui

Two more participants in the Ituri conflict, Germain Katanga and Mathieu Ngudjolo Chui, have also been surrendered to the Court by the Congolese authorities. Both men are charged with six counts of war crimes and three counts of crimes against humanity, relating to an attack on the village of Bogoro on 24 February 2003 in which at least 200 civilians were killed, survivors were imprisoned in a room filled with corpses, and women and girls were sexually enslaved. The charges against both men include murder, sexual slavery and using children under the age of fifteen years to participate actively in hostilities.

Katanga, the former leader of the Ngiti-majority Front for Patriotic Resistance of Ituri militia, was transferred to the Court on 17 October 2007; Ngudjolo, former leader of the National Integrationist Front, was transferred to the Court on 6 February 2008. The hearing to confirm the charges against them began on 27 June 2008. The trial against the two men started on 24 November 2009.

Callixte Mbarushimana

On 20 August 2010, the Prosecutor requested Pre-Trial Chamber I to issue a warrant of arrest against Callixte Mbarushimana. He is alleged to have been the Executive Secretary of the Forces démocratiques de libération du Rwanda – Forces Combattantes Abacunguzi (FDLR-FCA, FDLR). On 28 September 2010, the Pre-Trial Chamber complied with the request and issued a sealed warrant of arrest which was unsealed on 11 October 2010, the day French authorities arrested Mbarushimana. The suspect was transferred to the ICC on 25 January 2011. His confirmation of charges hearing was held from 16 to 21 September 2011. By a 2 to 1 majority, Pre-Trial Chamber I ruled on 16 December 2011 that the confirmation was declined. After the Prosecutor's appeal against the decision was rejected, Mbarushimana was released on 23 December 2011.

Central African Republic

In December 2004, the government of the Central African Republic, a state party, referred to the Prosecutor "the situation of crimes within the jurisdiction of the Court committed anywhere on the territory of the Central African Republic since 1 July 2002, the date of entry into force of the Rome Statute."

On 13 April 2006 the Court of Cassation of the Central African Republic investigating charges or murder and rape committed by former President Ange-Felix Patasse and Congolese Vice-President Jean-Pierre Bemba said that they could not secure the arrest of the suspects, despite international arrest warrants, and requested the ICC to take responsibility. The allegations against Bemba date to when his Movement for the Liberation of Congo rebel army was invited by Patasse into the capital Bangui to fight rebels who were fighting against Patasse. Also referred to the court were the cases of a French policeman and two aides of Patasse who were all involved in the alleged crimes, which human rights groups allege had about 400 victims.

Local activists from the Union of Central African Journalists (UJCA) have also accused the President, François Bozizé, of committing genocide against the inhabitants of northern Central African Republic – who supported the former regime – after seizing power in 2003, and asked the court to prosecute Bozizé.

In November 2005, the Office of the Prosecutor held meetings with the government, judiciary authorities, civil society and international community representatives in CAR to gather additional information for the preliminary analysis.

In September 2006 the government of the CAR filed a complaint with the court saying the Prosecutor had failed to decide within a reasonable time whether or not to investigate. In response the pre-trial chamber ordered the prosecutor to submit a report by 15 December 2006 as to the current status of the investigation and an estimate of when a decision on whether to investigate will be made.

On 22 May 2007, the Prosecutor announced his decision to open an investigation, focusing on allegations of killing and rape in 2002 and 2003, a period of intense fighting between government and rebel forces. The case has been allocated to Pre-Trial Chamber III.

On 24 May 2008, Jean-Pierre Bemba, the former Vice-President of the Democratic Republic of the Congo was arrested during a visit to Belgium under a sealed warrant under accusations of war crimes and crimes against humanity committed in CAR He was transferred to the ICC on 3 July 2008. His confirmation of charges hearing, taking place from 12–15 January 2009, resulted in the charges being confirmed on 15 June 2009. His trial began on 22 November 2010.

Darfur, Sudan

On 31 March 2005, the United Nations Security Council passed Resolution 1593, referring "the situation prevailing in Darfur since 1 July 2002" to the Prosecutor. The Prosecutor opened an investigation into this situation on 6 June, and the case was allocated to Pre-Trial Chamber I.

Ahmed Haroun and Ali Kushayb

In February 2007 the Prosecutor announced that two men – Sudanese humanitarian affairs minister Ahmad Muhammad Harun and Janjaweed militia leader Ali Kushayb – had been identified as key suspects, accused of war crimes and crimes against humanity. On 2 May 2007, the Court issued arrest warrants for the two men. However, Sudan claims the Court has no jurisdiction over this matter, and refuses to hand over the suspects.

In July 2008, the Chief Prosecutor applied to the Court for an arrest warrant for President of Sudan Omar al-Bashir on ten counts of genocide, crimes against humanity and war crimes. In October the Court asked the Prosecutor for more information to support the charges.

Omar al-Bashir

On 14 July 2008, the Prosecutor accused Sudanese President Omar al-Bashir of genocide, crimes against humanity and war crimes. The court issued an arrest warrant for al-Bashir on 4 March 2009 for war crimes and crimes against humanity, but ruled that there was insufficient evidence to prosecute him for genocide. Al-Bashir was the first sitting head of state indicted by the ICC. Al-Bashir denies all the charges, describing them as "not worth the ink they are written in". In July 2009, the member-states of the African Union agreed not to co-operate in his arrest. Nevertheless, several African Union members who are also States Parties of the ICC, including South

Africa and Uganda, let it be known that al-Bashir might be arrested if he entered their territory. However, in July and August 2010 al-Bashir traveled to Chad and Kenya, neither of which turned him over to the ICC despite being States Parties; the ICC has reported both member states to the UN Security Council and the ICC Assembly of States Parties.

On 3 February 2010, the Appeals Chamber of the ICC reversed the Pre-Trial Chamber's rejection of the genocide charge, ruling that the PTC had applied a too stringent standard of proof. Subsequently, the First Pre-Trial Chamber issued a second warrant of arrest against al-Bashir on 12 July 2010, in which he was charged with genocide against three ethnic groups in Darfur.

Bahr Idriss Abu Garda

On 17 May 2009, it was the first time that a suspect appeared voluntarily before the Court. Bahr Idriss Abu Garda, commander of the United Resistance Front, a Darfuri rebel group, was accused of responsibility for the attack on the African Union's peace mission in Haskanita (North-Darfur) on 29 September 2007. In this attack 12 soldiers were allegedly killed and eight injured. Abu Garda denies the charge, but reported voluntarily, stating that "every leader should co-operate with justice and observe the law". A summons was issued against Abu Garda, but no warrant of arrest. He was allowed to await the further proceedings while in liberty.

On 8 February 2010, Pre-Trial Chamber I of the Court ruled that there was insufficient evidence to proceed to trial on charges against Abu Garda. On 23 April 2010, this Chamber also declined the Prosecutor's application to appeal the decision. Under the Rome Statute, such a move to the Appeals Chamber can only be made once leave of the Pre-Trial Chamber has been granted. Both decisions do not preclude the Prosecution from subsequently requesting the confirmation of the charges against Abu Garda if such a request is supported by additional evidence.

Abdallah Banda and Saleh Jerbo

On 16 June 2010, two other rebel leaders came voluntarily to the Court. Abdallah Banda Abakaer Nourain (Banda) and Saleh Mohammed Jerbo Jamus (Jerbo), leaders of small Darfuri rebel groups, are also charged with war crimes for their alleged roles in the attack in Haskanita described above. Prosecutor Moreno Ocampo stated that their voluntary appearance was the culmination of months of efforts to secure their co-operation. On 17 June 2010, they faced Pre-Trial Chamber I, which ruled that there are reasonable grounds for their prosecution. Just as in the case against Abu Garda, the Prosecutor has not made a request for warrants of arrest against them.

On 20 November 2008, the Chief Prosecutor announced his intention also to prosecute three rebel commanders from the Justice and Equality Movement for the 2007 Haskanita raids, in which 12 AMIS peacekeepers were killed. In May 2009, the Court summoned the three to appear before the Court. One of these – Bahr Idriss Abu Garda – appeared voluntarily before the Court on 18 May 2009. Abu Garda has been charged with the war crimes of attacking peacekeepers, murder and pillage. The two other rebel commanders charged by the Prosecutor – Abdallah Banda Abakaer Nourain and Saleh Mohammed Jerbo Jamus – appeared voluntarily before the court on 17 June 2010. On 7 March 2011, Pre-Trial Chamber I confirmed the charges against the two and committed them to trial.

Kenya

On 31 March 2010, a Pre-Trial Chamber of the International Criminal Court authorized the Prosecutor to investigate the 2007–2008 Kenyan crisis. This was the first time the Prosecutor had requested such an authorization; all other investigations have been triggered by either the corresponding government or by the United Nations Security Council.

On 15 December 2010, the Prosecutor applied for summonses to appear for six alleged perpetrators: In the first case, William Ruto, Henry Kiprono Kosgey and Joshua Arap Sang are to stand trial for crimes against PNU supporters whereas, in the second case, Francis Muthaura, Uhuru Muigai Kenyatta and Mohamed Hussein Ali are to stand trial for crimes against ODM supporters. On 8 March 2011, the Pre-Trial Chamber issued summonses for all six alleged perpetrators to appear before the Court on 7 and 8 April 2011 respectively.

Libya

As a consequence of the 2011 Libyan civil war and its brutal suppression, the UN Security Council voted on 26 February 2011 in Resolution 1970 unanimously to refer the situation in Libya to the ICC. Other than the referral of the situation in Darfur, Sudan, to the ICC in March 2005, this is only the second time that the Security Council has referred a situation to the ICC, and the first time that it has done so unanimously. China and the United States had abstained in 2005, but this time voted in favor of referral to the

ICC.On 3 March 2011, just five days after the referral of the situation, the Prosecutor opened an investigation. On 16 May 2011, the Prosecutor requested a Pre-Trial Chamber of the Court to issue warrants of arrest against Muammar Gaddafi, his son Saif al-Islam, and the head of Libya's intelligence, Abdullah Senussi, for allegedly committed crimes against humanity. This request was granted on 27 June 2011, resulting in the second ICC warrant of arrest against an incumbent head of state, the other being Sudan's Omar al-Bashir.

Côte d'Ivoire

On 19 May 2011, the Prosecutor informed the Presidency of the Court of his intention to request the authorization to open a formal investigation into the situation in Côte d'Ivoire since 28 November 2010. A day later, the Presidency issued an order assigning the situation to Pre-Trial Chamber II which was on 22 June 2011 modified by establishing a Pre-Trial Chamber III and assigning the situation in Côte d'Ivoire to it. On 23 June 2011, the Prosecutor formally requested the authorization from a Pre-Trial Chamber to begin an investigation into crimes allegedly committed in Côte d'Ivoire.

While Côte d'Ivoire is not a state party to the Rome Statute, it has repeatedly and by different administrations accepted the ICC's jurisdiction.

On 3 October 2011, Pre-Trial Chamber III authorized the investigation to be conducted by the Prosecutor.

Preliminary Examinations

In addition to the seven situations where the Prosecutor has opened formal investigations, several other situations are under "preliminary examination", they are: Afghanistan, Colombia, Guinea, Georgia, Honduras, Korea, Mali, Nigeria, and Palestine.

Earlier preliminary examinations regarding Iraq and Venezuela were closed on 9 February 2006. The Prosecutor concluded that no investigation would be initiated because the necessary requirements had not been met.

With regard to the 2003 invasion of Iraq, the Prosecutor published a letter responding to complaints he had received. He noted that "the International Criminal Court has a mandate to examine the conduct during the conflict, but not whether the decision to engage in armed conflict was legal", and that the court's jurisdiction is limited to the actions of nationals of states parties. He concluded that there was a reasonable basis to believe that a limited number of war crimes had been committed in Iraq, but that the crimes allegedly committed by nationals of states parties did not appear to meet the required gravity threshold for an ICC investigation.

Other Complaints Received

As of end September 2010, the Office of the Prosecutor had received 8,874 communications about alleged crimes. After initial review, 4,002 of these communications were dismissed as "manifestly outside the jurisdiction of the Court".

National Proceedings under Complementarity

The Court is designed to complement existing national judicial systems: it can only exercise its jurisdiction when national courts are unwilling or unable to investigate or prosecute. States Parties are expected to implement national legislation to provide for the investigation and prosecution of crimes that fall under the jurisdiction of the Court.

Democratic Republic of the Congo

In February 2008, a Military Tribunal in Mbandaka sentenced Botuli Itofo, a policeman, to twenty years imprisonment after his conviction under ICC implementing legislation for the crime against humanity of mass rape and other "serious human rights violations". Over fifty women and girls had expressed that they had been raped as a part of a "punitive operation" by police sent to the area to restore order in March 2006.

Germany

Under the German complementarity law, crimes against humanity as defined in the Rome Statute can be prosecuted by German courts even if they are outside the jurisdiction of the court because they occur in a country that has not ratified the statute. This is under the principle of universal jurisdiction.

In December 2005, activists from Uzbekistan submitted a complaint against Uzbek Interior Minister Zokirjon Almatov in connection with the Andijan massacre. Almatov was visiting Germany at the time for hospital treatment. The prosecutor declined to act, saying chances of a successful prosecution were "non-existent" as the government of Uzbekistan would not cooperate in the gathering of evidence.

In May 2011, a trial against two alleged members of the FDLR began in Stuttgart, Germany. Ignace Murwanashyaka and Straton Musoni, both Rwandan citizens, are accused of 26 counts of crimes against humanity and 39 counts of war crimes, allegedly committed in the Democratic Republic of the Congo. This is the first trial in Germany under the Völkerstrafgesetzbuch in force since 2002.

United Kingdom

In 2007, Corporal Donald Payne became the first British person to be convicted of a war crime. He pleaded guilty under ICC implementing legislation for inhumane treatment of Baha Mousa, an Iraqi detainee following the 2003 invasion of Iraq. He was sentenced to one year in jail and dismissed from the army. Three other soldiers were acquitted of war crimes in the same trial.

References

Antonio Cassese, Paola Gaeta & John R.W.D. Jones (eds.), (2002). *The Rome Statute of the International Criminal Court: A Commentary*. Oxford: Oxford University Press

Bruce Broomhall, (2003). *International Justice and the International Criminal Court: Between Sovereignty and the Rule of Law*. Oxford: Oxford University Press.

Hans Köchler, (2003). *Global Justice or Global Revenge? International Criminal Justice at the Crossroads*. Vienna/New York: Springer.

Roy S Lee & Hakan Friman (eds.), (2001). *The International Criminal Court: Elements of Crimes and Rules of Procedure and Evidence*. Ardsley, NY: Transnational Publishers.

Steven C. Roach (ed.) (2009). *Governance, Order, and the International Criminal Court: Between Realpolitik and a Cosmopolitan Court*. Oxford: Oxford University Press.

William A Schabas, (2004). *An Introduction to the International Criminal Court* (2nd ed.). Cambridge: Cambridge University Press.

7

Vienna Declaration and Programme of Action

The Vienna Declaration and Programme of Action, also known as VDPA, is a human rights declaration adopted by consensus at the World Conference on Human Rights on 25 June 1993 in Vienna, Austria. The United Nations High Commissioner for Human Rights was created by this Declaration endorsed by General Assembly Resolution 48/121.

The text of the Vienna Declaration and Programme of Action, as adopted by the World Conference on Human Rights on 25 June 1993, is given below

The World Conference on Human Rights,

Considering that the promotion and protection of human rights is a matter of priority for the international community, and that the Conference affords a unique opportunity to carry out a comprehensive analysis of the international human rights system and of the machinery for the protection of human rights, in order to enhance and thus promote a fuller observance of those rights, in a just and balanced manner,

Recognizing and affirming that all human rights derive from the dignity and worth inherent in the human person, and that the human person is the central subject of human rights and fundamental freedoms, and consequently should be the principal beneficiary and should participate actively in the realization of these rights and freedoms,

Reaffirming their commitment to the purposes and principles contained in the Charter of the United Nations and the Universal Declaration of Human Rights,

Reaffirming the commitment contained in Article 56 of the Charter of the United Nations to take joint and separate action, placing proper emphasis on developing effective international cooperation for the realization of the purposes set out in Article 55, including universal respect for, and observance of, human rights and fundamental freedoms for all,

Emphasizing the responsibilities of all States, in conformity with the Charter of the United Nations, to develop and encourage respect for human rights and fundamental freedoms for all, without distinction as to race, sex, language or religion,

Recalling the Preamble to the Charter of the United Nations, in particular the determination to reaffirm faith in fundamental human rights, in the dignity and worth of the human person, and in the equal rights of men and women and of nations large and small,

Recalling also the determination expressed in the Preamble of the Charter of the United Nations to save succeeding generations from the scourge of war, to establish conditions under which justice and respect for obligations arising from treaties and other sources of international law can be maintained, to promote social progress and better standards of life in larger freedom, to practice tolerance and good neighbourliness, and to employ international machinery for the promotion of the economic and social advancement of all peoples,

Emphasizing that the Universal Declaration of Human Rights, which constitutes a common standard of achievement for all peoples and all nations, is the source of inspiration and has been the basis for the United Nations in making advances in standard setting as contained in the existing international human rights instruments, in particular the International Covenant on Civil and Political Rights and the International Covenant on Economic, Social and Cultural Rights.

Considering the major changes taking place on the international scene and the aspirations of all the peoples for an international order based on the principles enshrined in the Charter of the United Nations, including promoting and encouraging respect for human rights and fundamental freedoms for all and respect for the principle of equal rights and self - determination of peoples, peace, democracy, justice, equality, rule of law, pluralism, development, better standards of living and solidarity,

Deeply concerned by various forms of discrimination and violence, to which women continue to be exposed all over the world,

Recognizing that the activities of the United Nations in the field of human rights should be rationalized and enhanced in order to strengthen the United Nations machinery in this field and to further the objectives of universal respect for observance of international human rights standards,

Having taken into account the Declarations adopted by the three regional meetings at Tunis, San José and Bangkok and the contributions made by Governments, and bearing in mind the suggestions made by intergovernmental and non-governmental organizations, as well as the studies prepared by independent experts during the preparatory process leading to the World Conference on Human Rights,

Welcoming the International Year of the World's Indigenous People 1993 as a reaffirmation of the commitment of the international community to ensure their enjoyment of all human rights and fundamental freedoms and to respect the value and diversity of their cultures and identities,

Recognizing also that the international community should devise ways and means to remove the current obstacles and meet challenges to the full realization of all human rights and to prevent the continuation of human rights violations resulting thereof throughout the world,

Invoking the spirit of our age and the realities of our time which call upon the peoples of the world and all States Members of the United Nations to rededicate themselves to the global task of promoting and protecting all human rights and fundamental freedoms so as to secure full and universal enjoyment of these rights,

Determined to take new steps forward in the commitment of the international community with a view to achieving substantial progress in human rights endeavours by an increased and sustained effort of international cooperation and solidarity,

Solemnly adopts the Vienna Declaration and Programme of Action.

I

1. The World Conference on Human Rights reaffirms the solemn commitment of all States to fulfil their obligations to promote universal respect for, and observance and protection of, all human rights and fundamental freedoms for all in accordance with the Charter of the United

Nations, other instruments relating to human rights, and international law. The universal nature of these rights and freedoms is beyond question.

In this framework, enhancement of international cooperation in the field of human rights is essential for the full achievement of the purposes of the United Nations.

Human rights and fundamental freedoms are the birthright of all human beings; their protection and promotion is the first responsibility of Governments.

2. All peoples have the right of self-determination. By virtue of that right they freely determine their political status, and freely pursue their economic, social and cultural development.

Taking into account the particular situation of peoples under colonial or other forms of alien domination or foreign occupation, the World Conference on Human Rights recognizes the right of peoples to take any legitimate action, in accordance with the Charter of the United Nations, to realize their inalienable right of self-determination. The World Conference on Human Rights considers the denial of the right of self-determination as a violation of human rights and underlines the importance of the effective realization of this right.

In accordance with the Declaration on Principles of International Law concerning Friendly Relations and Cooperation Among States in accordance with the Charter of the United Nations, this shall not be construed as authorizing or encouraging any action which would dismember or impair, totally or in part, the territorial integrity or political unity of sovereign and independent States conducting themselves in compliance with the principle of equal rights and self-determination of peoples and thus possessed of a Government representing the whole people belonging to the territory without distinction of any kind.

3. Effective international measures to guarantee and monitor the implementation of human rights standards should be taken in respect of people under foreign occupation, and effective legal protection against the violation of their human rights should be provided, in accordance with human rights norms and international law, particularly the Geneva Convention relative to the Protection of Civilian Persons in Time of War, of 14 August 1949, and other applicable norms of humanitarian law.

4. The promotion and protection of all human rights and fundamental freedoms must be considered as a priority objective of the United Nations in accordance with its purposes and principles, in particular the purpose of international cooperation. In the framework of these purposes and principles, the promotion and protection of all human rights is a legitimate concern of the international community. The organs and specialized agencies related to human rights should therefore further enhance the coordination of their activities based on the consistent and objective application of international human rights instruments.

5. All human rights are universal, indivisible and interdependent and interrelated. The international community must treat human rights globally in a fair and equal manner, on the same footing, and with the same emphasis. While the significance of national and regional particularities and various historical, cultural and religious backgrounds must be borne in mind, it is the duty of States, regardless of their political, economic and cultural systems, to promote and protect all human rights and fundamental freedoms.

6. The efforts of the United Nations system towards the universal respect for, and observance of, human rights and fundamental freedoms for all, contribute to the stability and well-being necessary for peaceful and friendly relations among nations, and to improved conditions for peace and security as well as social and economic development, in conformity with the Charter of the United Nations.

7. The processes of promoting and protecting human rights should be conducted in conformity with the purposes and principles of the Charter of the United Nations, and international law.

8. Democracy, development and respect for human rights and fundamental freedoms are interdependent and mutually reinforcing. Democracy is based on the freely expressed will of the people to determine their own political, economic, social and cultural systems and their full participation in all aspects of their lives. In the context of the above, the promotion and protection of human rights and fundamental freedoms at the national and international levels should be universal and conducted without conditions attached. The international community should support the strengthening and promoting of democracy, development and respect for human rights and fundamental freedoms in the entire world.

9. The World Conference on Human Rights reaffirms that least developed countries committed to the process of democratization and economic reforms, many of which are in Africa, should be supported by the international community in order to succeed in their transition to democracy and economic development.

10. The World Conference on Human Rights reaffirms the right to development, as established in the Declaration on the Right to Development, as a universal and inalienable right and an integral part of fundamental human rights.

As stated in the Declaration on the Right to Development, the human person is the central subject of development.

While development facilitates the enjoyment of all human rights, the lack of development may not be invoked to justify the abridgement of internationally recognized human rights.

States should cooperate with each other in ensuring development and eliminating obstacles to development. The international community should promote an effective international cooperation for the realization of the right to development and the elimination of obstacles to development.

Lasting progress towards the implementation of the right to development requires effective development policies at the national level, as well as equitable economic relations and a favourable economic environment at the international level.

11. The right to development should be fulfilled so as to meet equitably the developmental and environmental needs of present and future generations. The World Conference on Human Rights recognizes that illicit dumping of toxic and dangerous substances and waste potentially constitutes a serious threat to the human rights to life and health of everyone.

Consequently, the World Conference on Human Rights calls on all States to adopt and vigorously implement existing conventions relating to the dumping of toxic and dangerous products and waste and to cooperate in the prevention of illicit dumping.

Everyone has the right to enjoy the benefits of scientific progress and its applications. The World Conference on Human Rights notes that certain advances, notably in the biomedical and life sciences as well as in information technology, may have potentially adverse consequences for the integrity, dignity and human rights of the individual, and calls for international cooperation to ensure that human rights and dignity are fully respected in this area of universal concern

12. The World Conference on Human Rights calls upon the international community to make all efforts to help alleviate the external debt burden of developing countries, in order to supplement the efforts of the Governments of such countries to attain the full realization of the economic, social and cultural rights of their people.

13. There is a need for States and international organizations, in cooperation with non-governmental organizations, to create favourable conditions at the national, regional and international levels to ensure the full and effective enjoyment of human rights. States should eliminate all violations of human rights and their causes, as well as obstacles to the enjoyment of these rights.

14. The existence of widespread extreme poverty inhibits the full and effective enjoyment of human rights; its immediate alleviation and eventual elimination must remain a high priority for the international community.

15. Respect for human rights and for fundamental freedoms without distinction of any kind is a fundamental rule of international human rights law. The speedy and comprehensive elimination of all forms of racism and racial discrimination, xenophobia and related intolerance is a priority task for the international community. Governments should take effective measures to prevent and combat them. Groups, institutions, intergovernmental and non-governmental organizations and individuals are urged to intensify their efforts in cooperating and coordinating their activities against these evils.

16. The World Conference on Human Rights welcomes the progress made in dismantling apartheid and calls upon the international community and the United Nations system to assist in this process.

The World Conference on Human Rights also deplores the continuing acts of violence aimed at undermining the quest for a peaceful dismantling of apartheid.

17. The acts, methods and practices of terrorism in all its forms and manifestations as well as linkage in some countries to drug trafficking are activities aimed at the destruction of human rights, fundamental freedoms and democracy, threatening territorial integrity, security of States and destabilizing legitimately constituted Governments. The international

community should take the necessary steps to enhance cooperation to prevent and combat terrorism.

18. The human rights of women and of the girl-child are an inalienable, integral and indivisible part of universal human rights. The full and equal participation of women in political, civil, economic, social and cultural life, at the national, regional and international levels, and the eradication of all forms of discrimination on grounds of sex are priority objectives of the international community.

Gender-based violence and all forms of sexual harassment and exploitation, including those resulting from cultural prejudice and international trafficking, are incompatible with the dignity and worth of the human person, and must be eliminated. This can be achieved by legal measures and through national action and international cooperation in such fields as economic and social development, education, safe maternity and health care, and social support.

The human rights of women should form an integral part of the United Nations human rights activities, including the promotion of all human rights instruments relating to women.

The World Conference on Human Rights urges Governments, institutions, intergovernmental and non-governmental organizations to intensify their efforts for the protection and promotion of human rights of women and the girl-child.

19. Considering the importance of the promotion and protection of the rights of persons belonging to minorities and the contribution of such promotion and protection to the political and social stability of the States in which such persons live,

The World Conference on Human Rights reaffirms the obligation of States to ensure that persons belonging to minorities may exercise fully and effectively all human rights and fundamental freedoms without any discrimination and in full equality before the law in accordance with the Declaration on the Rights of Persons Belonging to National or Ethnic, Religious and Linguistic Minorities.

The persons belonging to minorities have the right to enjoy their own culture, to profess and practise their own religion and to use their own language in private and in public, freely and without interference or any form of discrimination.

20. The World Conference on Human Rights recognizes the inherent dignity and the unique contribution of indigenous people to the development and plurality of society and strongly reaffirms the commitment of the international community to their economic, social and cultural well-being and their enjoyment of the fruits of sustainable development. States should ensure the full and free participation of indigenous people in all aspects of society, in particular in matters of concern to them. Considering the importance of the promotion and protection of the rights of indigenous people, and the contribution of such promotion and protection to the political and social stability of the States in which such people live, States should, in accordance with international law, take concerted positive steps to ensure respect for all human rights and fundamental freedoms of indigenous people, on the basis of equality and non-discrimination, and recognize the value and diversity of their distinct identities, cultures and social organization.

21. The World Conference on Human Rights, welcoming the early ratification of the Convention on the Rights of the Child by a large number of States and noting the recognition of the human rights of children in the World Declaration on the Survival, Protection and Development of Children and Plan of Action adopted by the World Summit for Children, urges universal ratification of the Convention by 1995 and its effective implementation by States parties through the adoption of all the necessary legislative, administrative and other measures and the allocation to the maximum extent of the available resources. In all actions concerning children, non-discrimination and the best interest of the child should be primary considerations and the views of the child given due weight. National and international mechanisms and programmes should be strengthened for the defence and protection of children, in particular, the girl-child, abandoned children, street children, economically and sexually exploited children, including through child pornography, child prostitution or sale of organs, children victims of diseases including acquired immunodeficiency syndrome, refugee and displaced children, children in detention, children in armed conflict, as well as children victims of famine and drought and other emergencies. International cooperation and solidarity should be promoted to support the implementation of the Convention and the rights of the child should be a priority in the United Nations system-wide action on human rights.

The World Conference on Human Rights also stresses that the child for the full and harmonious development of his or her personality should grow up in a family environment which accordingly merits broader protection.

22. Special attention needs to be paid to ensuring non-discrimination, and the equal enjoyment of all human rights and fundamental freedoms by disabled persons, including their active participation in all aspects of society.

23. The World Conference on Human Rights reaffirms that everyone, without distinction of any kind, is entitled to the right to seek and to enjoy in other countries asylum from persecution, as well as the right to return to one's own country. In this respect it stresses the importance of the Universal Declaration of Human Rights, the 1951 Convention relating to the Status of Refugees, its 1967 Protocol and regional instruments. It expresses its appreciation to States that continue to admit and host large numbers of refugees in their territories, and to the Office of the United Nations High Commissioner for Refugees for its dedication to its task. It also expresses its appreciation to the United Nations Relief and Works Agency for Palestine Refugees in the Near East.

The World Conference on Human Rights recognizes that gross violations of human rights, including in armed conflicts, are among the multiple and complex factors leading to displacement of people.

The World Conference on Human Rights recognizes that, in view of the complexities of the global refugee crisis and in accordance with the Charter of the United Nations, relevant international instruments and international solidarity and in the spirit of burden-sharing, a comprehensive approach by the international community is needed in coordination and cooperation with the countries concerned and relevant organizations, bearing in mind the mandate of the United Nations High Commissioner for Refugees. This should include the development of strategies to address the root causes and effects of movements of refugees and other displaced persons, the strengthening of emergency preparedness and response mechanisms, the provision of effective protection and assistance, bearing in mind the special needs of women and children, as well as the achievement of durable solutions, primarily through the preferred solution of dignified and safe voluntary repatriation, including solutions such as those adopted by the international refugee conferences. The World Conference on Human Rights underlines the responsibilities of States, particularly as they relate to the countries of origin.

In the light of the comprehensive approach, the World Conference on Human Rights emphasizes the importance of giving special attention including through intergovernmental and humanitarian organizations and finding lasting solutions to questions related to internally displaced persons including their voluntary and safe return and rehabilitation.

In accordance with the Charter of the United Nations and the principles of humanitarian law, the World Conference on Human Rights further emphasizes the importance of and the need for humanitarian assistance to victims of all natural and man-made disasters.

24. Great importance must be given to the promotion and protection of the human rights of persons belonging to groups which have been rendered vulnerable, including migrant workers, the elimination of all forms of discrimination against them, and the strengthening and more effective implementation of existing human rights instruments. States have an obligation to create and maintain adequate measures at the national level, in particular in the fields of education, health and social support, for the promotion and protection of the rights of persons in vulnerable sectors of their populations and to ensure the participation of those among them who are interested in finding a solution to their own problems.

25. The World Conference on Human Rights affirms that extreme poverty and social exclusion constitute a violation of human dignity and that urgent steps are necessary to achieve better knowledge of extreme poverty and its causes, including those related to the problem of development, in order to promote the human rights of the poorest, and to put an end to extreme poverty and social exclusion and to promote the enjoyment of the fruits of social progress. It is essential for States to foster participation by the poorest people in the decision-making process by the community in which they live, the promotion of human rights and efforts to combat extreme poverty.

26. The World Conference on Human Rights welcomes the progress made in the codification of human rights instruments, which is a dynamic and evolving process, and urges the universal ratification of human rights treaties. All States are encouraged to accede to these international instruments; all States are encouraged to avoid, as far as possible, the resort to reservations.

27. Every State should provide an effective framework of remedies to redress human rights grievances or violations. The administration of justice, including law enforcement and prosecutorial agencies and, especially, an independent judiciary and legal profession in full conformity with applicable standards contained in international human rights instruments, are essential to the full and non-discriminatory realization of human rights and indispensable to the processes of democracy and sustainable development. In this context, institutions concerned with the administration of justice should be properly funded, and an increased level of both technical and financial assistance should be provided by the international community. It is incumbent upon the United Nations to make use of special programmes of advisory services on a priority basis for the achievement of a strong and independent administration of justice.

28. The World Conference on Human Rights expresses its dismay at massive violations of human rights especially in the form of genocide, "ethnic cleansing" and systematic rape of women in war situations, creating mass exodus of refugees and displaced persons. While strongly condemning such abhorrent practices it reiterates the call that perpetrators of such crimes be punished and such practices immediately stopped.

29. The World Conference on Human Rights expresses grave concern about continuing human rights violations in all parts of the world in disregard of standards as contained in international human rights instruments and international humanitarian law and about the lack of sufficient and effective remedies for the victims.

The World Conference on Human Rights is deeply concerned about violations of human rights during armed conflicts, affecting the civilian population, especially women, children, the elderly and the disabled. The Conference therefore calls upon States and all parties to armed conflicts strictly to observe international humanitarian law, as set forth in the Geneva Conventions of 1949 and other rules and principles of international law, as well as minimum standards for protection of human rights, as laid down in international conventions.

The World Conference on Human Rights reaffirms the right of the victims to be assisted by humanitarian organizations, as set forth in the Geneva Conventions of 1949 and other relevant instruments of international humanitarian law, and calls for the safe and timely access for such assistance.

30. The World Conference on Human Rights also expresses its dismay and condemnation that gross and systematic violations and situations that constitute serious obstacles to the full enjoyment of all human rights continue to occur in different parts of the world. Such violations and obstacles include, as well as torture and cruel, inhuman and degrading treatment or punishment, summary and arbitrary executions, disappearances, arbitrary detentions, all forms of racism, racial discrimination and apartheid, foreign occupation and alien domination, xenophobia, poverty, hunger and other denials of economic, social and cultural rights, religious intolerance, terrorism, discrimination against women and lack of the rule of law.

31. The World Conference on Human Rights calls upon States to refrain from any unilateral measure not in accordance with international law and the Charter of the United Nations that creates obstacles to trade relations among States and impedes the full realization of the human rights set forth in the Universal Declaration of Human Rights and international human rights instruments, in particular the rights of everyone to a standard of living adequate for their health and well-being, including food and medical care, housing and the necessary social services. The World Conference on Human Rights affirms that food should not be used as a tool for political pressure.

32. The World Conference on Human Rights reaffirms the importance of ensuring the universality, objectivity and non-selectivity of the consideration of human rights issues.

33. The World Conference on Human Rights reaffirms that States are duty-bound, as stipulated in the Universal Declaration of Human Rights and the International Covenant on Economic, Social and Cultural Rights and in other international human rights instruments, to ensure that education is aimed at strengthening the respect of human rights and fundamental freedoms. The World Conference on Human Rights emphasizes the importance of incorporating the subject of human rights education programmes and calls upon States to do so. Education should promote understanding, tolerance, peace and friendly relations between the nations and all racial or religious groups and encourage the development of United Nations activities in pursuance of these objectives. Therefore, education on human rights and the dissemination of proper information, both theoretical and practical, play an important role in the promotion and respect of human rights with regard to all individuals without distinction of any kind such as race, sex, language or religion, and this should be integrated in the education

policies at the national as well as international levels. The World Conference on Human Rights notes that resource constraints and institutional inadequacies may impede the immediate realization of these objectives.

34. Increased efforts should be made to assist countries which so request to create the conditions whereby each individual can enjoy universal human rights and fundamental freedoms. Governments, the United Nations system as well as other multilateral organizations are urged to increase considerably the resources allocated to programmes aiming at the establishment and strengthening of national legislation, national institutions and related infrastructures which uphold the rule of law and democracy, electoral assistance, human rights awareness through training, teaching and education, popular participation and civil society.

The programmes of advisory services and technical cooperation under the Centre for Human Rights should be strengthened as well as made more efficient and transparent and thus become a major contribution to improving respect for human rights. States are called upon to increase their contributions to these programmes, both through promoting a larger allocation from the United Nations regular budget, and through voluntary contributions.

35. The full and effective implementation of United Nations activities to promote and protect human rights must reflect the high importance accorded to human rights by the Charter of the United Nations and the demands of the United Nations human rights activities, as mandated by Member States. To this end, United Nations human rights activities should be provided with increased resources.

36. The World Conference on Human Rights reaffirms the important and constructive role played by national institutions for the promotion and protection of human rights, in particular in their advisory capacity to the competent authorities, their role in remedying human rights violations, in the dissemination of human rights information, and education in human rights.

The World Conference on Human Rights encourages the establishment and strengthening of national institutions, having regard to the "Principles relating to the status of national institutions" and recognizing that it is the right of each State to choose the framework which is best suited to its particular needs at the national level.

37. Regional arrangements play a fundamental role in promoting and protecting human rights. They should reinforce universal human rights standards, as contained in international human rights instruments, and their protection. The World Conference on Human Rights endorses efforts under way to strengthen these arrangements and to increase their effectiveness, while at the same time stressing the importance of cooperation with the United Nations human rights activities.

The World Conference on Human Rights reiterates the need to consider the possibility of establishing regional and subregional arrangements for the promotion and protection of human rights where they do not already exist.

38. The World Conference on Human Rights recognizes the important role of non-governmental organizations in the promotion of all human rights and in humanitarian activities at national, regional and international levels. The World Conference on Human Rights appreciates their contribution to increasing public awareness of human rights issues, to the conduct of education, training and research in this field, and to the promotion and protection of all human rights and fundamental freedoms. While recognizing that the primary responsibility for standard-setting lies with States, the conference also appreciates the contribution of non-governmental organizations to this process. In this respect, the World Conference on Human Rights emphasizes the importance of continued dialogue and cooperation between Governments and non-governmental organizations. Non-governmental organizations and their members genuinely involved in the field of human rights should enjoy the rights and freedoms recognized in the Universal Declaration of Human Rights, and the protection of the national law. These rights and freedoms may not be exercised contrary to the purposes and principles of the United Nations. Non-governmental organizations should be free to carry out their human rights activities, without interference, within the framework of national law and the Universal Declaration of Human Rights.

39. Underlining the importance of objective, responsible and impartial information about human rights and humanitarian issues, the World Conference on Human Rights encourages the increased involvement of the media, for whom freedom and protection should be guaranteed within the framework of national law.

II

A. Increased Coordination on Human Rights within the United Nations System

1. The World Conference on Human Rights recommends increased coordination in support of human rights and fundamental freedoms within the United Nations system. To this end, the World Conference on Human Rights urges all United Nations organs, bodies and the specialized agencies whose activities deal with human rights to cooperate in order to strengthen, rationalize and streamline their activities, taking into account the need to avoid unnecessary duplication. The World Conference on Human Rights also recommends to the Secretary-General that high-level officials of relevant United Nations bodies and specialized agencies at their annual meeting, besides coordinating their activities, also assess the impact of their strategies and policies on the enjoyment of all human rights.

2. Furthermore, the World Conference on Human Rights calls on regional organizations and prominent international and regional finance and development institutions to assess also the impact of their policies and programmes on the enjoyment of human rights.

3. The World Conference on Human Rights recognizes that relevant specialized agencies and bodies and institutions of the United Nations system as well as other relevant intergovernmental organizations whose activities deal with human rights play a vital role in the formulation, promotion and implementation of human rights standards, within their respective mandates, and should take into account the outcome of the World Conference on Human Rights within their fields of competence.

4. The World Conference on Human Rights strongly recommends that a concerted effort be made to encourage and facilitate the ratification of and accession or succession to international human rights treaties and protocols adopted within the framework of the United Nations system with the aim of universal acceptance. The Secretary-General, in consultation with treaty bodies, should consider opening a dialogue with States not having acceded to these human rights treaties, in order to identify obstacles and to seek ways of overcoming them.

5. The World Conference on Human Rights encourages States to consider limiting the extent of any reservations they lodge to international

human rights instruments, formulate any reservations as precisely and narrowly as possible, ensure that none is incompatible with the object and purpose of the relevant treaty and regularly review any reservations with a view to withdrawing them.

6. The World Conference on Human Rights, recognizing the need to maintain consistency with the high quality of existing international standards and to avoid proliferation of human rights instruments, reaffirms the guidelines relating to the elaboration of new international instruments contained in General Assembly resolution 41/120 of 4 December 1986 and calls on the United Nations human rights bodies, when considering the elaboration of new international standards, to keep those guidelines in mind, to consult with human rights treaty bodies on the necessity for drafting new standards and to request the Secretariat to carry out technical reviews of proposed new instruments.

7. The World Conference on Human Rights recommends that human rights officers be assigned if and when necessary to regional offices of the United Nations Organization with the purpose of disseminating information and offering training and other technical assistance in the field of human rights upon the request of concerned Member States. Human rights training for international civil servants who are assigned to work relating to human rights should be organized.

8. The World Conference on Human Rights welcomes the convening of emergency sessions of the Commission on Human Rights as a positive initiative and that other ways of responding to acute violations of human rights be considered by the relevant organs of the United Nations system.

Resources

9. The World Conference on Human Rights, concerned by the growing disparity between the activities of the Centre for Human Rights and the human, financial and other resources available to carry them out, and bearing in mind the resources needed for other important United Nations programmes, requests the Secretary-General and the General Assembly to take immediate steps to increase substantially the resources for the human rights programme from within the existing and future regular budgets of the United Nations, and to take urgent steps to seek increased extrabudgetary resources.

10. Within this framework, an increased proportion of the regular budget should be allocated directly to the Centre for Human Rights to cover its costs and all other costs borne by the Centre for Human Rights, including those related to the United Nations human rights bodies. Voluntary funding of the Centre's technical cooperation activities should reinforce this enhanced budget; the World Conference on Human Rights calls for generous contributions to the existing trust funds.

11. The World Conference on Human Rights requests the Secretary-General and the General Assembly to provide sufficient human, financial and other resources to the Centre for Human Rights to enable it effectively, efficiently and expeditiously to carry out its activities.

12. The World Conference on Human Rights, noting the need to ensure that human and financial resources are available to carry out the human rights activities, as mandated by intergovernmental bodies, urges the Secretary-General, in accordance with Article 101 of the Charter of the United Nations, and Member States to adopt a coherent approach aimed at securing that resources commensurate to the increased mandates are allocated to the Secretariat. The World Conference on Human Rights invites the Secretary-General to consider whether adjustments to procedures in the programme budget cycle would be necessary or helpful to ensure the timely and effective implementation of human rights activities as mandated by Member States.

Centre for Human Rights

13. The World Conference on Human Rights stresses the importance of strengthening the United Nations Centre for Human Rights.

14. The Centre for Human Rights should play an important role in coordinating system-wide attention for human rights. The focal role of the Centre can best be realized if it is enabled to cooperate fully with other United Nations bodies and organs. The coordinating role of the Centre for Human Rights also implies that the office of the Centre for Human Rights in New York is strengthened.

15. The Centre for Human Rights should be assured adequate means for the system of thematic and country rapporteurs, experts, working groups and treaty bodies. Follow-up on recommendations should become a priority matter for consideration by the Commission on Human Rights.

16. The Centre for Human Rights should assume a larger role in the promotion of human rights. This role could be given shape through

cooperation with Member States and by an enhanced programme of advisory services and technical assistance. The existing voluntary funds will have to be expanded substantially for these purposes and should be managed in a more efficient and coordinated way. All activities should follow strict and transparent project management rules and regular programme and project evaluations should be held periodically. To this end, the results of such evaluation exercises and other relevant information should be made available regularly. The Centre should, in particular, organize at least once a year information meetings open to all Member States and organizations directly involved in these projects and programmes.

Adaptation and strengthening of the United Nations machinery for human rights, including the question of the establishment of a United Nations High Commissioner for Human Rights

17. The World Conference on Human Rights recognizes the necessity for a continuing adaptation of the United Nations human rights machinery to the current and future needs in the promotion and protection of human rights, as reflected in the present Declaration and within the framework of a balanced and sustainable development for all people. In particular, the United Nations human rights organs should improve their coordination, efficiency and effectiveness.

18. The World Conference on Human Rights recommends to the General Assembly that when examining the report of the Conference at its forty-eighth session, it begin, as a matter of priority, consideration of the question of the establishment of a High Commissioner for Human Rights for the promotion and protection of all human rights.

B. Equality, Dignity and Tolerance

1. Racism, racial discrimination, xenophobia and other forms of intolerance

19. The World Conference on Human Rights considers the elimination of racism and racial discrimination, in particular in their institutionalized forms such as apartheid or resulting from doctrines of racial superiority or exclusivity or contemporary forms and manifestations of racism, as a primary objective for the international community and a worldwide promotion programme in the field of human rights. United Nations organs and agencies

should strengthen their efforts to implement such a programme of action related to the third decade to combat racism and racial discrimination as well as subsequent mandates to the same end. The World Conference on Human Rights strongly appeals to the international community to contribute generously to the Trust Fund for the Programme for the Decade for Action to Combat Racism and Racial Discrimination.

20. The World Conference on Human Rights urges all Governments to take immediate measures and to develop strong policies to prevent and combat all forms and manifestations of racism, xenophobia or related intolerance, where necessary by enactment of appropriate legislation, including penal measures, and by the establishment of national institutions to combat such phenomena.

21. The World Conference on Human Rights welcomes the decision of the Commission on Human Rights to appoint a Special Rapporteur on contemporary forms of racism, racial discrimination, xenophobia and related intolerance. The World Conference on Human Rights also appeals to all States parties to the International Convention on the Elimination of All Forms of Racial Discrimination to consider making the declaration under article 14 of the Convention.

22. The World Conference on Human Rights calls upon all Governments to take all appropriate measures in compliance with their international obligations and with due regard to their respective legal systems to counter intolerance and related violence based on religion or belief, including practices of discrimination against women and including the desecration of religious sites, recognizing that every individual has the right to freedom of thought, conscience, expression and religion. The Conference also invites all States to put into practice the provisions of the Declaration on the Elimination of All Forms of Intolerance and of Discrimination Based on Religion or Belief.

23. The World Conference on Human Rights stresses that all persons who perpetrate or authorize criminal acts associated with ethnic cleansing are individually responsible and accountable for such human rights violations, and that the international community should exert every effort to bring those legally responsible for such violations to justice.

24. The World Conference on Human Rights calls on all States to take immediate measures, individually and collectively, to combat the practice

of ethnic cleansing to bring it quickly to an end. Victims of the abhorrent practice of ethnic cleansing are entitled to appropriate and effective remedies.

2. Persons belonging to national or ethnic, religious and linguistic minorities

25. The World Conference on Human Rights calls on the Commission on Human Rights to examine ways and means to promote and protect effectively the rights of persons belonging to minorities as set out in the Declaration on the Rights of Persons belonging to National or Ethnic, Religious and Linguistic Minorities. In this context, the World Conference on Human Rights calls upon the Centre for Human Rights to provide, at the request of Governments concerned and as part of its programme of advisory services and technical assistance, qualified expertise on minority issues and human rights, as well as on the prevention and resolution of disputes, to assist in existing or potential situations involving minorities.

26. The World Conference on Human Rights urges States and the international community to promote and protect the rights of persons belonging to national or ethnic, religious and linguistic minorities in accordance with the Declaration on the Rights of Persons belonging to National or Ethnic, Religious and Linguistic Minorities.

27. Measures to be taken, where appropriate, should include facilitation of their full participation in all aspects of the political, economic, social, religious and cultural life of society and in the economic progress and development in their country.

Indigenous people

28. The World Conference on Human Rights calls on the Working Group on Indigenous Populations of the Sub-Commission on Prevention of Discrimination and Protection of Minorities to complete the drafting of a declaration on the rights of indigenous people at its eleventh session.

29. The World Conference on Human Rights recommends that the Commission on Human Rights consider the renewal and updating of the mandate of the Working Group on Indigenous Populations upon completion of the drafting of a declaration on the rights of indigenous people.

30. The World Conference on Human Rights also recommends that advisory services and technical assistance programmes within the United Nations system respond positively to requests by States for assistance which

would be of direct benefit to indigenous people. The World Conference on Human Rights further recommends that adequate human and financial resources be made available to the Centre for Human Rights within the overall framework of strengthening the Centre's activities as envisaged by this document.

31. The World Conference on Human Rights urges States to ensure the full and free participation of indigenous people in all aspects of society, in particular in matters of concern to them.

32. The World Conference on Human Rights recommends that the General Assembly proclaim an international decade of the world's indigenous people, to begin from January 1994, including action-orientated programmes, to be decided upon in partnership with indigenous people. An appropriate voluntary trust fund should be set up for this purpose. In the framework of such a decade, the establishment of a permanent forum for indigenous people in the United Nations system should be considered.

Migrant Workers

33. The World Conference on Human Rights urges all States to guarantee the protection of the human rights of all migrant workers and their families.

34. The World Conference on Human Rights considers that the creation of conditions to foster greater harmony and tolerance between migrant workers and the rest of the society of the State in which they reside is of particular importance.

35. The World Conference on Human Rights invites States to consider the possibility of signing and ratifying, at the earliest possible time, the International Convention on the Rights of All Migrant Workers and Members of Their Families.

3. The equal status and human rights of women

36. The World Conference on Human Rights urges the full and equal enjoyment by women of all human rights and that this be a priority for Governments and for the United Nations. The World Conference on Human Rights also underlines the importance of the integration and full participation of women as both agents and beneficiaries in the development process, and reiterates the objectives established on global action for women towards sustainable and equitable development set forth in the Rio Declaration on Environment and Development and chapter 24 of Agenda 21, adopted by

the United Nations Conference on Environment and Development (Rio de Janeiro, Brazil, 3-14 June 1992).

37. The equal status of women and the human rights of women should be integrated into the mainstream of United Nations system-wide activity. These issues should be regularly and systematically addressed throughout relevant United Nations bodies and mechanisms. In particular, steps should be taken to increase cooperation and promote further integration of objectives and goals between the Commission on the Status of Women, the Commission on Human Rights, the Committee for the Elimination of Discrimination against Women, the United Nations Development Fund for Women, the United Nations Development Programme and other United Nations agencies. In this context, cooperation and coordination should be strengthened between the Centre for Human Rights and the Division for the Advancement of Women.

38. In particular, the World Conference on Human Rights stresses the importance of working towards the elimination of violence against women in public and private life, the elimination of all forms of sexual harassment, exploitation and trafficking in women, the elimination of gender bias in the administration of justice and the eradication of any conflicts which may arise between the rights of women and the harmful effects of certain traditional or customary practices, cultural prejudices and religious extremism. The World Conference on Human Rights calls upon the General Assembly to adopt the draft declaration on violence against women and urges States to combat violence against women in accordance with its provisions. Violations of the human rights of women in situations of armed conflict are violations of the fundamental principles of international human rights and humanitarian law. All violations of this kind, including in particular murder, systematic rape, sexual slavery, and forced pregnancy, require a particularly effective response.

39. The World Conference on Human Rights urges the eradication of all forms of discrimination against women, both hidden and overt. The United Nations should encourage the goal of universal ratification by all States of the Convention on the Elimination of All Forms of Discrimination against Women by the year 2000. Ways and means of addressing the particularly large number of reservations to the Convention should be encouraged. Inter alia, the Committee on the Elimination of Discrimination against Women should continue its review of reservations to the Convention.

States are urged to withdraw reservations that are contrary to the object and purpose of the Convention or which are otherwise incompatible with international treaty law.

40. Treaty monitoring bodies should disseminate necessary information to enable women to make more effective use of existing implementation procedures in their pursuits of full and equal enjoyment of human rights and non-discrimination. New procedures should also be adopted to strengthen implementation of the commitment to women's equality and the human rights of women. The Commission on the Status of Women and the Committee on the Elimination of Discrimination against Women should quickly examine the possibility of introducing the right of petition through the preparation of an optional protocol to the Convention on the Elimination of All Forms of Discrimination against Women. The World Conference on Human Rights welcomes the decision of the Commission on Human Rights to consider the appointment of a special rapporteur on violence against women at its fiftieth session.

41. The World Conference on Human Rights recognizes the importance of the enjoyment by women of the highest standard of physical and mental health throughout their life span. In the context of the World Conference on Women and the Convention on the Elimination of All Forms of Discrimination against Women, as well as the Proclamation of Tehran of 1968, the World Conference on Human Rights reaffirms, on the basis of equality between women and men, a woman's right to accessible and adequate health care and the widest range of family planning services, as well as equal access to education at all levels.

42. Treaty monitoring bodies should include the status of women and the human rights of women in their deliberations and findings, making use of gender-specific data. States should be encouraged to supply information on the situation of women de jure and de facto in their reports to treaty monitoring bodies. The World Conference on Human Rights notes with satisfaction that the Commission on Human Rights adopted at its forty-ninth session resolution 1993/46 of 8 March 1993 stating that rapporteurs and working groups in the field of human rights should also be encouraged to do so. Steps should also be taken by the Division for the Advancement of Women in cooperation with other United Nations bodies, specifically the Centre for Human Rights, to ensure that the human rights activities of the United Nations regularly address violations of women's human rights,

including gender-specific abuses. Training for United Nations human rights and humanitarian relief personnel to assist them to recognize and deal with human rights abuses particular to women and to carry out their work without gender bias should be encouraged.

43. The World Conference on Human Rights urges Governments and regional and international organizations to facilitate the access of women to decision-making posts and their greater participation in the decision-making process. It encourages further steps within the United Nations Secretariat to appoint and promote women staff members in accordance with the Charter of the United Nations, and encourages other principal and subsidiary organs of the United Nations to guarantee the participation of women under conditions of equality.

44. The World Conference on Human Rights welcomes the World Conference on Women to be held in Beijing in 1995 and urges that human rights of women should play an important role in its deliberations, in accordance with the priority themes of the World Conference on Women of equality, development and peace.

4. The rights of the child

45. The World Conference on Human Rights reiterates the principle of "First Call for Children" and, in this respect, underlines the importance of major national and international efforts, especially those of the United Nations Children's Fund, for promoting respect for the rights of the child to survival, protection, development and participation.

46. Measures should be taken to achieve universal ratification of the Convention on the Rights of the Child by 1995 and the universal signing of the World Declaration on the Survival, Protection and Development of Children and Plan of Action adopted by the World Summit for Children, as well as their effective implementation. The World Conference on Human Rights urges States to withdraw reservations to the Convention on the Rights of the Child contrary to the object and purpose of the Convention or otherwise contrary to international treaty law.

47. The World Conference on Human Rights urges all nations to undertake measures to the maximum extent of their available resources, with the support of international cooperation, to achieve the goals in the World Summit Plan of Action. The Conference calls on States to integrate the Convention on the Rights of the Child into their national action plans. By

means of these national action plans and through international efforts, particular priority should be placed on reducing infant and maternal mortality rates, reducing malnutrition and illiteracy rates and providing access to safe drinking water and to basic education. Whenever so called for, national plans of action should be devised to combat devastating emergencies resulting from natural disasters and armed conflicts and the equally grave problem of children in extreme poverty.

48. The World Conference on Human Rights urges all States, with the support of international cooperation, to address the acute problem of children under especially difficult circumstances. Exploitation and abuse of children should be actively combated, including by addressing their root causes. Effective measures are required against female infanticide, harmful child labour, sale of children and organs, child prostitution, child pornography, as well as other forms of sexual abuse.

49. The World Conference on Human Rights supports all measures by the United Nations and its specialized agencies to ensure the effective protection and promotion of human rights of the girl child. The World Conference on Human Rights urges States to repeal existing laws and regulations and remove customs and practices which discriminate against and cause harm to the girl child.

50. The World Conference on Human Rights strongly supports the proposal that the Secretary-General initiate a study into means of improving the protection of children in armed conflicts. Humanitarian norms should be implemented and measures taken in order to protect and facilitate assistance to children in war zones. Measures should include protection for children against indiscriminate use of all weapons of war, especially anti-personnel mines. The need for aftercare and rehabilitation of children traumatized by war must be addressed urgently. The Conference calls on the Committee on the Rights of the Child to study the question of raising the minimum age of recruitment into armed forces.

51. The World Conference on Human Rights recommends that matters relating to human rights and the situation of children be regularly reviewed and monitored by all relevant organs and mechanisms of the United Nations system and by the supervisory bodies of the specialized agencies in accordance with their mandates.

52. The World Conference on Human Rights recognizes the important role played by non-governmental organizations in the effective

implementation of all human rights instruments and, in particular, the Convention on the Rights of the Child.

53. The World Conference on Human Rights recommends that the Committee on the Rights of the Child, with the assistance of the Centre for Human Rights, be enabled expeditiously and effectively to meet its mandate, especially in view of the unprecedented extent of ratification and subsequent submission of country reports.

5. Freedom from torture

54. The World Conference on Human Rights welcomes the ratification by many Member States of the Convention against Torture and Other Cruel, Inhuman or Degrading Treatment or Punishment and encourages its speedy ratification by all other Member States.

55. The World Conference on Human Rights emphasizes that one of the most atrocious violations against human dignity is the act of torture, the result of which destroys the dignity and impairs the capability of victims to continue their lives and their activities.

56. The World Conference on Human Rights reaffirms that under human rights law and international humanitarian law, freedom from torture is a right which must be protected under all circumstances, including in times of internal or international disturbance or armed conflicts.

57. The World Conference on Human Rights therefore urges all States to put an immediate end to the practice of torture and eradicate this evil forever through full implementation of the Universal Declaration of Human Rights as well as the relevant conventions and, where necessary, strengthening of existing mechanisms. The World Conference on Human Rights calls on all States to cooperate fully with the Special Rapporteur on the question of torture in the fulfilment of his mandate.

58. Special attention should be given to ensure universal respect for, and effective implementation of, the Principles of Medical Ethics relevant to the Role of Health Personnel, particularly Physicians, in the Protection of Prisoners and Detainees against Torture and other Cruel, Inhuman or Degrading Treatment or Punishment adopted by the General Assembly of the United Nations.

59. The World Conference on Human Rights stresses the importance of further concrete action within the framework of the United Nations with

the view to providing assistance to victims of torture and ensure more effective remedies for their physical, psychological and social rehabilitation. Providing the necessary resources for this purpose should be given high priority, inter alia, by additional contributions to the United Nations Voluntary Fund for the Victims of Torture.

60. States should abrogate legislation leading to impunity for those responsible for grave violations of human rights such as torture and prosecute such violations, thereby providing a firm basis for the rule of law.

61. The World Conference on Human Rights reaffirms that efforts to eradicate torture should, first and foremost, be concentrated on prevention and, therefore, calls for the early adoption of an optional protocol to the Convention against Torture and Other Cruel, Inhuman and Degrading Treatment or Punishment, which is intended to establish a preventive system of regular visits to places of detention.

Enforced disappearances

62. The World Conference on Human Rights, welcoming the adoption by the General Assembly of the Declaration on the Protection of All Persons from Enforced Disappearance, calls upon all States to take effective legislative, administrative, judicial or other measures to prevent, terminate and punish acts of enforced disappearances. The World Conference on Human Rights reaffirms that it is the duty of all States, under any circumstances, to make investigations whenever there is reason to believe that an enforced disappearance has taken place on a territory under their jurisdiction and, if allegations are confirmed, to prosecute its perpetrators.

6. The rights of the disabled person

63. The World Conference on Human Rights reaffirms that all human rights and fundamental freedoms are universal and thus unreservedly include persons with disabilities. Every person is born equal and has the same rights to life and welfare, education and work, living independently and active participation in all aspects of society. Any direct discrimination or other negative discriminatory treatment of a disabled person is therefore a violation of his or her rights. The World Conference on Human Rights calls on Governments, where necessary, to adopt or adjust legislation to assure access to these and other rights for disabled persons.

64. The place of disabled persons is everywhere. Persons with disabilities should be guaranteed equal opportunity through the elimination of all socially determined barriers, be they physical, financial, social or psychological, which exclude or restrict full participation in society.

65. Recalling the World Programme of Action concerning Disabled Persons, adopted by the General Assembly at its thirty-seventh session, the World Conference on Human Rights calls upon the General Assembly and the Economic and Social Council to adopt the draft standard rules on the equalization of opportunities for persons with disabilities, at their meetings in 1993.

C. Cooperation, Development and Strengthening of Human Rights

66. The World Conference on Human Rights recommends that priority be given to national and international action to promote democracy, development and human rights.

67. Special emphasis should be given to measures to assist in the strengthening and building of institutions relating to human rights, strengthening of a pluralistic civil society and the protection of groups which have been rendered vulnerable. In this context, assistance provided upon the request of Governments for the conduct of free and fair elections, including assistance in the human rights aspects of elections and public information about elections, is of particular importance. Equally important is the assistance to be given to the strengthening of the rule of law, the promotion of freedom of expression and the administration of justice, and to the real and effective participation of the people in the decision-making processes.

68. The World Conference on Human Rights stresses the need for the implementation of strengthened advisory services and technical assistance activities by the Centre for Human Rights. The Centre should make available to States upon request assistance on specific human rights issues, including the preparation of reports under human rights treaties as well as for the implementation of coherent and comprehensive plans of action for the promotion and protection of human rights. Strengthening the institutions of human rights and democracy, the legal protection of human rights, training of officials and others, broad-based education and public information aimed at promoting respect for human rights should all be available as components of these programmes.

69. The World Conference on Human Rights strongly recommends that a comprehensive programme be established within the United Nations in order to help States in the task of building and strengthening adequate national structures which have a direct impact on the overall observance of human rights and the maintenance of the rule of law. Such a programme, to be coordinated by the Centre for Human Rights, should be able to provide, upon the request of the interested Government, technical and financial assistance to national projects in reforming penal and correctional establishments, education and training of lawyers, judges and security forces in human rights, and any other sphere of activity relevant to the good functioning of the rule of law. That programme should make available to States assistance for the implementation of plans of action for the promotion and protection of human rights.

70. The World Conference on Human Rights requests the Secretary-General of the United Nations to submit proposals to the United Nations General Assembly, containing alternatives for the establishment, structure, operational modalities and funding of the proposed programme.

71. The World Conference on Human Rights recommends that each State consider the desirability of drawing up a national action plan identifying steps whereby that State would improve the promotion and protection of human rights.

72. The World Conference on Human Rights on Human Rights reaffirms that the universal and inalienable right to development, as established in the Declaration on the Right to Development, must be implemented and realized. In this context, the World Conference on Human Rights welcomes the appointment by the Commission on Human Rights of a thematic working group on the right to development and urges that the Working Group, in consultation and cooperation with other organs and agencies of the United Nations system, promptly formulate, for early consideration by the United Nations General Assembly, comprehensive and effective measures to eliminate obstacles to the implementation and realization of the Declaration on the Right to Development and recommending ways and means towards the realization of the right to development by all States.

73. The World Conference on Human Rights recommends that non-governmental and other grass-roots organizations active in development and/or human rights should be enabled to play a major role on the national and

international levels in the debate, activities and implementation relating to the right to development and, in cooperation with Governments, in all relevant aspects of development cooperation.

74. The World Conference on Human Rights appeals to Governments, competent agencies and institutions to increase considerably the resources devoted to building well-functioning legal systems able to protect human rights, and to national institutions working in this area. Actors in the field of development cooperation should bear in mind the mutually reinforcing interrelationship between development, democracy and human rights. Cooperation should be based on dialogue and transparency. The World Conference on Human Rights also calls for the establishment of comprehensive programmes, including resource banks of information and personnel with expertise relating to the strengthening of the rule of law and of democratic institutions.

75. The World Conference on Human Rights encourages the Commission on Human Rights, in cooperation with the Committee on Economic, Social and Cultural Rights, to continue the examination of optional protocols to the International Covenant on Economic, Social and Cultural Rights.

76. The World Conference on Human Rights recommends that more resources be made available for the strengthening or the establishment of regional arrangements for the promotion and protection of human rights under the programmes of advisory services and technical assistance of the Centre for Human Rights. States are encouraged to request assistance for such purposes as regional and subregional workshops, seminars and information exchanges designed to strengthen regional arrangements for the promotion and protection of human rights in accord with universal human rights standards as contained in international human rights instruments.

77. The World Conference on Human Rights supports all measures by the United Nations and its relevant specialized agencies to ensure the effective promotion and protection of trade union rights, as stipulated in the International Covenant on Economic, Social and Cultural Rights and other relevant international instruments. It calls on all States to abide fully by their obligations in this regard contained in international instruments.

D. Human Rights Education

78. The World Conference on Human Rights considers human rights

education, training and public information essential for the promotion and achievement of stable and harmonious relations among communities and for fostering mutual understanding, tolerance and peace.

79. States should strive to eradicate illiteracy and should direct education towards the full development of the human personality and to the strengthening of respect for human rights and fundamental freedoms. The World Conference on Human Rights calls on all States and institutions to include human rights, humanitarian law, democracy and rule of law as subjects in the curricula of all learning institutions in formal and non-formal settings.

80. Human rights education should include peace, democracy, development and social justice, as set forth in international and regional human rights instruments, in order to achieve common understanding and awareness with a view to strengthening universal commitment to human rights.

81. Taking into account the World Plan of Action on Education for Human Rights and Democracy, adopted in March 1993 by the International Congress on Education for Human Rights and Democracy of the United Nations Educational, Scientific and Cultural Organization, and other human rights instruments, the World Conference on Human Rights recommends that States develop specific programmes and strategies for ensuring the widest human rights education and the dissemination of public information, taking particular account of the human rights needs of women.

82. Governments, with the assistance of intergovernmental organizations, national institutions and non-governmental organizations, should promote an increased awareness of human rights and mutual tolerance. The World Conference on Human Rights underlines the importance of strengthening the World Public Information Campaign for Human Rights carried out by the United Nations. They should initiate and support education in human rights and undertake effective dissemination of public information in this field. The advisory services and technical assistance programmes of the United Nations system should be able to respond immediately to requests from States for educational and training activities in the field of human rights as well as for special education concerning standards as contained in international human rights instruments and in humanitarian law and their application to special groups such as military forces, law enforcement personnel, police and the health profession.

The proclamation of a United Nations decade for human rights education in order to promote, encourage and focus these educational activities should be considered.

E. Implementation and Monitoring Methods

83. The World Conference on Human Rights urges Governments to incorporate standards as contained in international human rights instruments in domestic legislation and to strengthen national structures, institutions and organs of society which play a role in promoting and safeguarding human rights.

84. The World Conference on Human Rights recommends the strengthening of United Nations activities and programmes to meet requests for assistance by States which want to establish or strengthen their own national institutions for the promotion and protection of human rights.

85. The World Conference on Human Rights also encourages the strengthening of cooperation between national institutions for the promotion and protection of human rights, particularly through exchanges of information and experience, as well as cooperation with regional organizations and the United Nations.

86. The World Conference on Human Rights strongly recommends in this regard that representatives of national institutions for the promotion and protection of human rights convene periodic meetings under the auspices of the Centre for Human Rights to examine ways and means of improving their mechanisms and sharing experiences.

87. The World Conference on Human Rights recommends to the human rights treaty bodies, to the meetings of chairpersons of the treaty bodies and to the meetings of States parties that they continue to take steps aimed at coordinating the multiple reporting requirements and guidelines for preparing State reports under the respective human rights conventions and study the suggestion that the submission of one overall report on treaty obligations undertaken by each State would make these procedures more effective and increase their impact.

88. The World Conference on Human Rights recommends that the States parties to international human rights instruments, the General Assembly and the Economic and Social Council should consider studying the existing human rights treaty bodies and the various thematic mechanisms

and procedures with a view to promoting greater efficiency and effectiveness through better coordination of the various bodies, mechanisms and procedures, taking into account the need to avoid unnecessary duplication and overlapping of their mandates and tasks.

89. The World Conference on Human Rights recommends continued work on the improvement of the functioning, including the monitoring tasks, of the treaty bodies, taking into account multiple proposals made in this respect, in particular those made by the treaty bodies themselves and by the meetings of the chairpersons of the treaty bodies. The comprehensive national approach taken by the Committee on the Rights of the Child should also be encouraged.

90. The World Conference on Human Rights recommends that States parties to human rights treaties consider accepting all the available optional communication procedures.

91. The World Conference on Human Rights views with concern the issue of impunity of perpetrators of human rights violations, and supports the efforts of the Commission on Human Rights and the Sub-Commission on Prevention of Discrimination and Protection of Minorities to examine all aspects of the issue.

92. The World Conference on Human Rights recommends that the Commission on Human Rights examine the possibility for better implementation of existing human rights instruments at the international and regional levels and encourages the International Law Commission to continue its work on an international criminal court.

93. The World Conference on Human Rights appeals to States which have not yet done so to accede to the Geneva Conventions of 12 August 1949 and the Protocols thereto, and to take all appropriate national measures, including legislative ones, for their full implementation.

94. The World Conference on Human Rights recommends the speedy completion and adoption of the draft declaration on the right and responsibility of individuals, groups and organs of society to promote and protect universally recognized human rights and fundamental freedoms.

95. The World Conference on Human Rights underlines the importance of preserving and strengthening the system of special procedures, rapporteurs, representatives, experts and working groups of the Commission on Human Rights and the Sub-Commission on the Prevention of

Discrimination and Protection of Minorities, in order to enable them to carry out their mandates in all countries throughout the world, providing them with the necessary human and financial resources. The procedures and mechanisms should be enabled to harmonize and rationalize their work through periodic meetings. All States are asked to cooperate fully with these procedures and mechanisms.

96. The World Conference on Human Rights recommends that the United Nations assume a more active role in the promotion and protection of human rights in ensuring full respect for international humanitarian law in all situations of armed conflict, in accordance with the purposes and principles of the Charter of the United Nations.

97. The World Conference on Human Rights, recognizing the important role of human rights components in specific arrangements concerning some peace-keeping operations by the United Nations, recommends that the Secretary-General take into account the reporting, experience and capabilities of the Centre for Human Rights and human rights mechanisms, in conformity with the Charter of the United Nations.

98. To strengthen the enjoyment of economic, social and cultural rights, additional approaches should be examined, such as a system of indicators to measure progress in the realization of the rights set forth in the International Covenant on Economic, Social and Cultural Rights. There must be a concerted effort to ensure recognition of economic, social and cultural rights at the national, regional and international levels.

F. Follow-up to the World Conference on Human Rights

99. The World Conference on Human Rights on Human Rights recommends that the General Assembly, the Commission on Human Rights and other organs and agencies of the United Nations system related to human rights consider ways and means for the full implementation, without delay, of the recommendations contained in the present Declaration, including the possibility of proclaiming a United Nations decade for human rights. The World Conference on Human Rights further recommends that the Commission on Human Rights annually review the progress towards this end.

100. The World Conference on Human Rights requests the Secretary-General of the United Nations to invite on the occasion of the fiftieth

anniversary of the Universal Declaration of Human Rights all States, all organs and agencies of the United Nations system related to human rights, to report to him on the progress made in the implementation of the present Declaration and to submit a report to the General Assembly at its fifty-third session, through the Commission on Human Rights and the Economic and Social Council. Likewise, regional and, as appropriate, national human rights institutions, as well as non-governmental organizations, may present their views to the Secretary-General on the progress made in the implementation of the present Declaration. Special attention should be paid to assessing the progress towards the goal of universal ratification of international human rights treaties and protocols adopted within the framework of the United Nations system.

References

Glendon, Mary Ann (2002). *A world made new: Eleanor Roosevelt and the Universal Declaration of Human Rights*. Random House.

Ignatieff, Michael (2001). *Human rights as politics and idolatry* (3. print. ed.). Princeton, N.J.: Princeton University Press.

Morsink, Johannes (1999). *The Universal Declaration of Human Rights: origins, drafting, and intent*. University of Pennsylvania Press.

Williams, Paul; United Nations. General Assembly (1981). *The International bill of human rights*. Entwhistle Books.

Bibliography

Abouharb, R. and D. Cingranelli (2007). "Human Rights and Structural Adjustment". New York: Cambridge University Press.

Antonio Cassese, Paola Gaeta & John R.W.D. Jones (eds.), (2002). *The Rome Statute of the International Criminal Court: A Commentary*. Oxford: Oxford University Press

Ball, Olivia; Gready, Paul (2006). *The no-nonsense guide to human rights*. Oxford: New Internationalist.

Barsh, R. (1993). "Measuring Human Rights: Problems of Methodology and Purpose." Human Rights Quarterly 15: 87-121.

Beitz, Charles R. (2009). *The idea of human rights*. Oxford: Oxford University Press.

Brownlie, Ian (2003). *Principles of Public International Law*. OUP.

Bruce Broomhall, (2003). *International Justice and the International Criminal Court: Between Sovereignty and the Rule of Law*. Oxford: Oxford University Press.

Chauhan, O.P. (2004). *Human Rights: Promotion and Protection*. Anmol Publications PVT. LTD.

Doebbler, Curtis (2006). *Introduction to international human rights law.*. Cd Publishing.

Donnelly, Jack (2003). *Universal human rights in theory and practice* (2nd ed.). Ithaca: Cornell University Press.

Forsythe, David P. (2000). *Human Rights in International Relations*. Cambridge: Cambridge University Press. International Progress Organization.

Freeman, Michael (2002). *Human rights : an interdisciplinary approach*. Cambridge: Polity Press.

Gerald M. Steinberg, Anne Herzberg and Jordan Berman (2012). *Best Practices for Human Rights and Humanitarian NGO Fact-Finding*. Martinus Nijhoff Publishers.

Gerald M. Steinberg, Anne Herzberg and Jordan Berman (2012). *Best Practices for Human Rights and Humanitarian NGO Fact-Finding*. Martinus Nijhoff Publisher.

Glendon, Mary Ann (2001). *A world made new : Eleanor Roosevelt and the Universal Declaration of Human Rights*. New York: Random House.

Glendon, Mary Ann (2002). *A world made new: Eleanor Roosevelt and the Universal Declaration of Human Rights*. Random House.

Hans Köchler, (2003). *Global Justice or Global Revenge? International Criminal Justice at the Crossroads*. Vienna/New York: Springer.

Hashmi, Sohail H. (2002). *Islamic political ethics: civil society, pluralism, and conflict*. Princeton University Press.

Ignatieff, Michael (2001). *Human rights as politics and idolatry* (3. print. ed.). Princeton, N.J.: Princeton University Press.

Ishay, Micheline R. (2008). *The history of human rights : from ancient times to the globalization era*. Berkeley, Calif.: University of California Press.

Morsink, Johannes (1999). *The Universal Declaration of Human Rights: origins, drafting, and intent*. University of Pennsylvania Press.

Moyn, Samuel (2010). *The last utopia: human rights in history*. Cambridge, Mass.: Belknap Press of Harvard University Press.

Price, Daniel E. (1999). *Islamic political culture, democracy, and human rights: a comparative study*. Greenwood Publishing Group.

Robertson, Arthur Henry; Merrills, John Graham (1996). *Human Rights in the World: An Introduction to the Study of the International Protection of Human Rights*. Manchester University Press.

Rosenne S., (2003)."Rosenne's the world court: what it is and how it works *6th ed* (Leiden: Martinus Nijhoff.

Roy S Lee & Hakan Friman (eds.), (2001). *The International Criminal Court: Elements of Crimes and Rules of Procedure and Evidence*. Ardsley, NY: Transnational Publishers.

Shaw, Malcom (2008). *International Law*. Leiden: Cambridge University Press.

Shute, Stephen & Hurley, Susan (eds.). (1993). *On Human Rights: The Oxford Amnesty Lectures.* New York: BasicBooks.

Steiner, J. & Alston, Philip. (1996). *International Human Rights in Context: Law, Politics, Morals.* Oxford: Clarendon Press.

Steven C. Roach (ed.) (2009). *Governance, Order, and the International Criminal Court: Between Realpolitik and a Cosmopolitan Court.* Oxford: Oxford University Press.

Van Der Wolf W. & De Ruiter D., (2011). "The International Court of Justice: Facts and Documents About the History and Work of the Court". *International Courts Association.*

Universal Declaration of Human Rights, UN General Assembly, December 10, 1948, 217 A (III)

William A Schabas, (2004). *An Introduction to the International Criminal Court* (2nd ed.). Cambridge: Cambridge University Press.

Williams, Paul; United Nations. General Assembly (1981). *The International bill of human rights*. Entwhistle Books.